Y THE LAST MAN – Paper Dolls

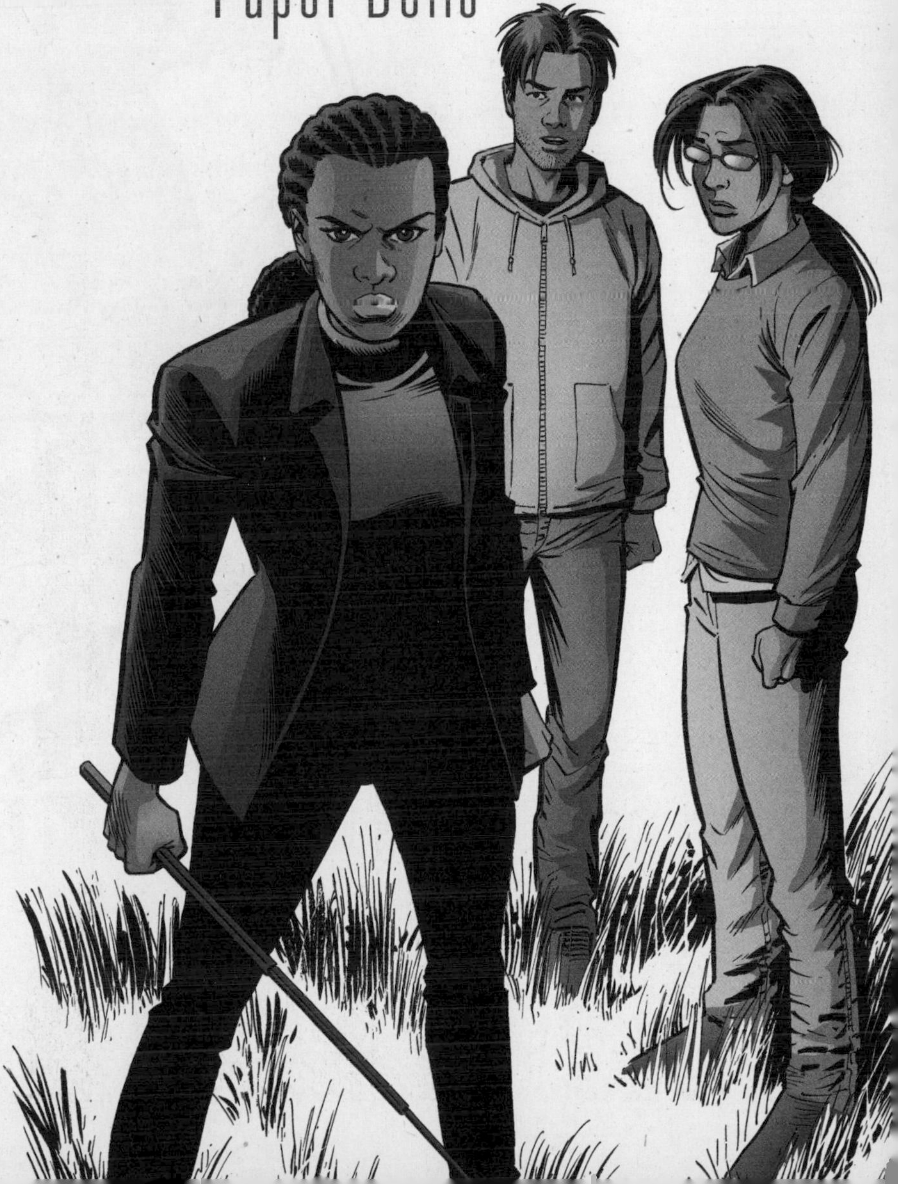

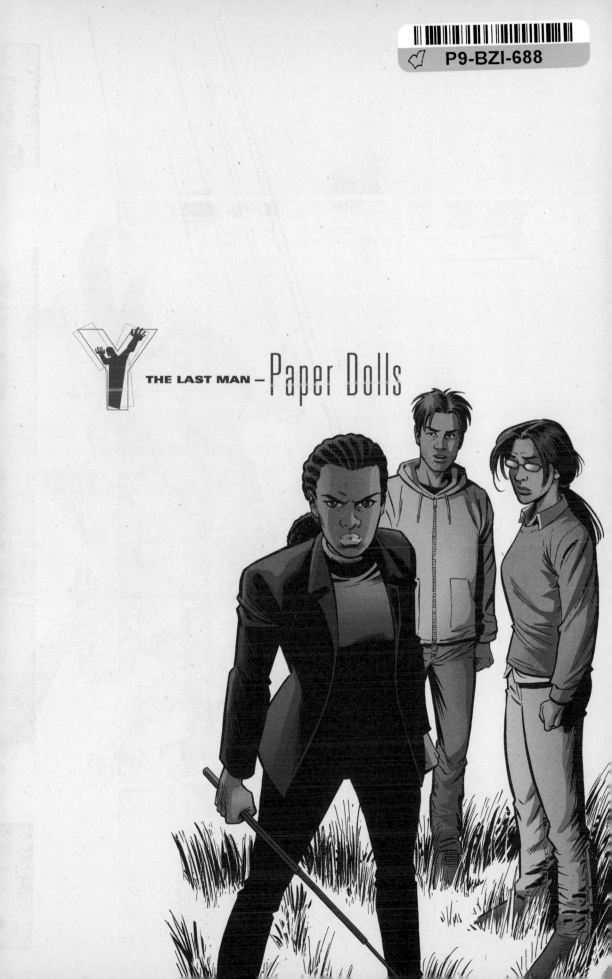

THE LAST MAN — Paper Dolls

Brian K. Vaughan
Writer

Pia Guerra
Goran Sudžuka
Pencillers

José Marzán, Jr.
Inker

Zylonol
Colorist

Clem Robins
Letterer

Massimo Carnevale
Original series covers

Y: THE LAST MAN created by Brian K. Vaughan and Pia Guerra

Will Dennis
Editor – Original Series

Casey Seijas
Assistant Editor – Original Series

Scott Nybakken
Editor

Robbin Brosterman
Design Director – Books

Louis Prandi
Publication Design

Shelly Bond
Executive Editor – Vertigo

Hank Kanalz
Senior VP – Vertigo & Integrated Publishing

Diane Nelson
President

Dan DiDio and **Jim Lee**
Co-Publishers

Geoff Johns
Chief Creative Officer

John Rood
Executive VP – Sales, Marketing & Business Development

Amy Genkins
Senior VP – Business & Legal Affairs

Nairi Gardiner
Senior VP – Finance

Jeff Boison
VP – Publishing Planning

Mark Chiarello
VP – Art Direction & Design

John Cunningham
VP – Marketing

Terri Cunningham
VP – Editorial Administration

Alison Gill
Senior VP – Manufacturing & Operations

Jay Kogan
VP – Business & Legal Affairs, Publishing

Jack Mahan
VP – Business Affairs, Talent

Nick Napolitano
VP – Manufacturing Administration

Sue Pohja
VP – Book Sales

Courtney Simmons
Senior VP – Publicity

Bob Wayne
Senior VP – Sales

Y: THE LAST MAN — PAPER DOLLS

Originally published in single magazine form as Y: THE LAST MAN 37-42.
Copyright © 2006 Brian K. Vaughan and Pia Guerra. All Rights Reserved.
All characters, their distinctive likenesses and related elements featured in
this publication are trademarks of Brian K. Vaughan and Pia Guerra.
VERTIGO is a trademark of DC Comics. The stories, characters and incidents
featured in this publication are entirely fictional. DC Comics does not read
or accept unsolicited submissions of ideas, stories or artwork.

DC Comics, 1700 Broadway, New York, NY 10019
A Warner Bros. Entertainment Company.
Printed in the USA. Fourth Printing.
ISBN: 978-1-4012-1009-0
Cover illustrations by Massimo Carnevale.
Logo design by Terry Marks.

SUSTAINABLE FORESTRY INITIATIVE

Certified Chain of Custody
Promoting Sustainable Forestry
www.sfiprogram.org
SFI-01042
APPLIES TO TEXT STOCK ONLY

Y THE LAST MAN – Contents

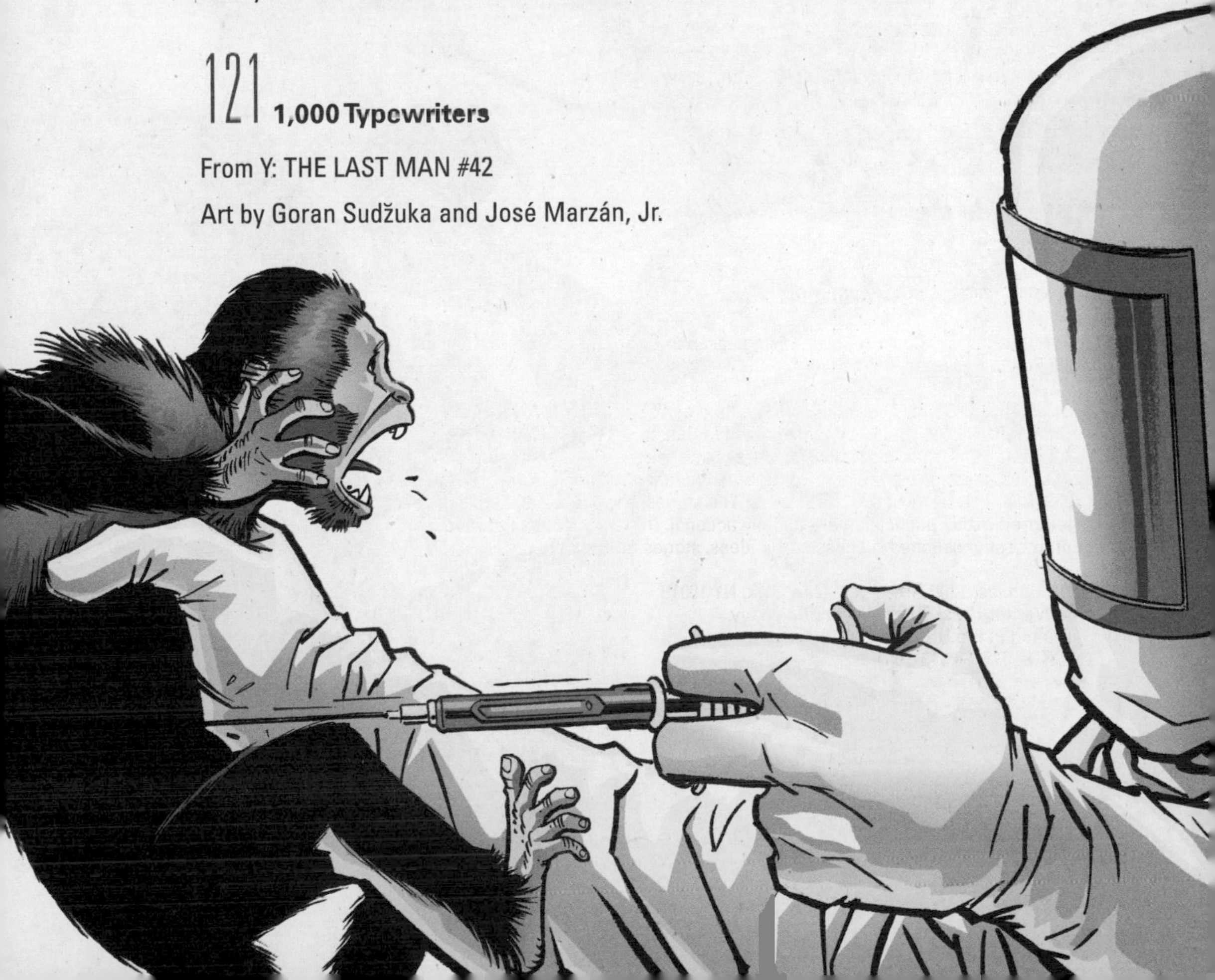

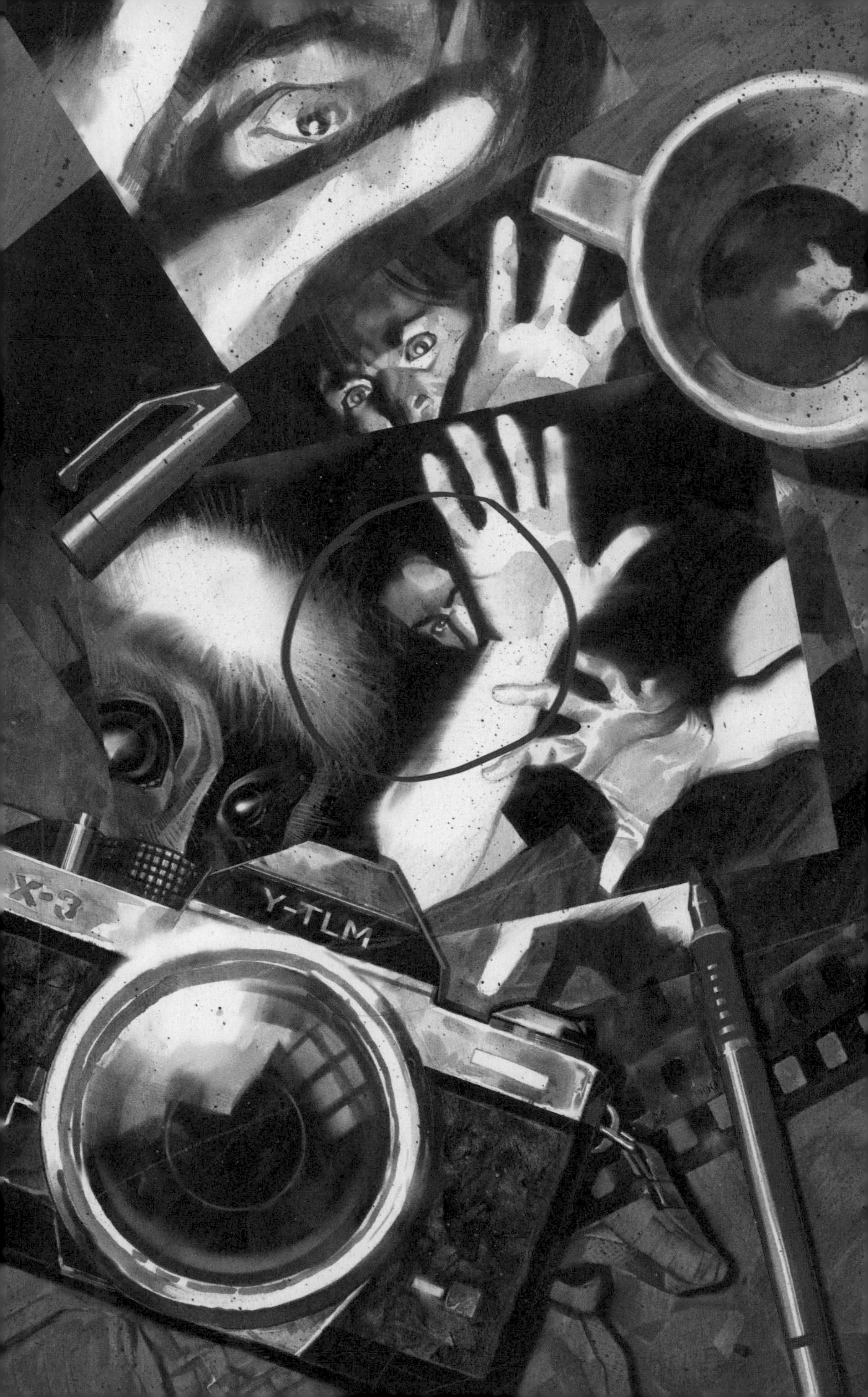
X-3
Y-TLM

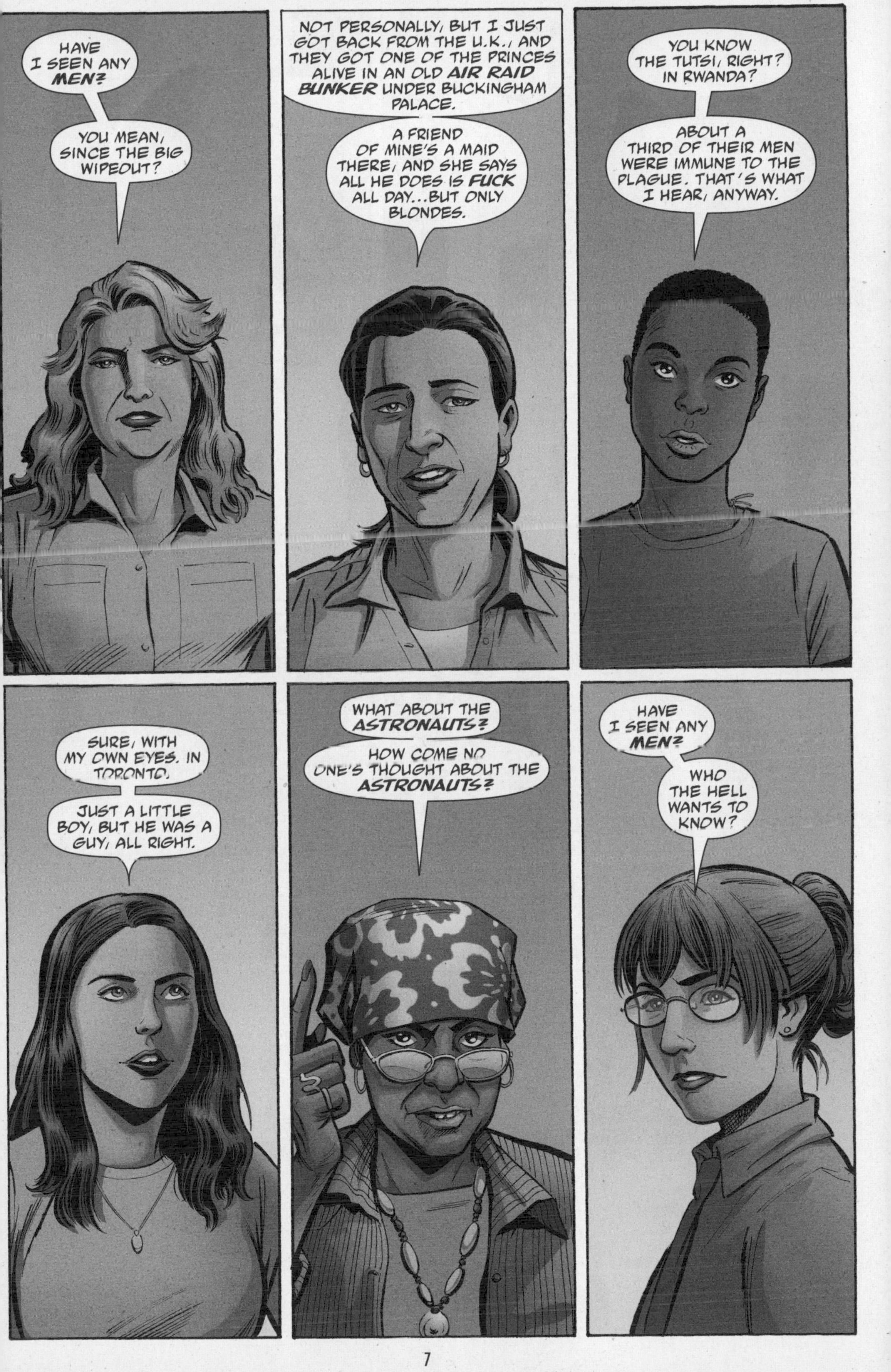
HAVE I SEEN ANY **MEN**?
YOU MEAN, SINCE THE BIG WIPEOUT?
NOT PERSONALLY, BUT I JUST GOT BACK FROM THE U.K., AND THEY GOT ONE OF THE PRINCES ALIVE IN AN OLD **AIR RAID BUNKER** UNDER BUCKINGHAM PALACE.
A FRIEND OF MINE'S A MAID THERE, AND SHE SAYS ALL HE DOES IS **FUCK** ALL DAY...BUT ONLY BLONDES.
YOU KNOW THE TUTSI, RIGHT? IN RWANDA?
ABOUT A THIRD OF THEIR MEN WERE IMMUNE TO THE PLAGUE. THAT'S WHAT I HEAR, ANYWAY.
SURE, WITH MY OWN EYES. IN TORONTO.
JUST A LITTLE BOY, BUT HE WAS A GUY, ALL RIGHT.
WHAT ABOUT THE **ASTRONAUTS**?
HOW COME NO ONE'S THOUGHT ABOUT THE **ASTRONAUTS**?
HAVE I SEEN ANY **MEN**?
WHO THE HELL WANTS TO KNOW?

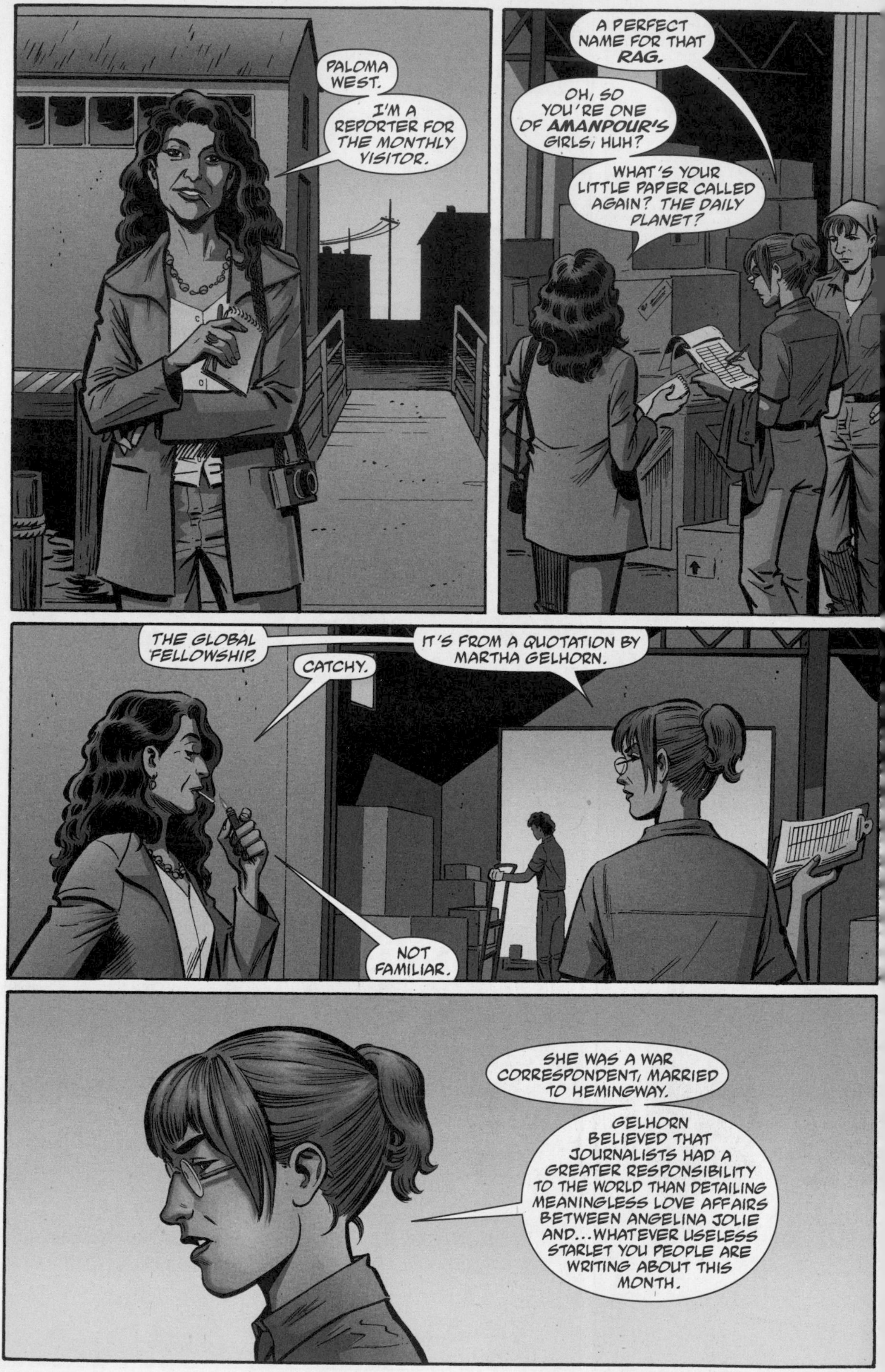

PALOMA WEST.
I'M A REPORTER FOR THE MONTHLY VISITOR.
A PERFECT NAME FOR THAT RAG.
OH, SO YOU'RE ONE OF AMANPOUR'S GIRLS, HUH?
WHAT'S YOUR LITTLE PAPER CALLED AGAIN? THE DAILY PLANET?
THE GLOBAL FELLOWSHIP.
CATCHY.
IT'S FROM A QUOTATION BY MARTHA GELHORN.
NOT FAMILIAR.
SHE WAS A WAR CORRESPONDENT, MARRIED TO HEMINGWAY.
GELHORN BELIEVED THAT JOURNALISTS HAD A GREATER RESPONSIBILITY TO THE WORLD THAN DETAILING MEANINGLESS LOVE AFFAIRS BETWEEN ANGELINA JOLIE AND...WHATEVER USELESS STARLET YOU PEOPLE ARE WRITING ABOUT THIS MONTH.

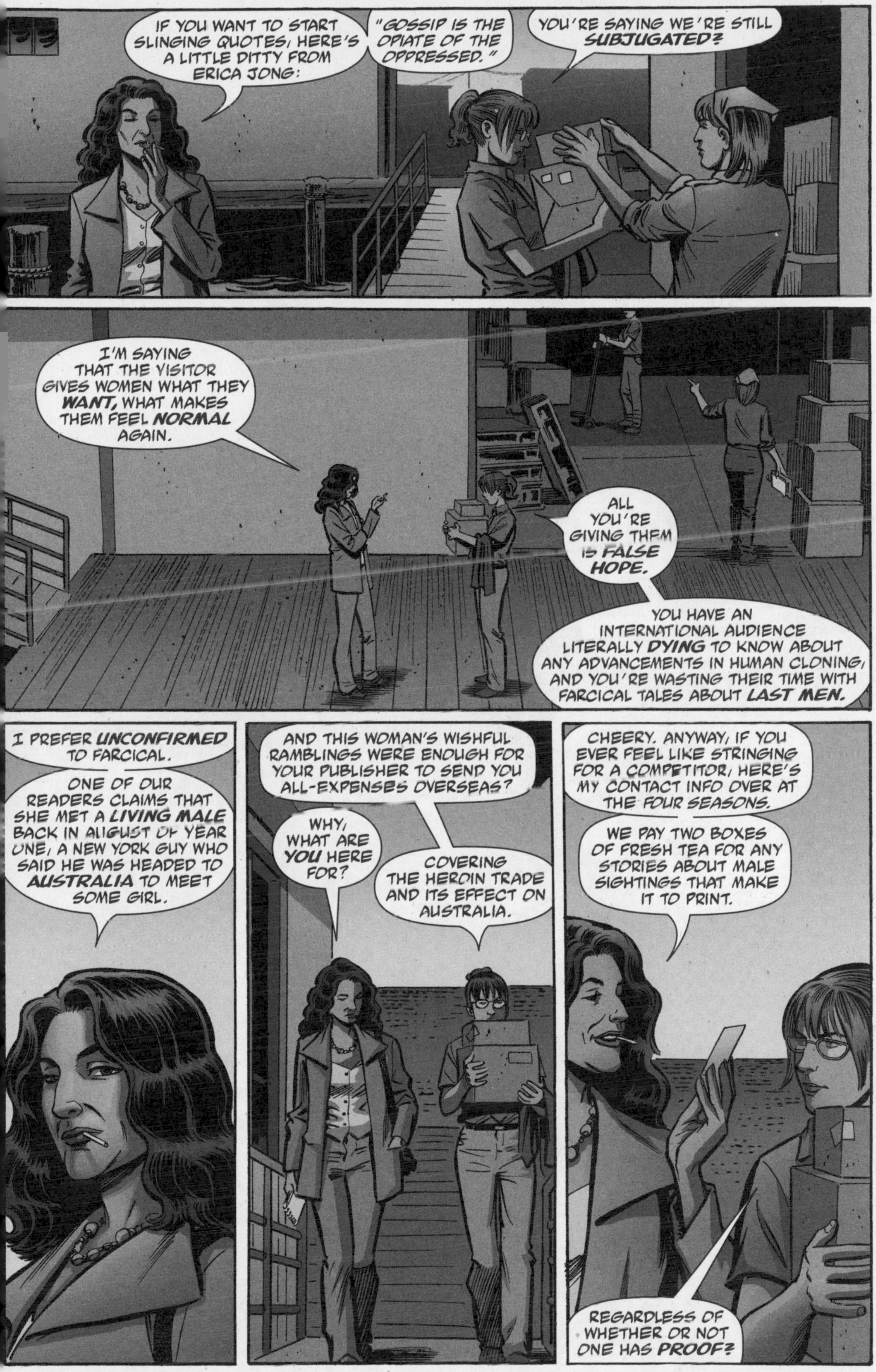
IF YOU WANT TO START SLINGING QUOTES, HERE'S A LITTLE DITTY FROM ERICA JONG:
"GOSSIP IS THE OPIATE OF THE OPPRESSED."
YOU'RE SAYING WE'RE STILL SUBJUGATED?
I'M SAYING THAT THE VISITOR GIVES WOMEN WHAT THEY WANT, WHAT MAKES THEM FEEL NORMAL AGAIN.
ALL YOU'RE GIVING THEM IS FALSE HOPE.
YOU HAVE AN INTERNATIONAL AUDIENCE LITERALLY DYING TO KNOW ABOUT ANY ADVANCEMENTS IN HUMAN CLONING, AND YOU'RE WASTING THEIR TIME WITH FARCICAL TALES ABOUT LAST MEN.
I PREFER UNCONFIRMED TO FARCICAL.
ONE OF OUR READERS CLAIMS THAT SHE MET A LIVING MALE BACK IN AUGUST OF YEAR ONE, A NEW YORK GUY WHO SAID HE WAS HEADED TO AUSTRALIA TO MEET SOME GIRL.
AND THIS WOMAN'S WISHFUL RAMBLINGS WERE ENOUGH FOR YOUR PUBLISHER TO SEND YOU ALL-EXPENSES OVERSEAS?
WHY, WHAT ARE YOU HERE FOR?
COVERING THE HEROIN TRADE AND ITS EFFECT ON AUSTRALIA.
CHEERY. ANYWAY, IF YOU EVER FEEL LIKE STRINGING FOR A COMPETITOR, HERE'S MY CONTACT INFO OVER AT THE FOUR SEASONS.
WE PAY TWO BOXES OF FRESH TEA FOR ANY STORIES ABOUT MALE SIGHTINGS THAT MAKE IT TO PRINT.
REGARDLESS OF WHETHER OR NOT ONE HAS PROOF?

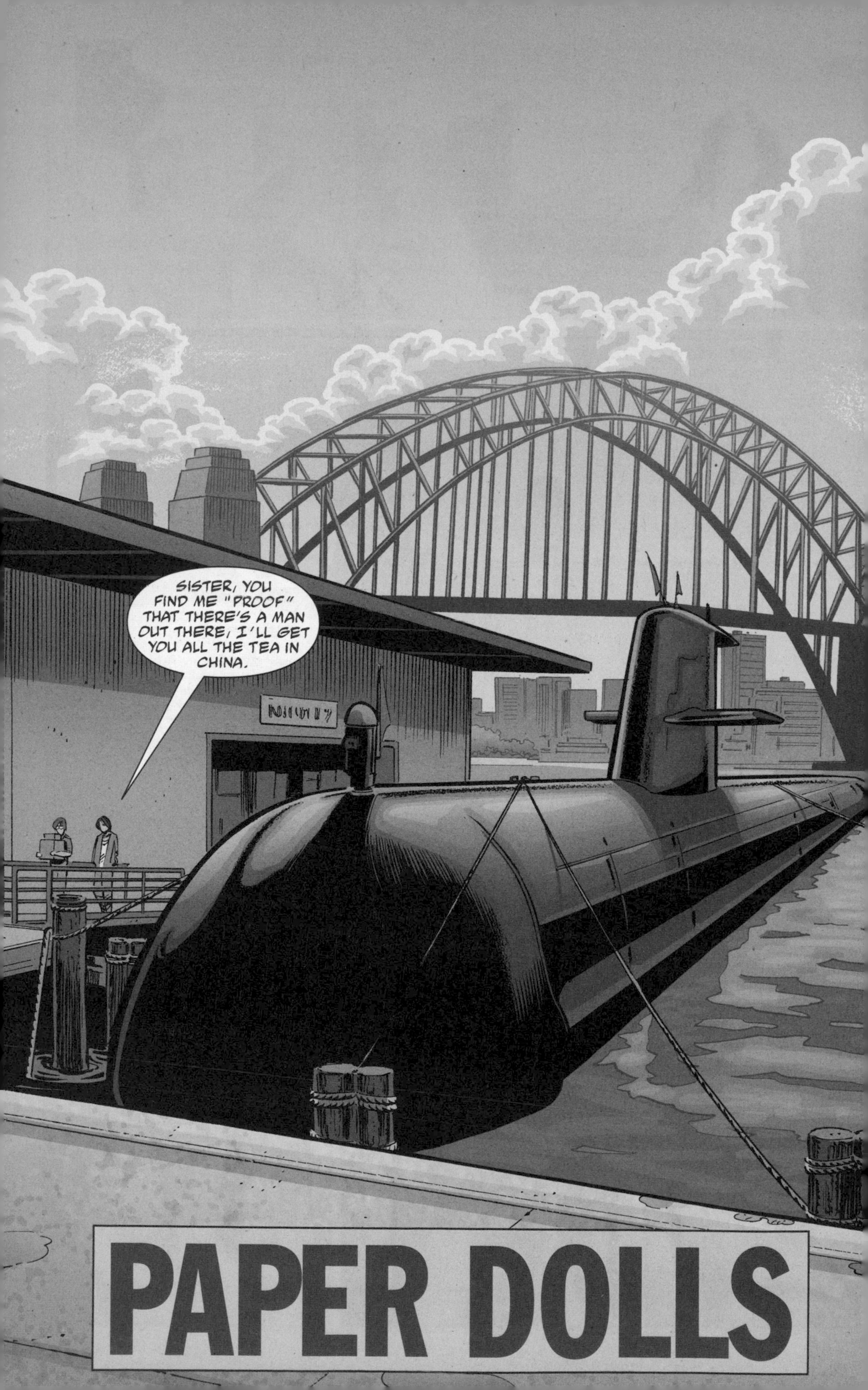
SISTER, YOU FIND ME "PROOF" THAT THERE'S A MAN OUT THERE, I'LL GET YOU ALL THE TEA IN CHINA.
PAPER DOLLS

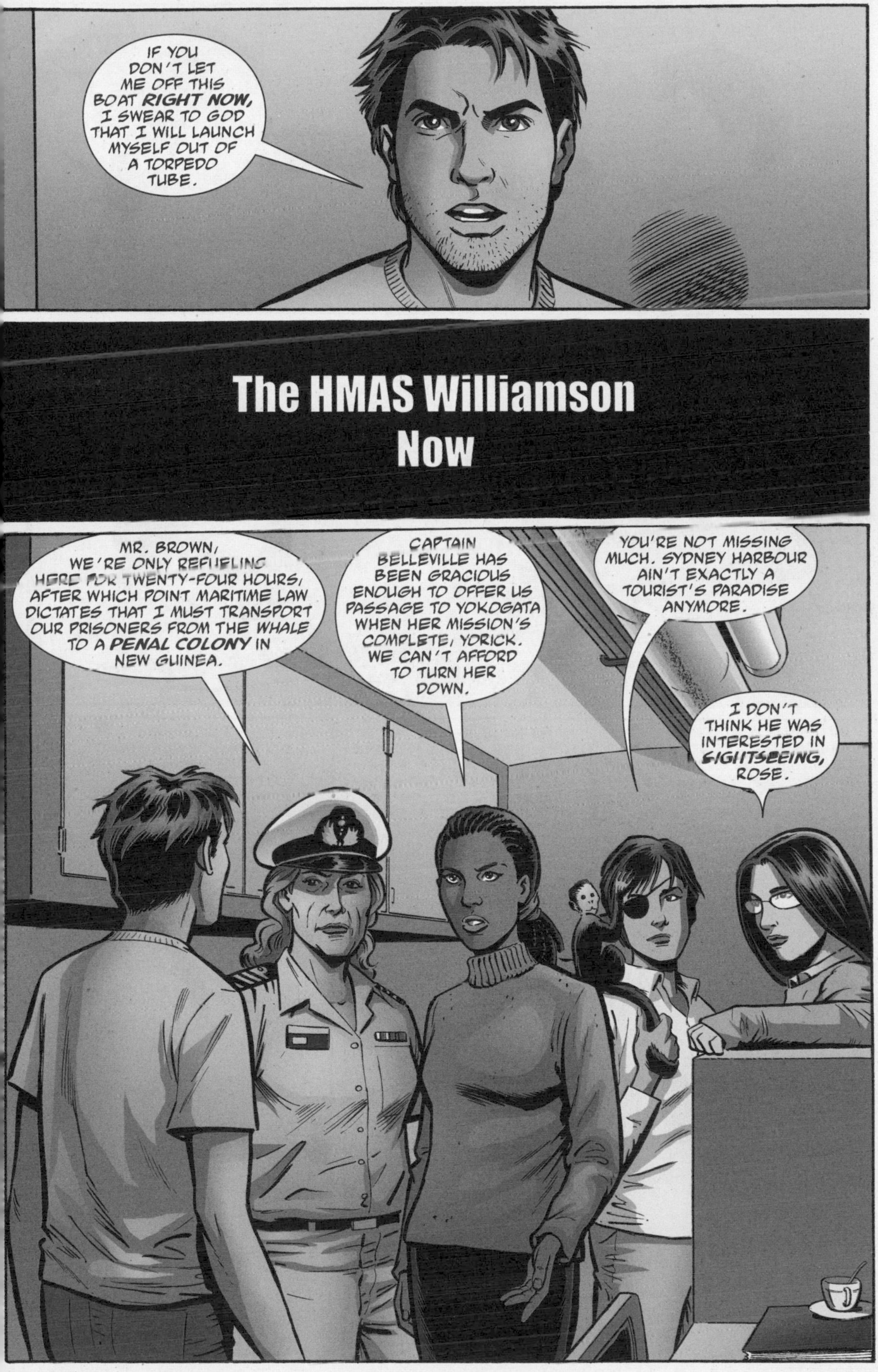
IF YOU DON'T LET ME OFF THIS BOAT RIGHT NOW, I SWEAR TO GOD THAT I WILL LAUNCH MYSELF OUT OF A TORPEDO TUBE.
The HMAS Williamson
Now
MR. BROWN, WE'RE ONLY REFUELING HERE FOR TWENTY-FOUR HOURS, AFTER WHICH POINT MARITIME LAW DICTATES THAT I MUST TRANSPORT OUR PRISONERS FROM THE WHALE TO A PENAL COLONY IN NEW GUINEA.
CAPTAIN BELLEVILLE HAS BEEN GRACIOUS ENOUGH TO OFFER US PASSAGE TO YOKOGATA WHEN HER MISSION'S COMPLETE, YORICK. WE CAN'T AFFORD TO TURN HER DOWN.
YOU'RE NOT MISSING MUCH. SYDNEY HARBOUR AIN'T EXACTLY A TOURIST'S PARADISE ANYMORE.
I DON'T THINK HE WAS INTERESTED IN SIGHTSEEING, ROSE.

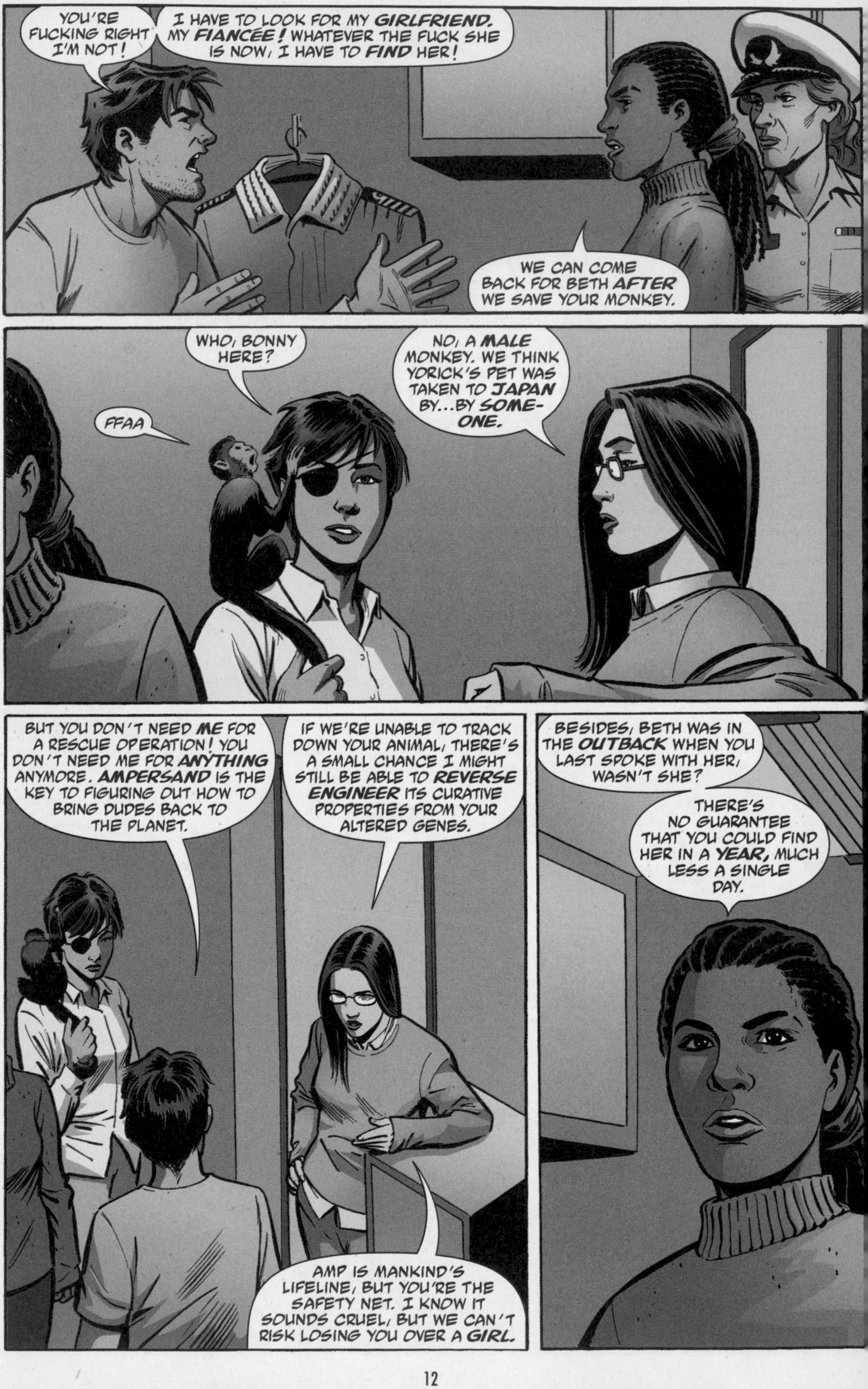
YOU'RE FUCKING RIGHT I'M NOT!
I HAVE TO LOOK FOR MY GIRLFRIEND. MY FIANCÉE! WHATEVER THE FUCK SHE IS NOW, I HAVE TO FIND HER!
WE CAN COME BACK FOR BETH AFTER WE SAVE YOUR MONKEY.
WHO, BONNY HERE?
FFAA
NO, A MALE MONKEY. WE THINK YORICK'S PET WAS TAKEN TO JAPAN BY...BY SOME-ONE.
BUT YOU DON'T NEED ME FOR A RESCUE OPERATION! YOU DON'T NEED ME FOR ANYTHING ANYMORE. AMPERSAND IS THE KEY TO FIGURING OUT HOW TO BRING DUDES BACK TO THE PLANET.
IF WE'RE UNABLE TO TRACK DOWN YOUR ANIMAL, THERE'S A SMALL CHANCE I MIGHT STILL BE ABLE TO REVERSE ENGINEER ITS CURATIVE PROPERTIES FROM YOUR ALTERED GENES.
AMP IS MANKIND'S LIFELINE, BUT YOU'RE THE SAFETY NET. I KNOW IT SOUNDS CRUEL, BUT WE CAN'T RISK LOSING YOU OVER A GIRL.
BESIDES, BETH WAS IN THE OUTBACK WHEN YOU LAST SPOKE WITH HER, WASN'T SHE?
THERE'S NO GUARANTEE THAT YOU COULD FIND HER IN A YEAR, MUCH LESS A SINGLE DAY.

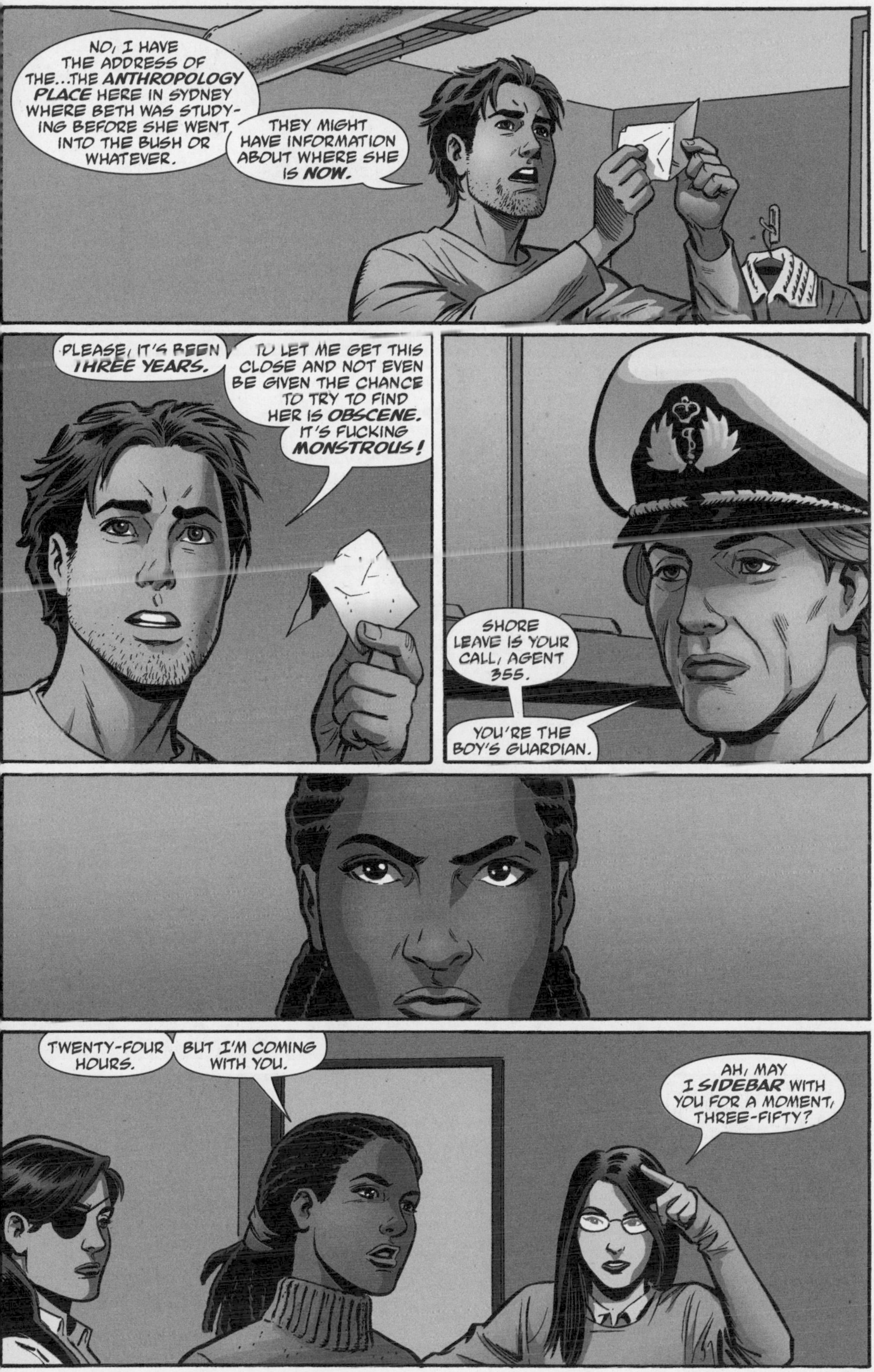
NO, I HAVE THE ADDRESS OF THE...THE ANTHROPOLOGY PLACE HERE IN SYDNEY WHERE BETH WAS STUDYING BEFORE SHE WENT INTO THE BUSH OR WHATEVER.
THEY MIGHT HAVE INFORMATION ABOUT WHERE SHE IS NOW.
PLEASE, IT'S BEEN THREE YEARS.
TO LET ME GET THIS CLOSE AND NOT EVEN BE GIVEN THE CHANCE TO TRY TO FIND HER IS OBSCENE. IT'S FUCKING MONSTROUS!
SHORE LEAVE IS YOUR CALL, AGENT 355.
YOU'RE THE BOY'S GUARDIAN.
TWENTY-FOUR HOURS.
BUT I'M COMING WITH YOU.
AH, MAY I SIDEBAR WITH YOU FOR A MOMENT, THREE-FIFTY?

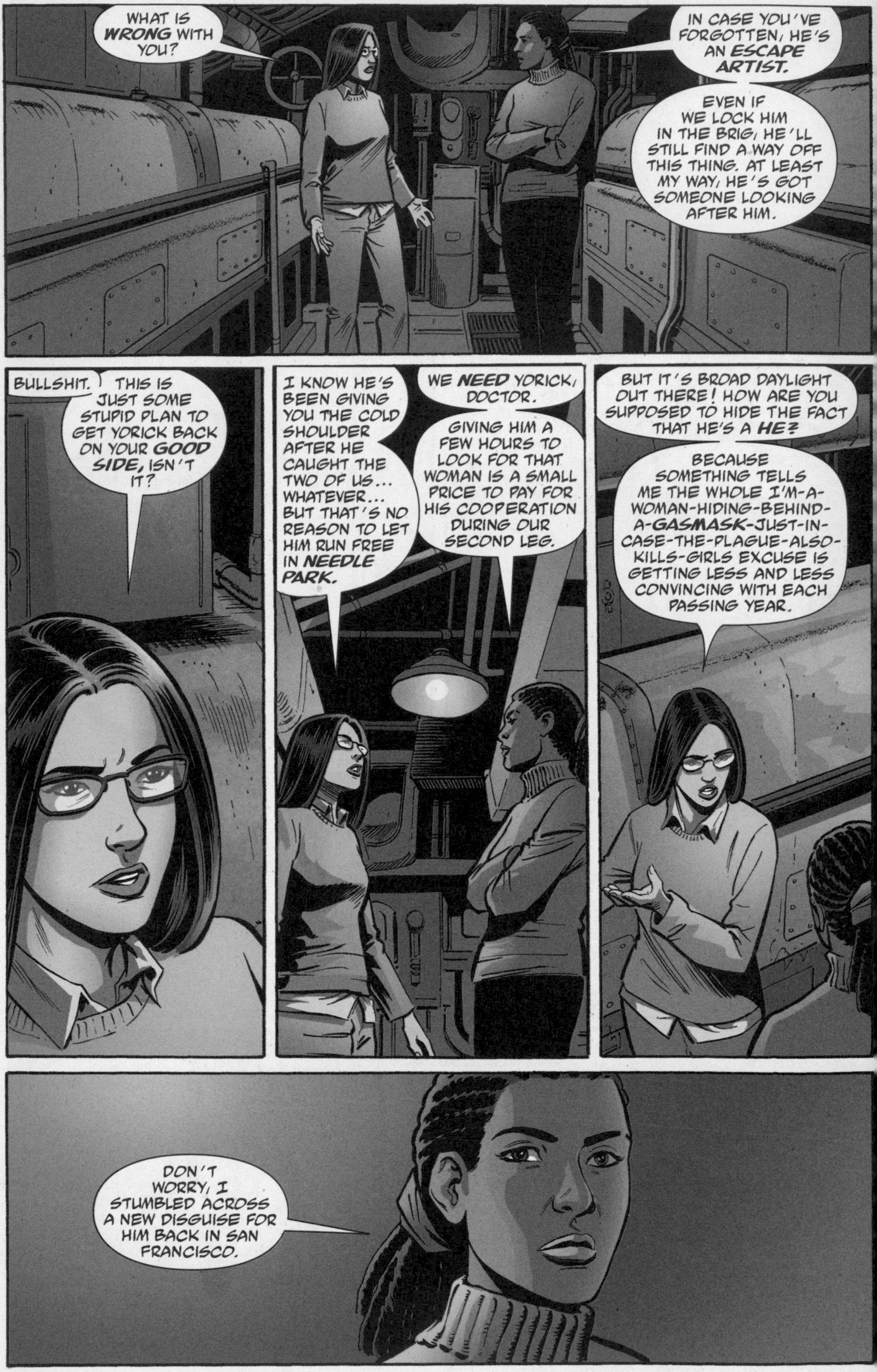

WHAT IS WRONG WITH YOU?
IN CASE YOU'VE FORGOTTEN, HE'S AN ESCAPE ARTIST.
EVEN IF WE LOCK HIM IN THE BRIG, HE'LL STILL FIND A WAY OFF THIS THING. AT LEAST MY WAY, HE'S GOT SOMEONE LOOKING AFTER HIM.
BULLSHIT.
THIS IS JUST SOME STUPID PLAN TO GET YORICK BACK ON YOUR GOOD SIDE, ISN'T IT?
WE NEED YORICK, DOCTOR.
GIVING HIM A FEW HOURS TO LOOK FOR THAT WOMAN IS A SMALL PRICE TO PAY FOR HIS COOPERATION DURING OUR SECOND LEG.
I KNOW HE'S BEEN GIVING YOU THE COLD SHOULDER AFTER HE CAUGHT THE TWO OF US... WHATEVER... BUT THAT'S NO REASON TO LET HIM RUN FREE IN NEEDLE PARK.
BUT IT'S BROAD DAYLIGHT OUT THERE! HOW ARE YOU SUPPOSED TO HIDE THE FACT THAT HE'S A HE?
BECAUSE SOMETHING TELLS ME THE WHOLE I'M-A-WOMAN-HIDING-BEHIND-A-GASMASK-JUST-IN-CASE-THE-PLAGUE-ALSO-KILLS-GIRLS EXCUSE IS GETTING LESS AND LESS CONVINCING WITH EACH PASSING YEAR.
DON'T WORRY, I STUMBLED ACROSS A NEW DISGUISE FOR HIM BACK IN SAN FRANCISCO.

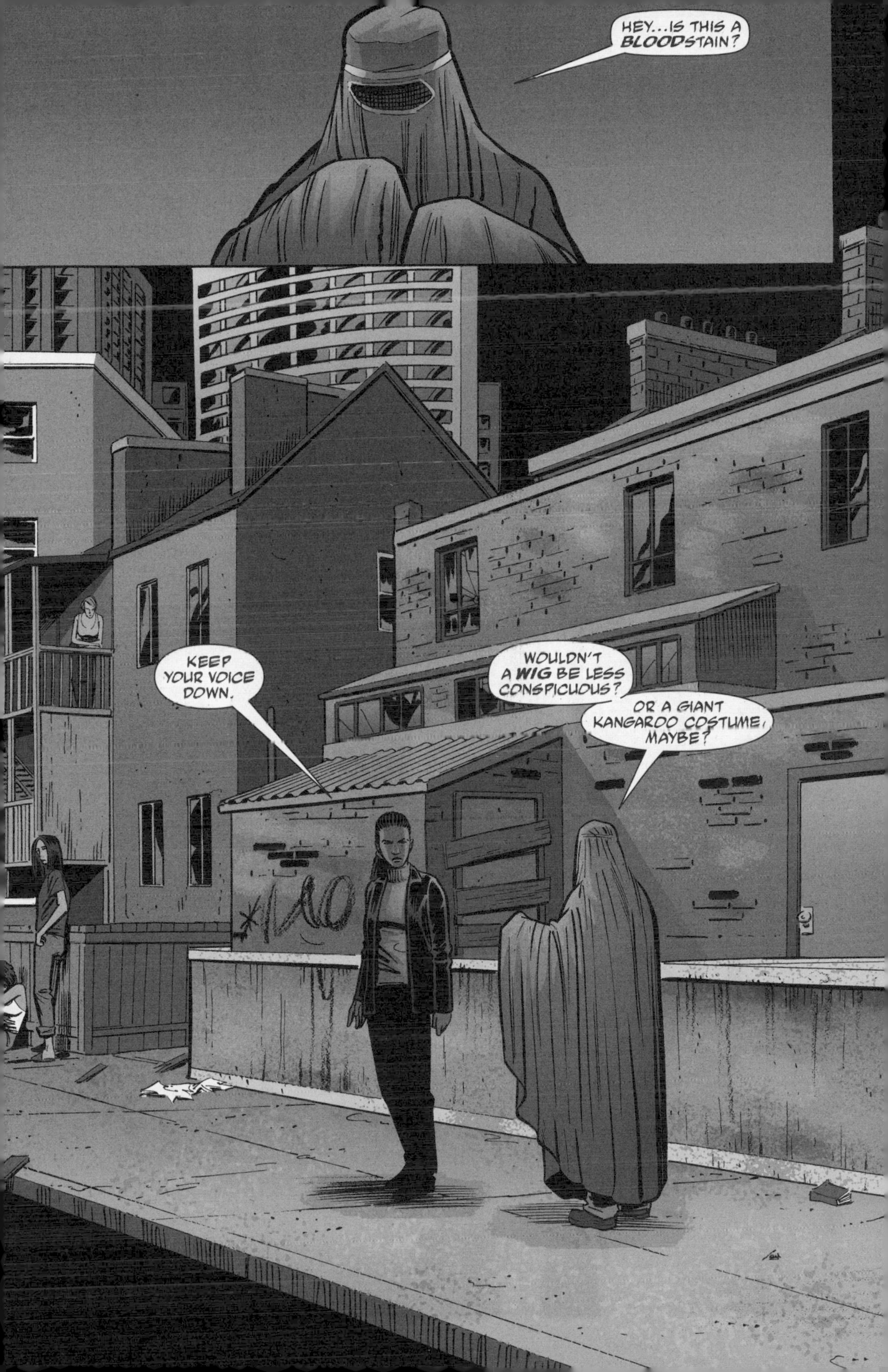
HEY...IS THIS A BLOODSTAIN?
KEEP YOUR VOICE DOWN.
WOULDN'T A WIG BE LESS CONSPICUOUS?
OR A GIANT KANGAROO COSTUME, MAYBE?

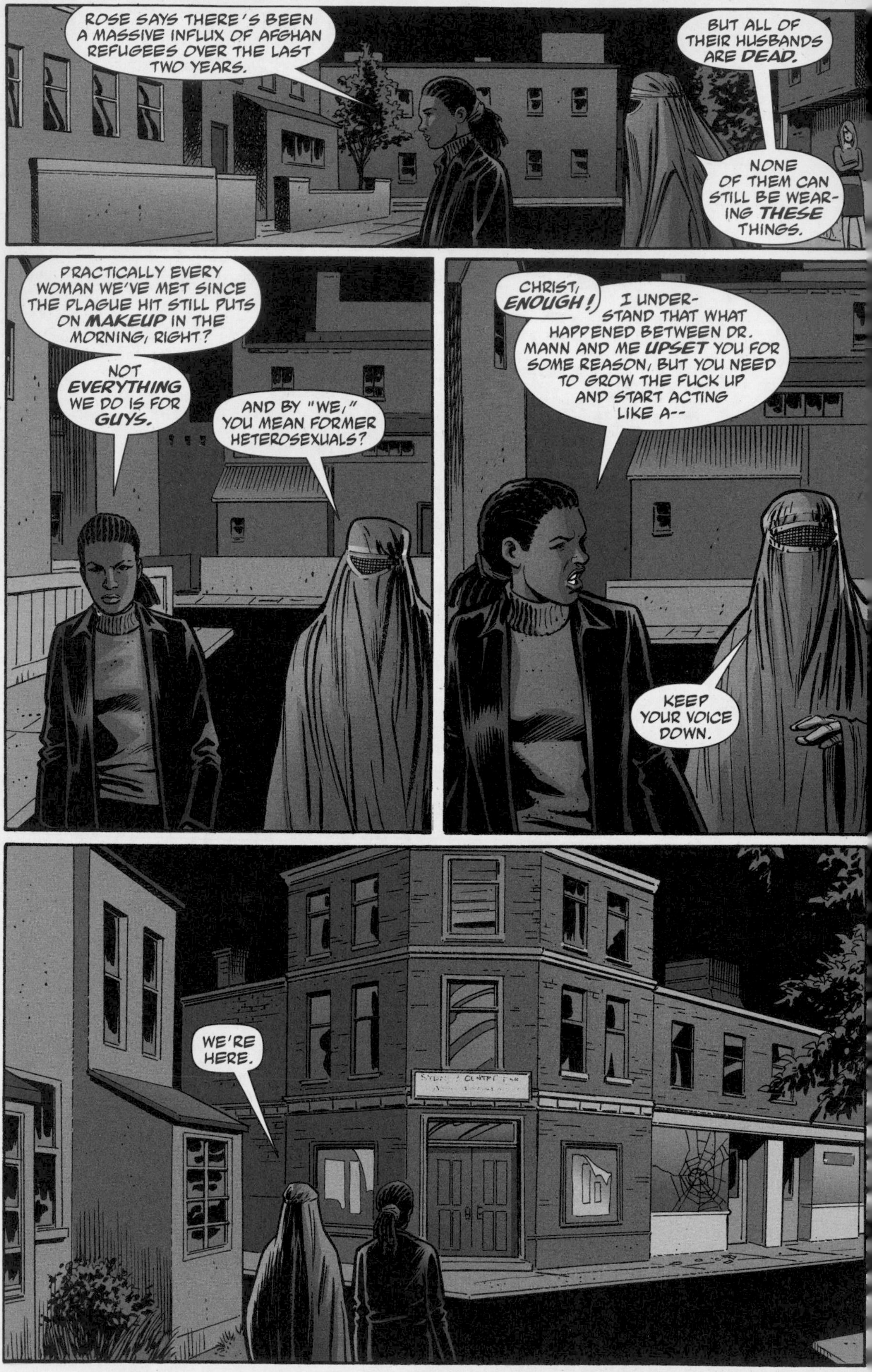
ROSE SAYS THERE'S BEEN A MASSIVE INFLUX OF AFGHAN REFUGEES OVER THE LAST TWO YEARS.
BUT ALL OF THEIR HUSBANDS ARE DEAD.
NONE OF THEM CAN STILL BE WEARING THESE THINGS.
PRACTICALLY EVERY WOMAN WE'VE MET SINCE THE PLAGUE HIT STILL PUTS ON MAKEUP IN THE MORNING, RIGHT?
NOT EVERYTHING WE DO IS FOR GUYS.
AND BY "WE," YOU MEAN FORMER HETEROSEXUALS?
CHRIST, ENOUGH!
I UNDERSTAND THAT WHAT HAPPENED BETWEEN DR. MANN AND ME UPSET YOU FOR SOME REASON, BUT YOU NEED TO GROW THE FUCK UP AND START ACTING LIKE A--
KEEP YOUR VOICE DOWN.
WE'RE HERE.

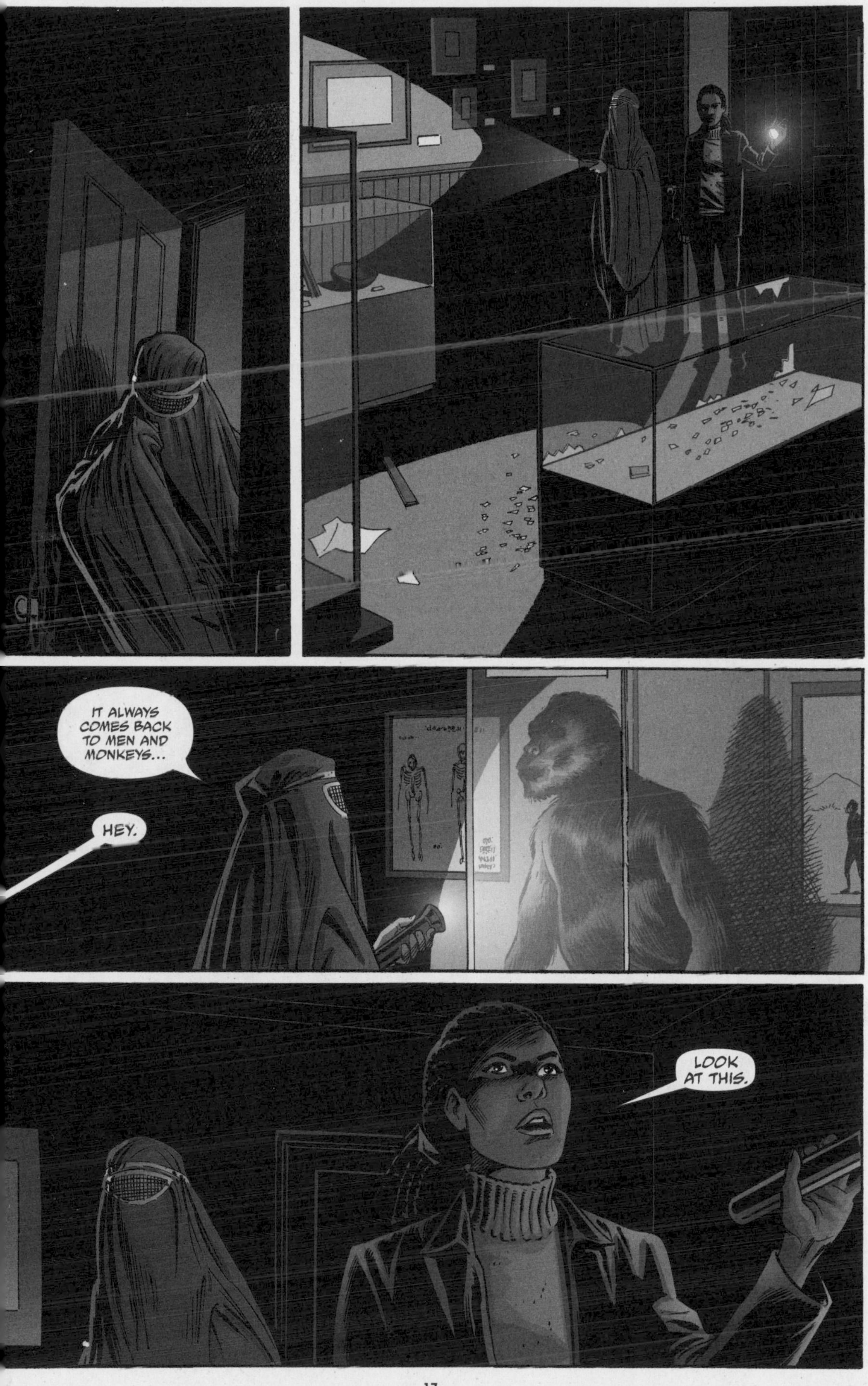
IT ALWAYS COMES BACK TO MEN AND MONKEYS...
HEY.
LOOK AT THIS.

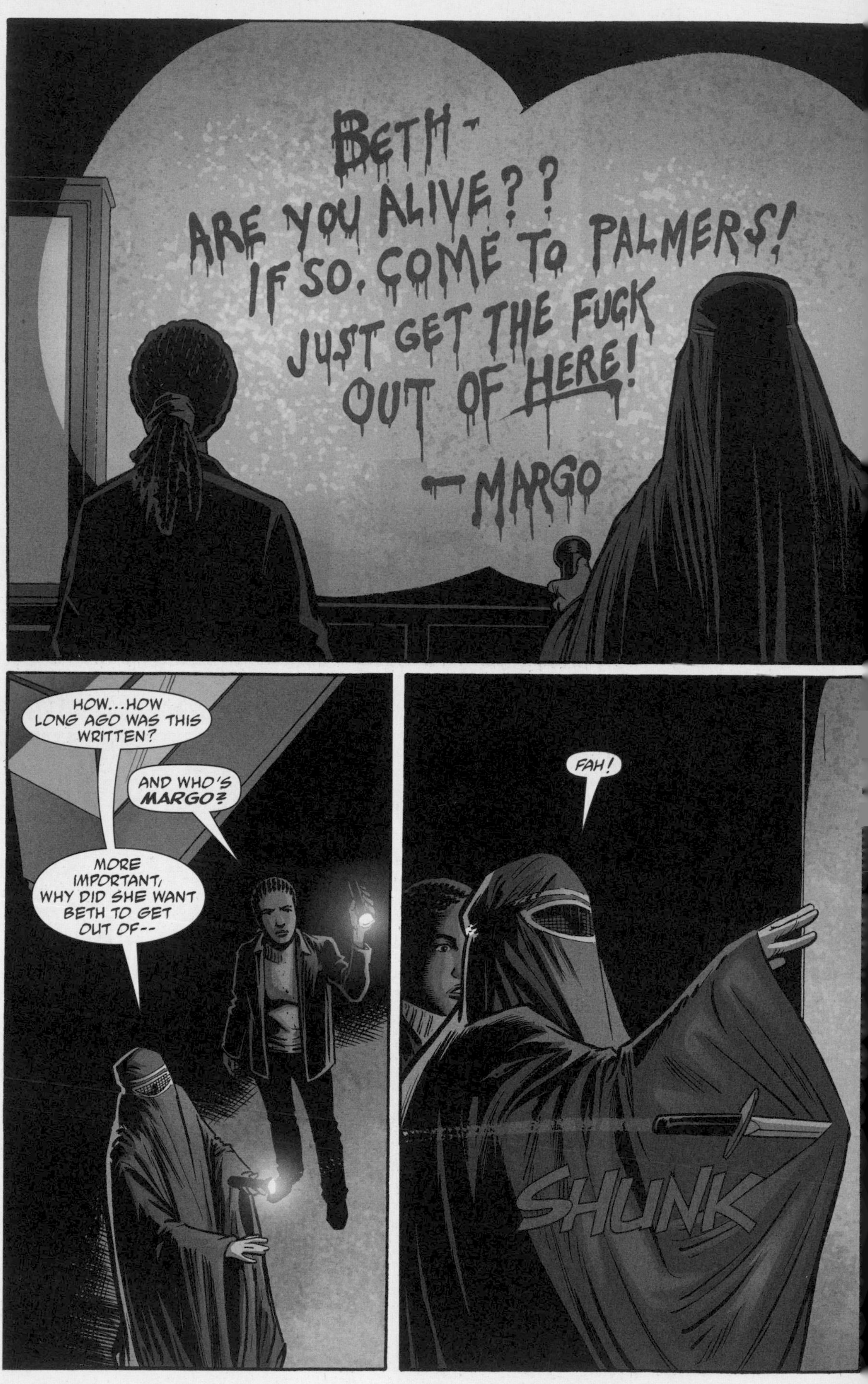
BETH -
ARE YOU ALIVE??
IF SO, COME TO PALMERS!
JUST GET THE FUCK
OUT OF HERE!
- MARGO
HOW...HOW LONG AGO WAS THIS WRITTEN?
AND WHO'S MARGO?
MORE IMPORTANT, WHY DID SHE WANT BETH TO GET OUT OF--
FAH!
SHUNK

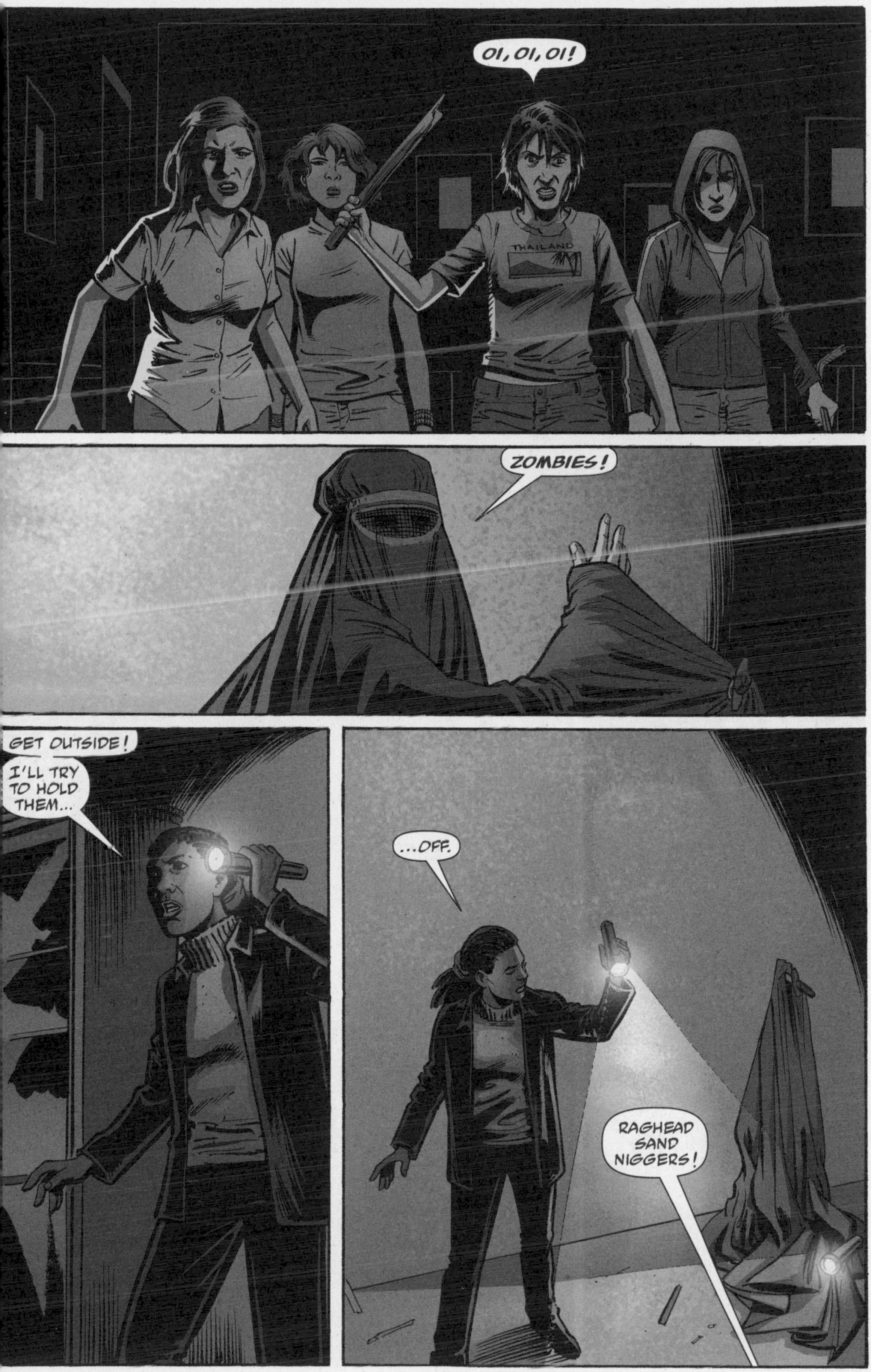
OI, OI, OI!
ZOMBIES!
GET OUTSIDE! I'LL TRY TO HOLD THEM...
...OFF.
RAGHEAD SAND NIGGERS!

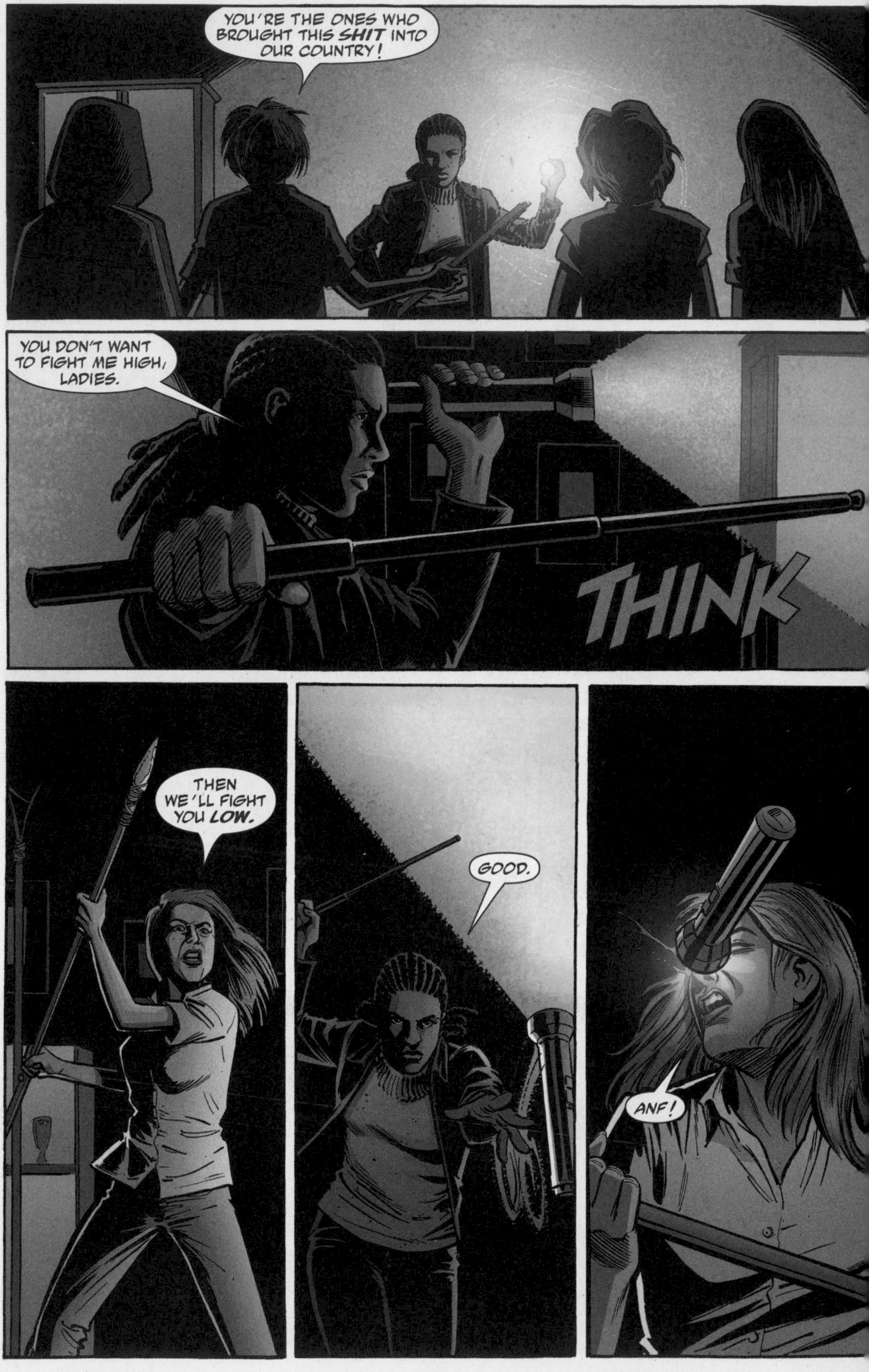
YOU'RE THE ONES WHO BROUGHT THIS SHIT INTO OUR COUNTRY!
YOU DON'T WANT TO FIGHT ME HIGH, LADIES.
THINK
THEN WE'LL FIGHT YOU LOW.
GOOD.
ANF!

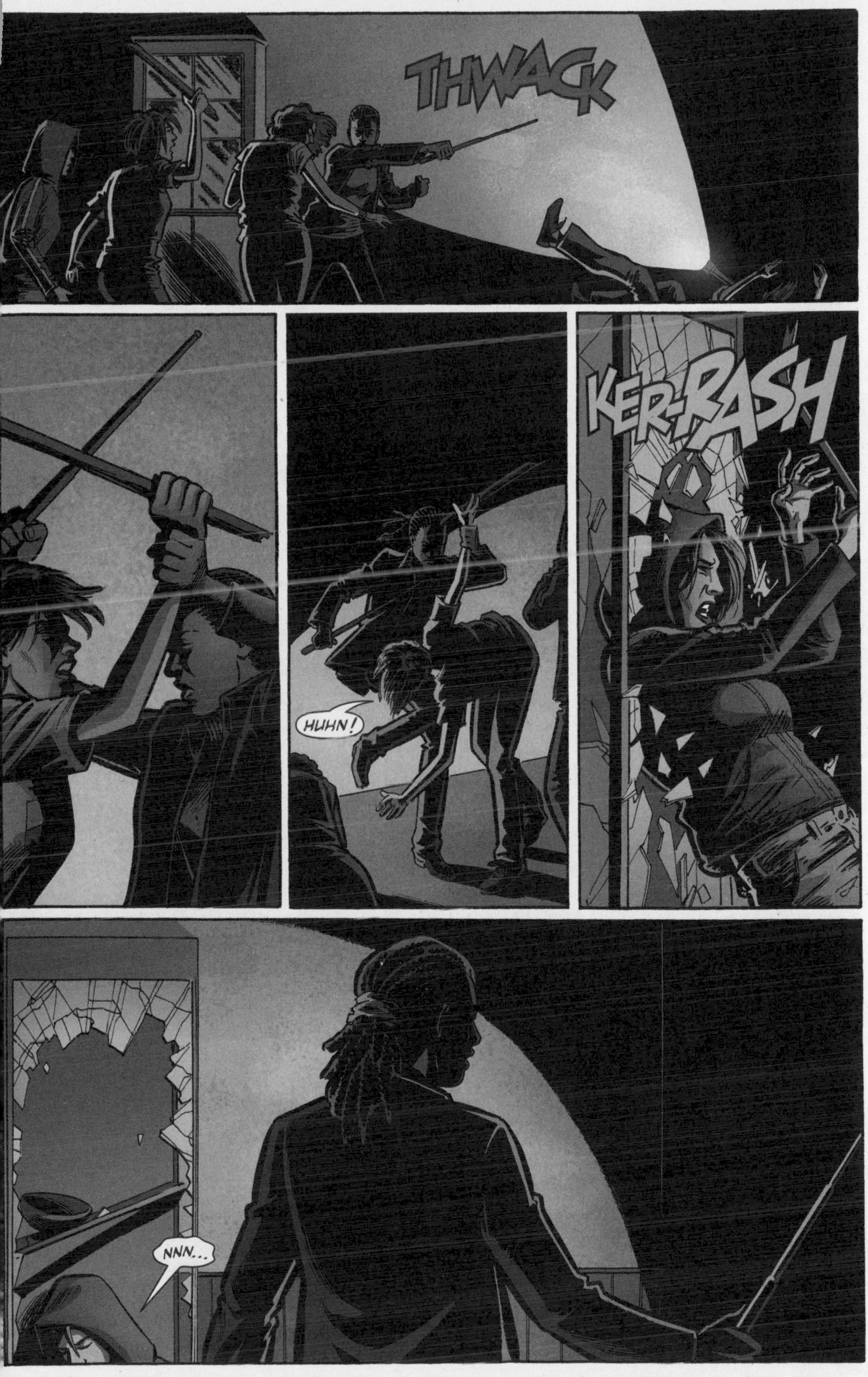
THWACK
HUHN!
KER-RASH
NNN...

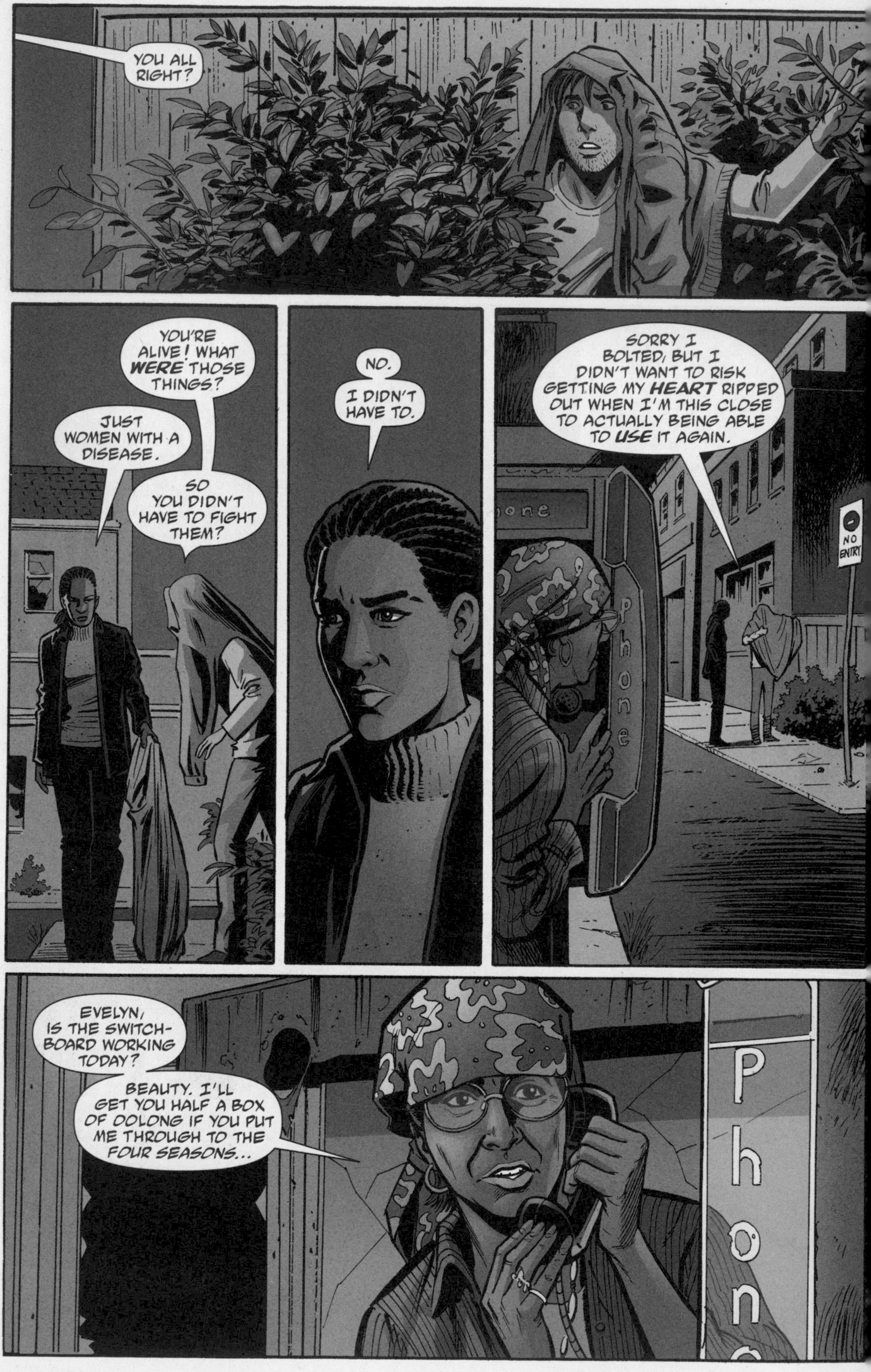
YOU ALL RIGHT?
YOU'RE ALIVE! WHAT WERE THOSE THINGS?
JUST WOMEN WITH A DISEASE.
SO YOU DIDN'T HAVE TO FIGHT THEM?
NO.
I DIDN'T HAVE TO.
SORRY I BOLTED, BUT I DIDN'T WANT TO RISK GETTING MY HEART RIPPED OUT WHEN I'M THIS CLOSE TO ACTUALLY BEING ABLE TO USE IT AGAIN.
NO ENTRY
phone
EVELYN, IS THE SWITCH-BOARD WORKING TODAY?
BEAUTY. I'LL GET YOU HALF A BOX OF OOLONG IF YOU PUT ME THROUGH TO THE FOUR SEASONS...

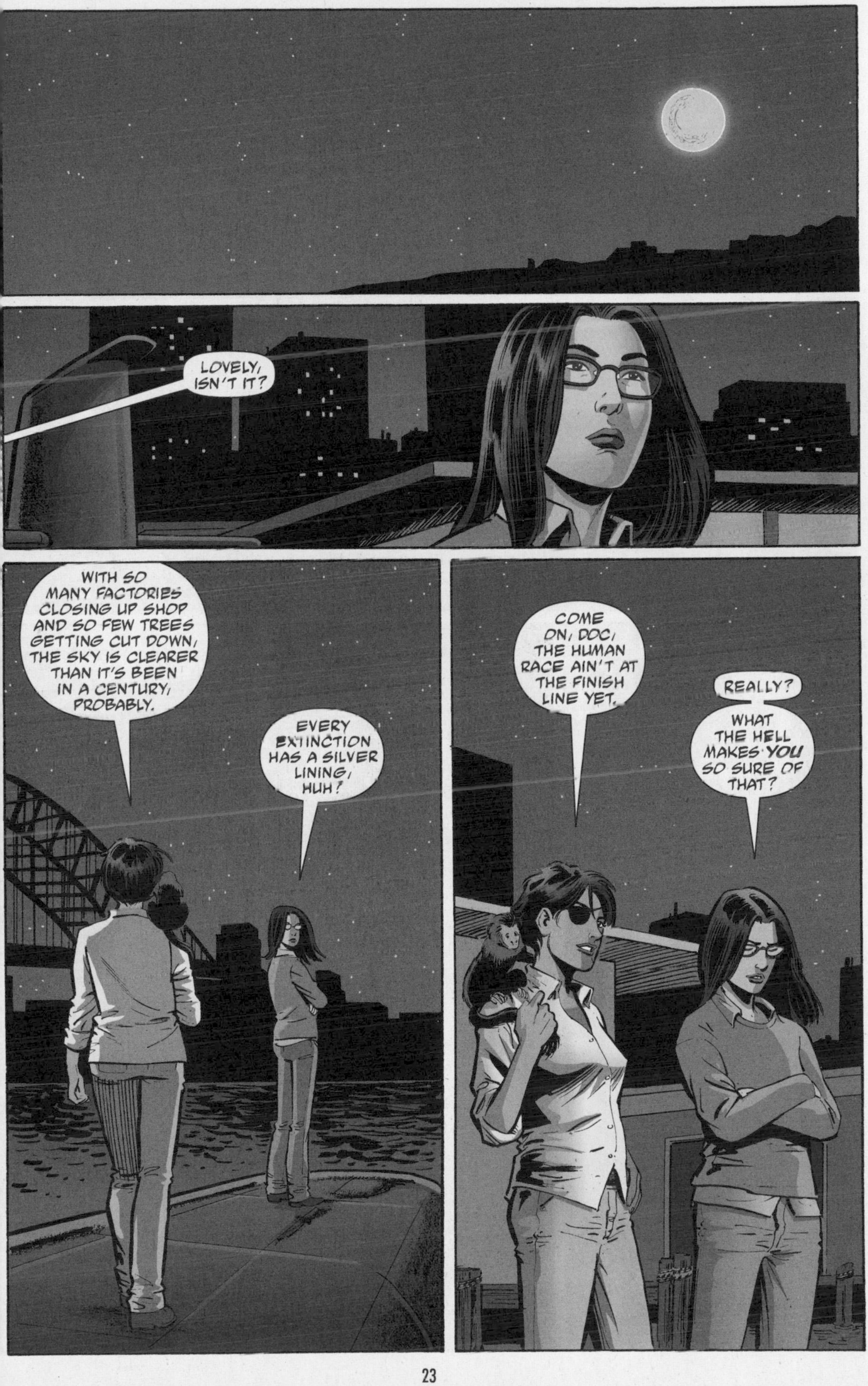
LOVELY, ISN'T IT?
WITH SO MANY FACTORIES CLOSING UP SHOP AND SO FEW TREES GETTING CUT DOWN, THE SKY IS CLEARER THAN IT'S BEEN IN A CENTURY, PROBABLY.
EVERY EXTINCTION HAS A SILVER LINING, HUH?
COME ON, DOC, THE HUMAN RACE AIN'T AT THE FINISH LINE YET.
REALLY?
WHAT THE HELL MAKES YOU SO SURE OF THAT?

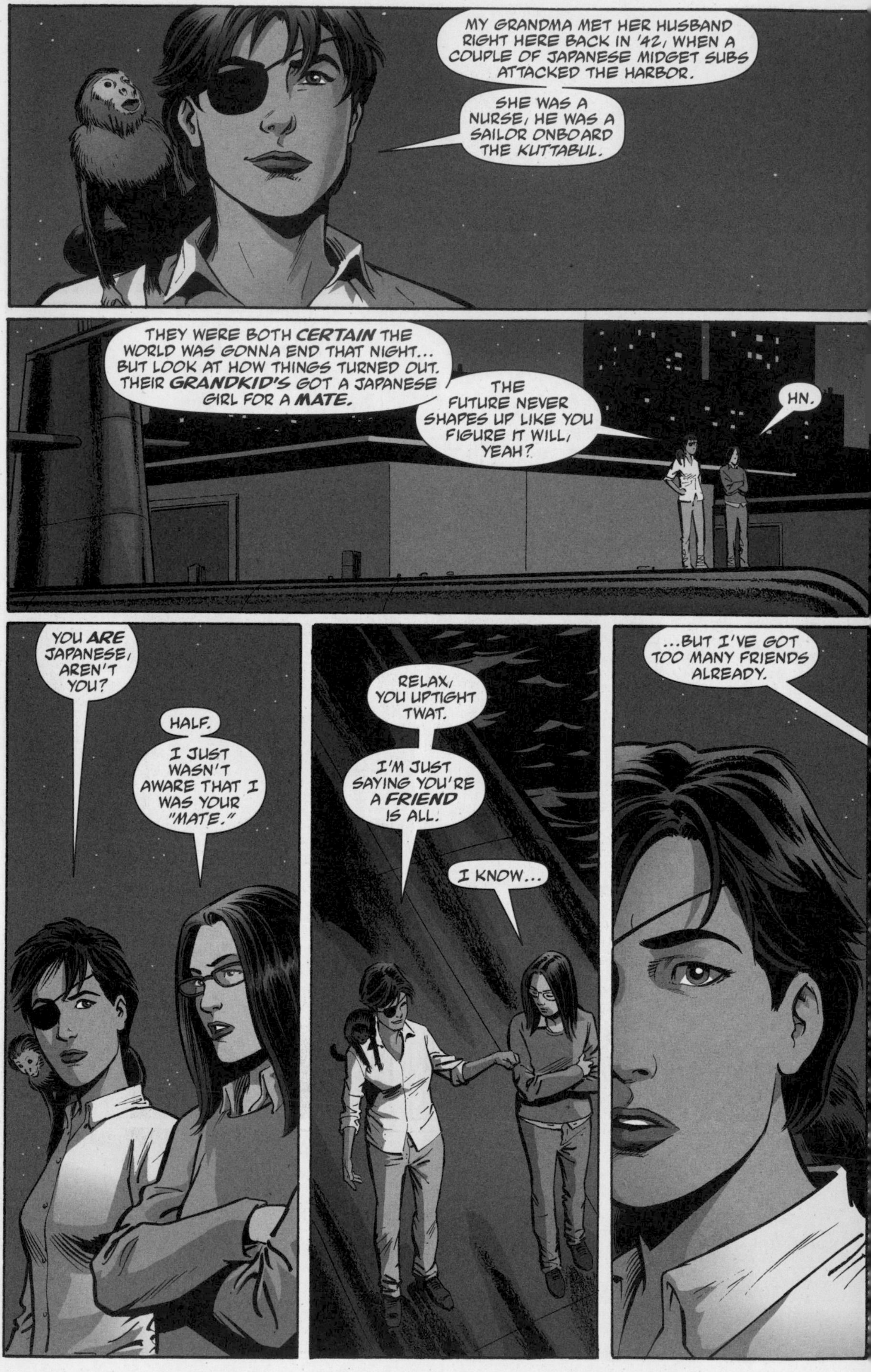
MY GRANDMA MET HER HUSBAND RIGHT HERE BACK IN '42, WHEN A COUPLE OF JAPANESE MIDGET SUBS ATTACKED THE HARBOR.
SHE WAS A NURSE, HE WAS A SAILOR ONBOARD THE KUTTABUL.
THEY WERE BOTH CERTAIN THE WORLD WAS GONNA END THAT NIGHT... BUT LOOK AT HOW THINGS TURNED OUT. THEIR GRANDKID'S GOT A JAPANESE GIRL FOR A MATE.
THE FUTURE NEVER SHAPES UP LIKE YOU FIGURE IT WILL, YEAH?
HN.
YOU ARE JAPANESE, AREN'T YOU?
HALF.
I JUST WASN'T AWARE THAT I WAS YOUR "MATE."
RELAX, YOU UPTIGHT TWAT.
I'M JUST SAYING YOU'RE A FRIEND IS ALL.
I KNOW...
...BUT I'VE GOT TOO MANY FRIENDS ALREADY.

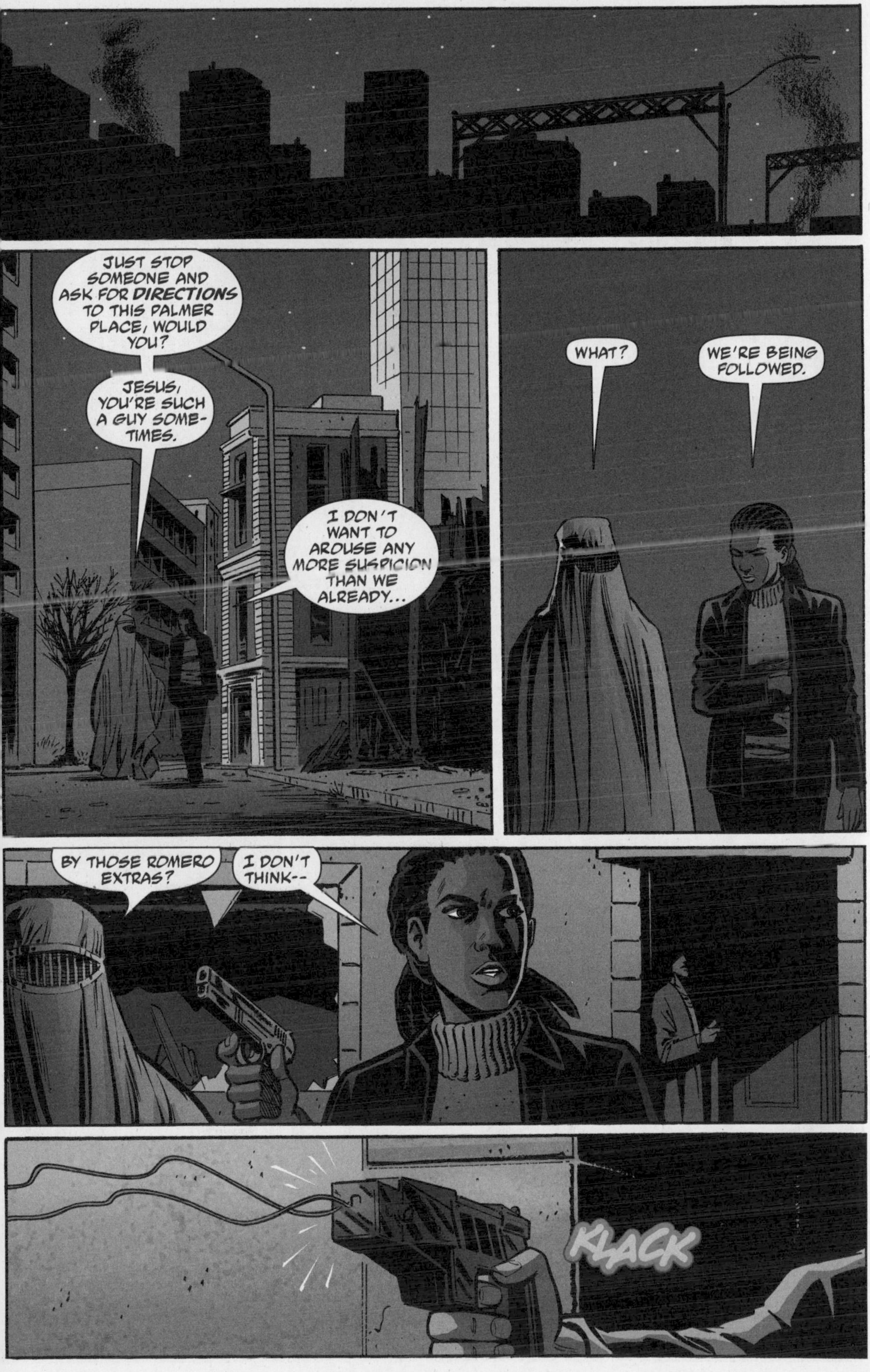
JUST STOP SOMEONE AND ASK FOR DIRECTIONS TO THIS PALMER PLACE, WOULD YOU?
JESUS, YOU'RE SUCH A GUY SOME-TIMES.
I DON'T WANT TO AROUSE ANY MORE SUSPICION THAN WE ALREADY...
WHAT?
WE'RE BEING FOLLOWED.
BY THOSE ROMERO EXTRAS?
I DON'T THINK--
KLACK

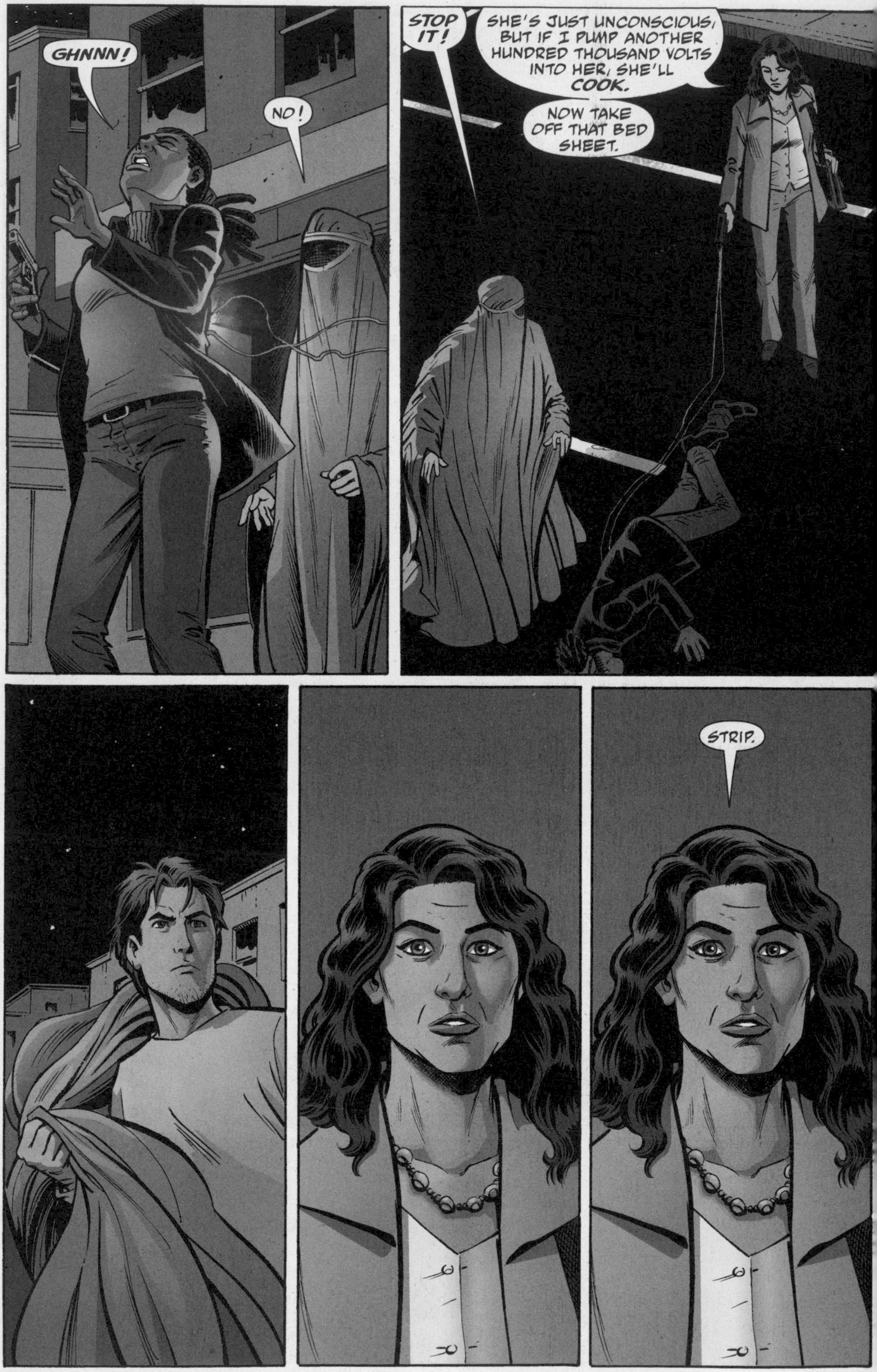
GHNNN!
NO!
STOP IT!
SHE'S JUST UNCONSCIOUS, BUT IF I PUMP ANOTHER HUNDRED THOUSAND VOLTS INTO HER, SHE'LL COOK.
NOW TAKE OFF THAT BED SHEET.
STRIP.

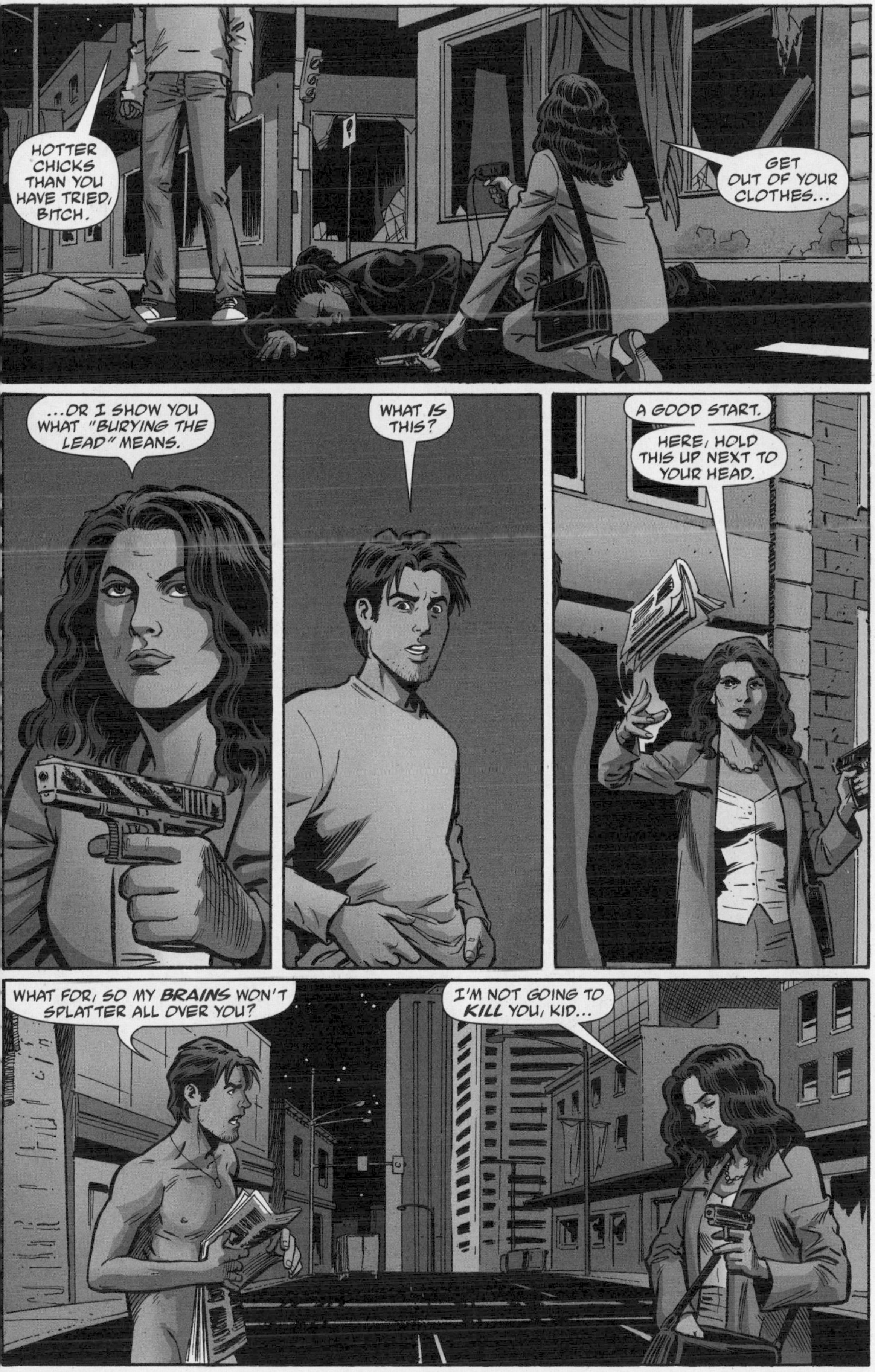

HOTTER CHICKS THAN YOU HAVE TRIED, BITCH.
GET OUT OF YOUR CLOTHES...
...OR I SHOW YOU WHAT "BURYING THE LEAD" MEANS.
WHAT IS THIS?
A GOOD START.
HERE, HOLD THIS UP NEXT TO YOUR HEAD.
WHAT FOR, SO MY BRAINS WON'T SPLATTER ALL OVER YOU?
I'M NOT GOING TO KILL YOU, KID...

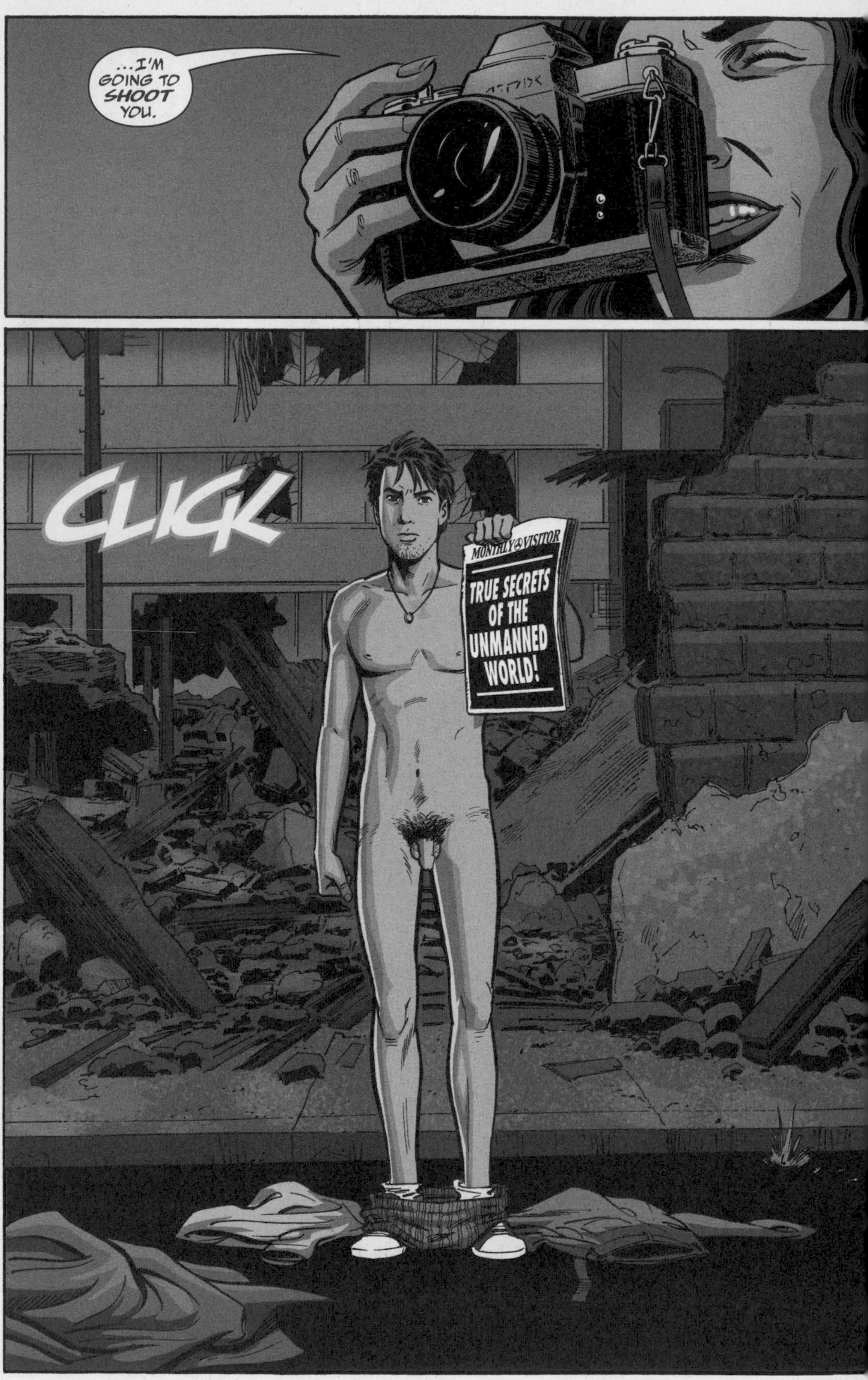
...I'M GOING TO SHOOT YOU.
CLICK
MONTHLY VISITOR
TRUE SECRETS OF THE UNMANNED WORLD!

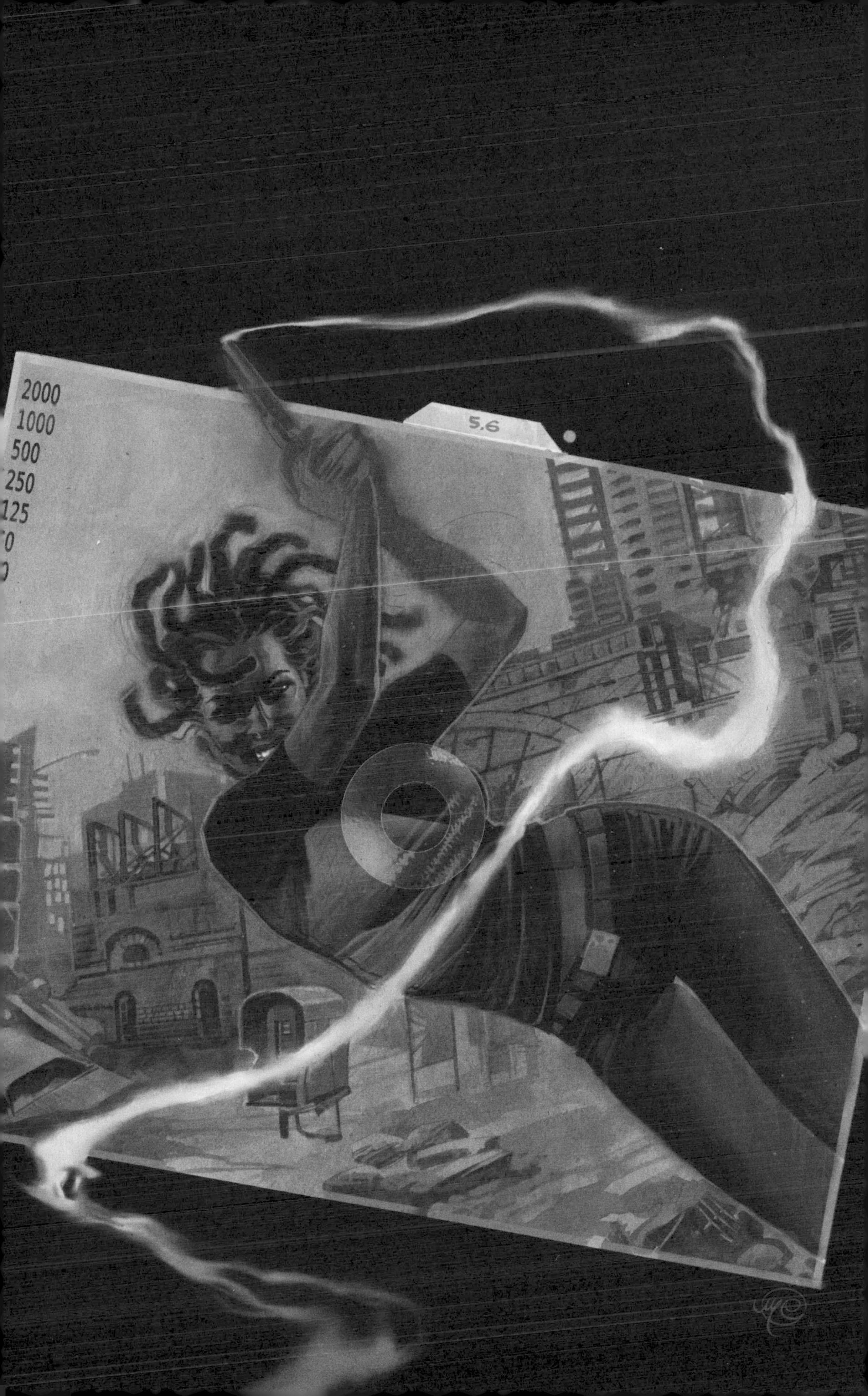
2000
1000
500
250
125
5.6

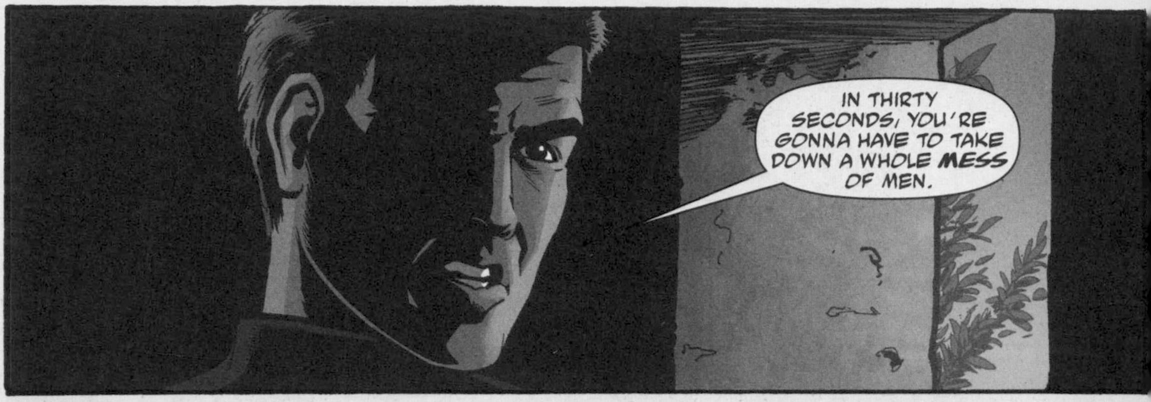
IN THIRTY SECONDS, YOU'RE GONNA HAVE TO TAKE DOWN A WHOLE MESS OF MEN.

Adis Ababa, Ethiopia
Thirteen Years Ago

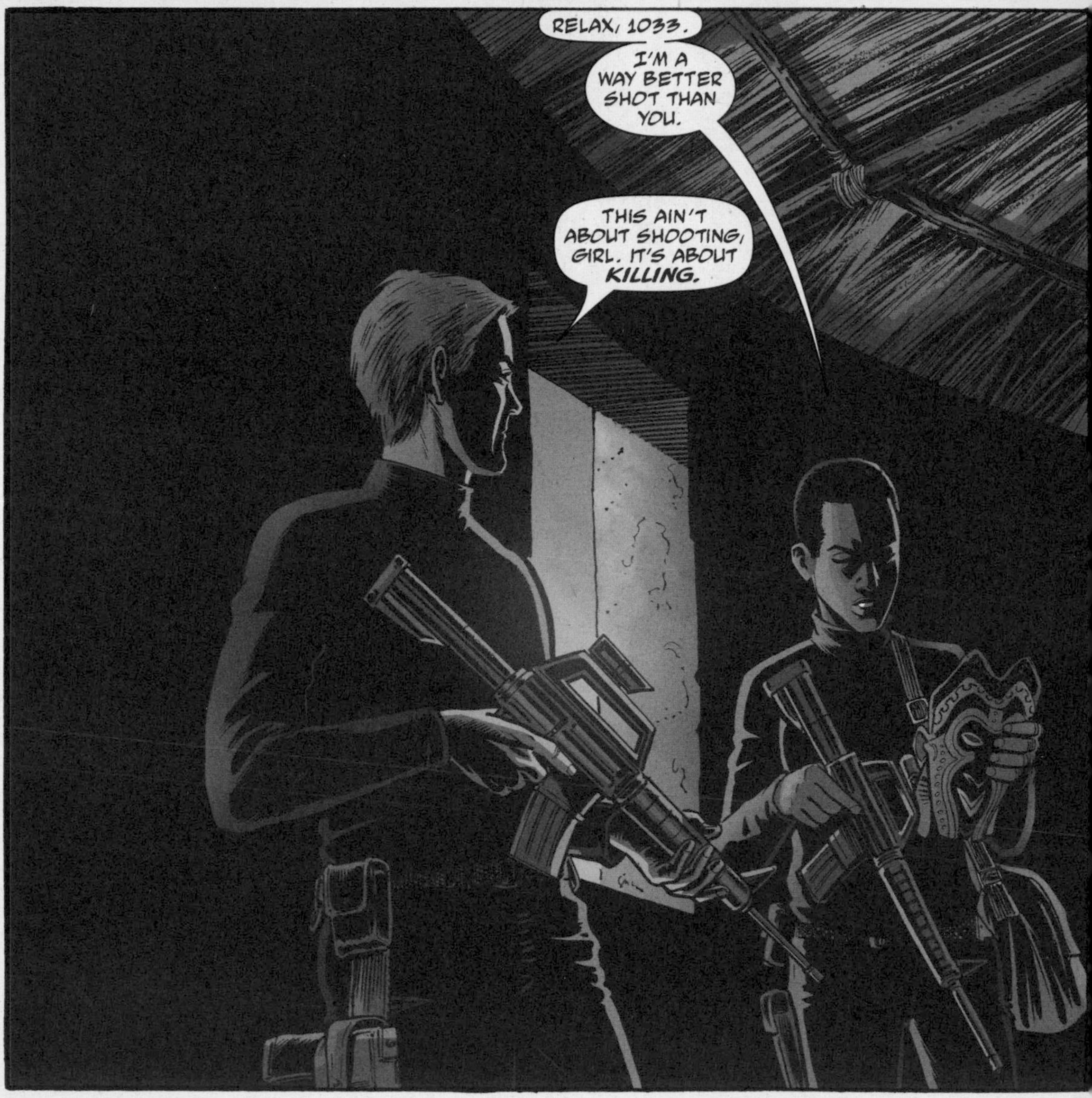
RELAX, 1033.
I'M A WAY BETTER SHOT THAN YOU.
THIS AIN'T ABOUT SHOOTING, GIRL. IT'S ABOUT KILLING.

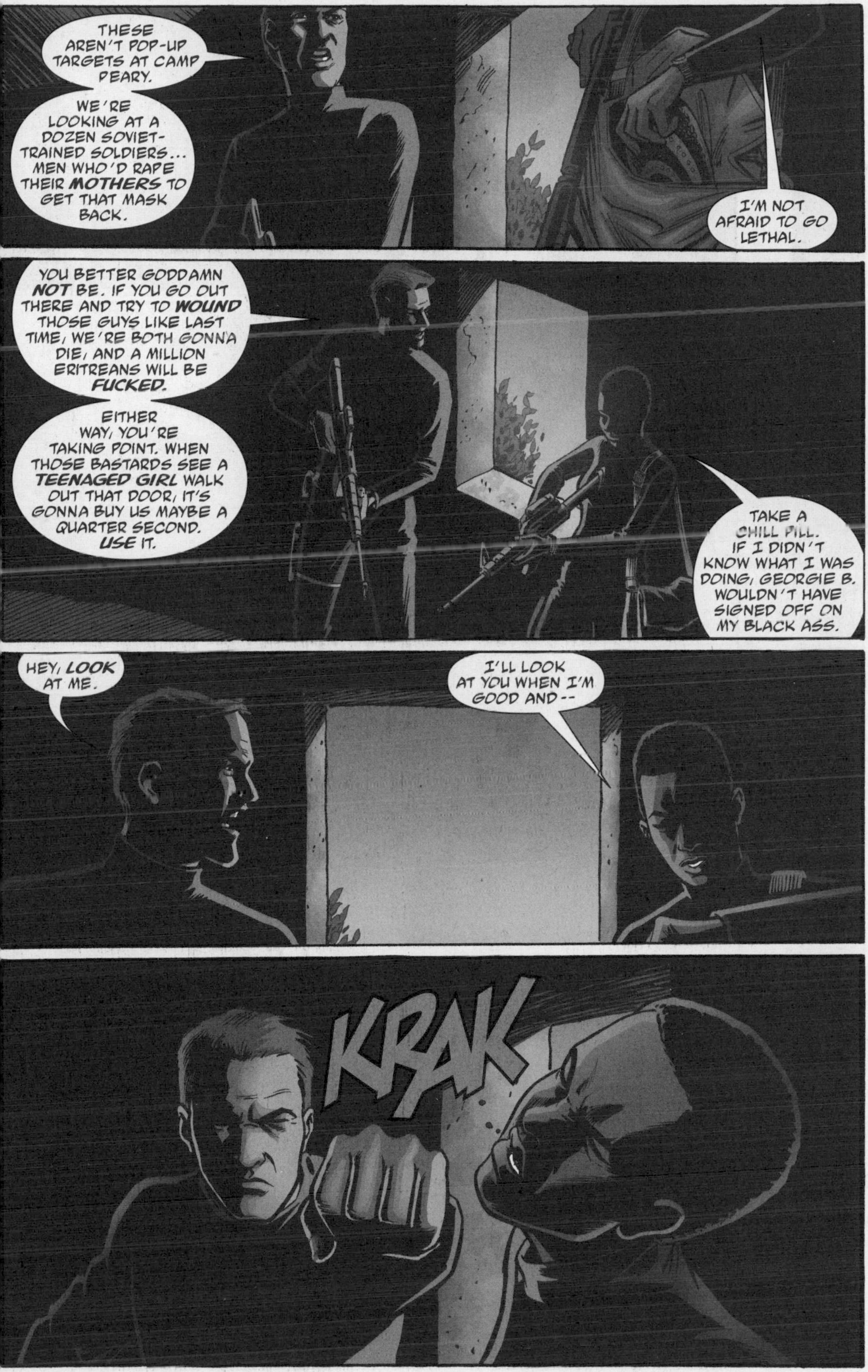
THESE AREN'T POP-UP TARGETS AT CAMP PEARY.
WE'RE LOOKING AT A DOZEN SOVIET-TRAINED SOLDIERS... MEN WHO'D RAPE THEIR **MOTHERS** TO GET THAT MASK BACK.
I'M NOT AFRAID TO GO LETHAL.
YOU BETTER GODDAMN **NOT** BE. IF YOU GO OUT THERE AND TRY TO **WOUND** THOSE GUYS LIKE LAST TIME, WE'RE BOTH GONNA DIE, AND A MILLION ERITREANS WILL BE **FUCKED.**
EITHER WAY, YOU'RE TAKING POINT. WHEN THOSE BASTARDS SEE A **TEENAGED GIRL** WALK OUT THAT DOOR, IT'S GONNA BUY US MAYBE A QUARTER SECOND. **USE** IT.
TAKE A CHILL PILL. IF I DIDN'T KNOW WHAT I WAS DOING, GEORGIE B. WOULDN'T HAVE SIGNED OFF ON MY BLACK ASS.
HEY, **LOOK** AT ME.
I'LL LOOK AT YOU WHEN I'M GOOD AND --
KRAK

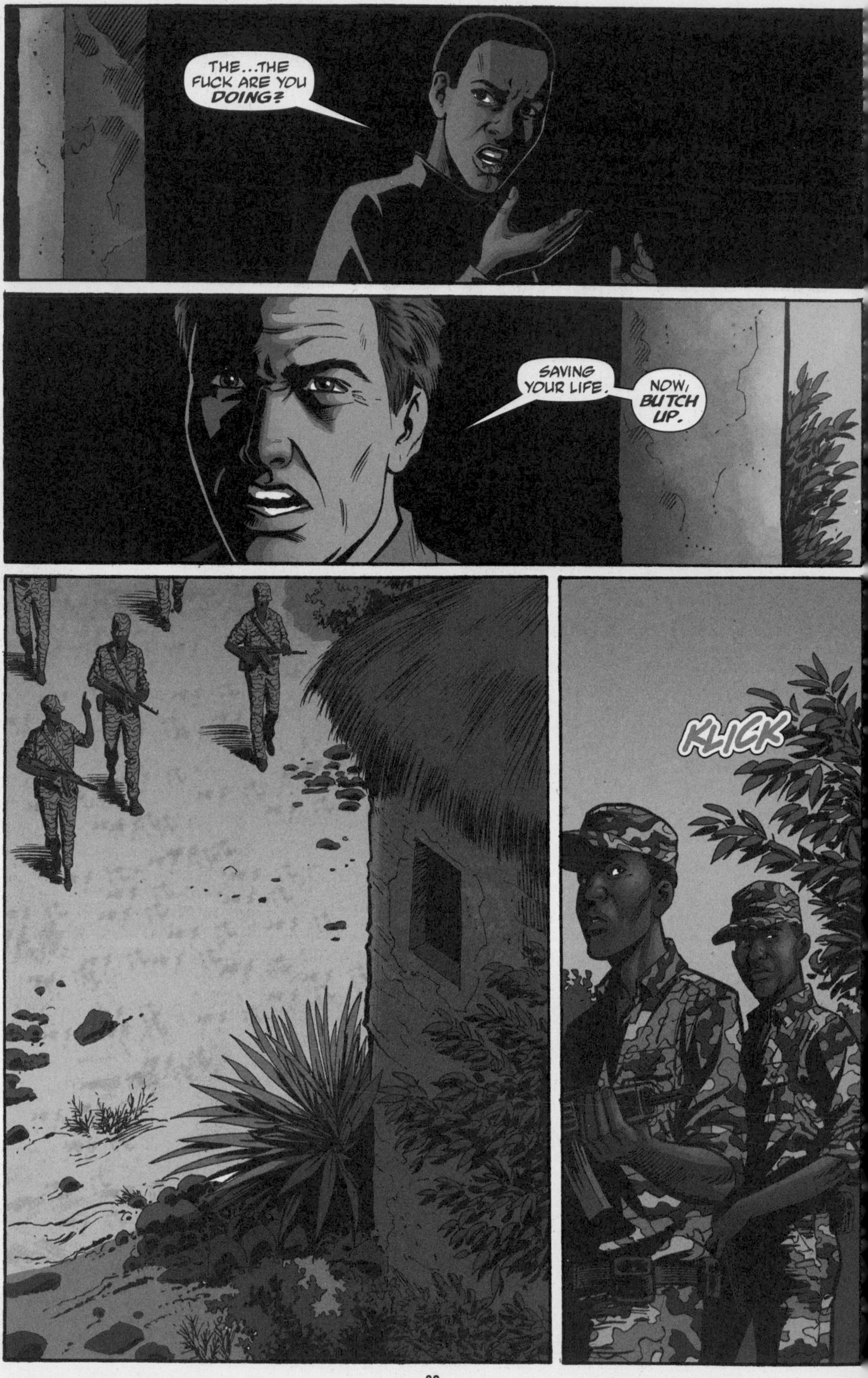
THE...THE FUCK ARE YOU DOING?
SAVING YOUR LIFE.
NOW, BUTCH UP.
KLICK

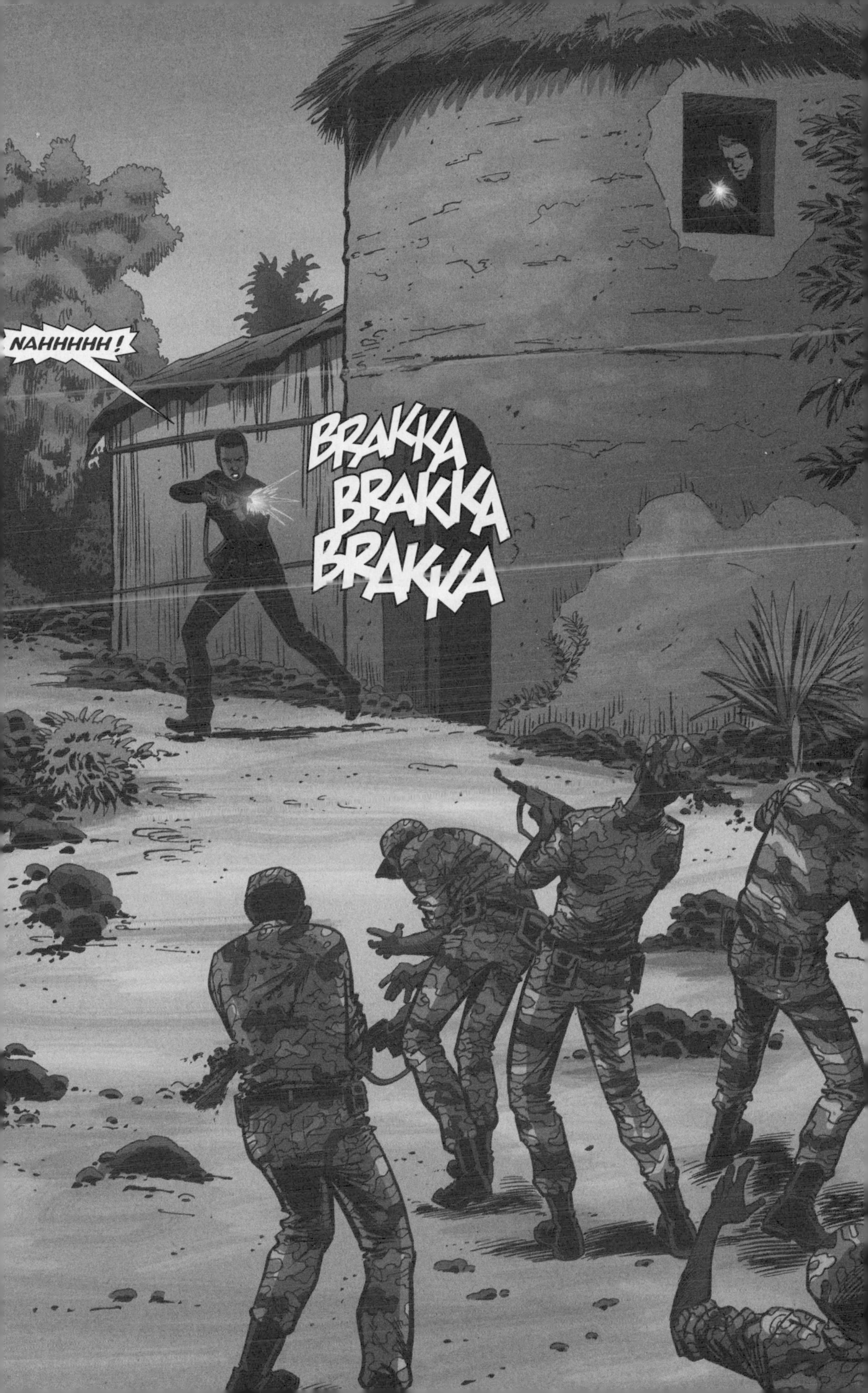
NAHHHHH!
BRAKKA
BRAKKA
BRAKKA

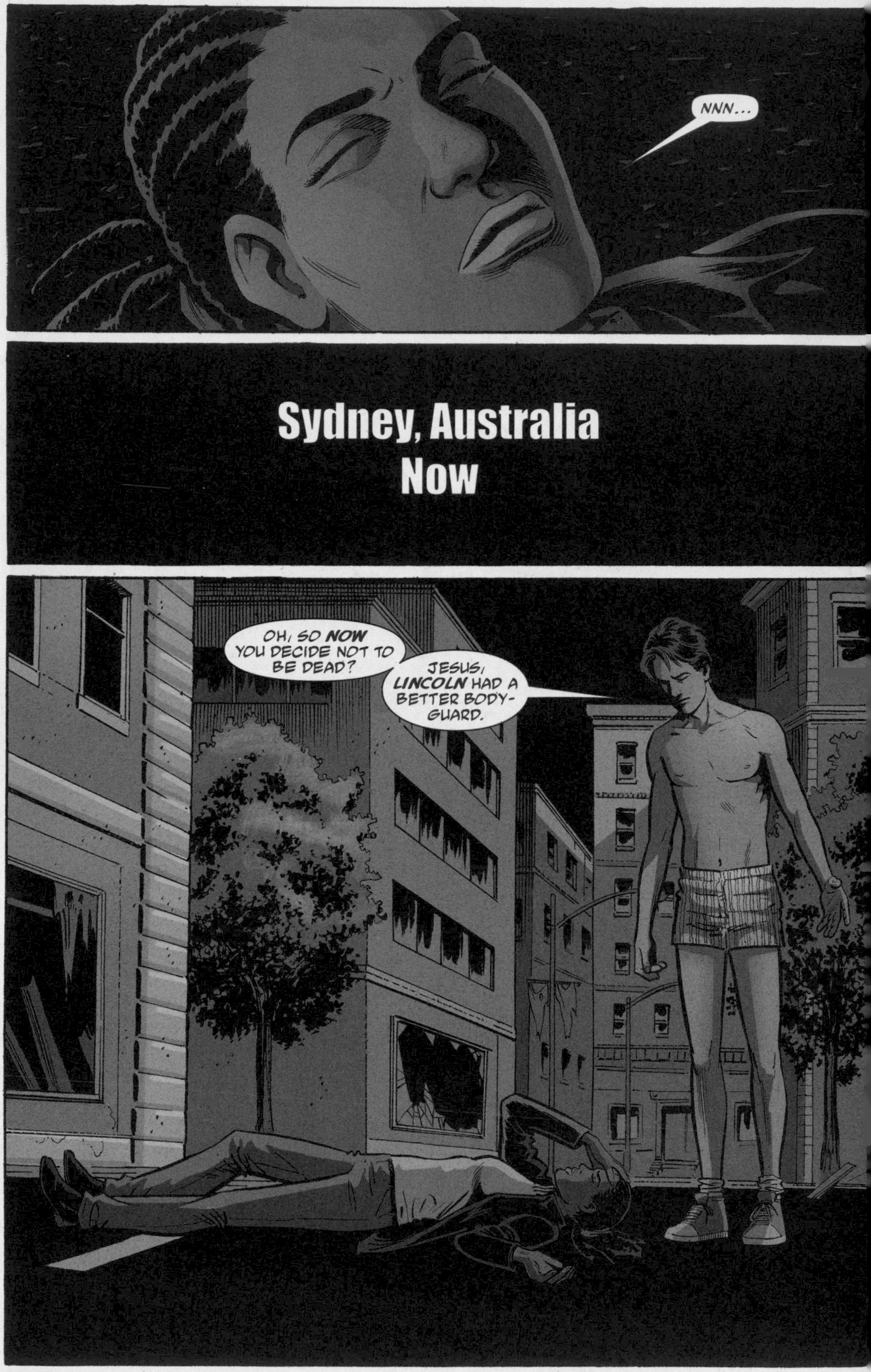
NNN...
Sydney, Australia
Now
OH, SO NOW YOU DECIDE NOT TO BE DEAD?
JESUS, LINCOLN HAD A BETTER BODY-GUARD.

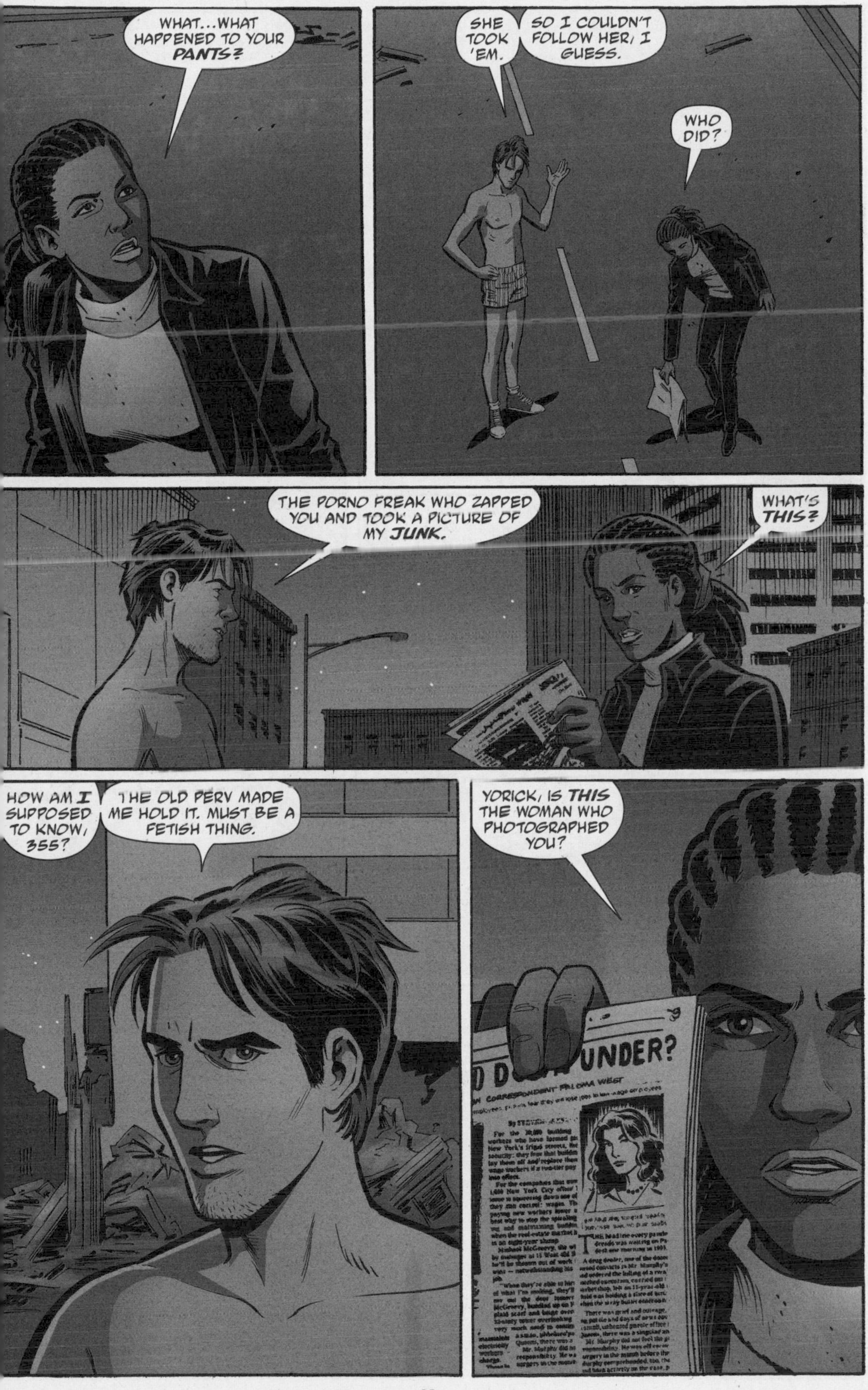
WHAT...WHAT HAPPENED TO YOUR PANTS?
SHE TOOK 'EM.
SO I COULDN'T FOLLOW HER, I GUESS.
WHO DID?
THE PORNO FREAK WHO ZAPPED YOU AND TOOK A PICTURE OF MY JUNK.
WHAT'S THIS?
HOW AM I SUPPOSED TO KNOW, 355?
THE OLD PERV MADE ME HOLD IT. MUST BE A FETISH THING.
YORICK, IS THIS THE WOMAN WHO PHOTOGRAPHED YOU?
UNDER?
CORRESPONDENT PALOMA WEST

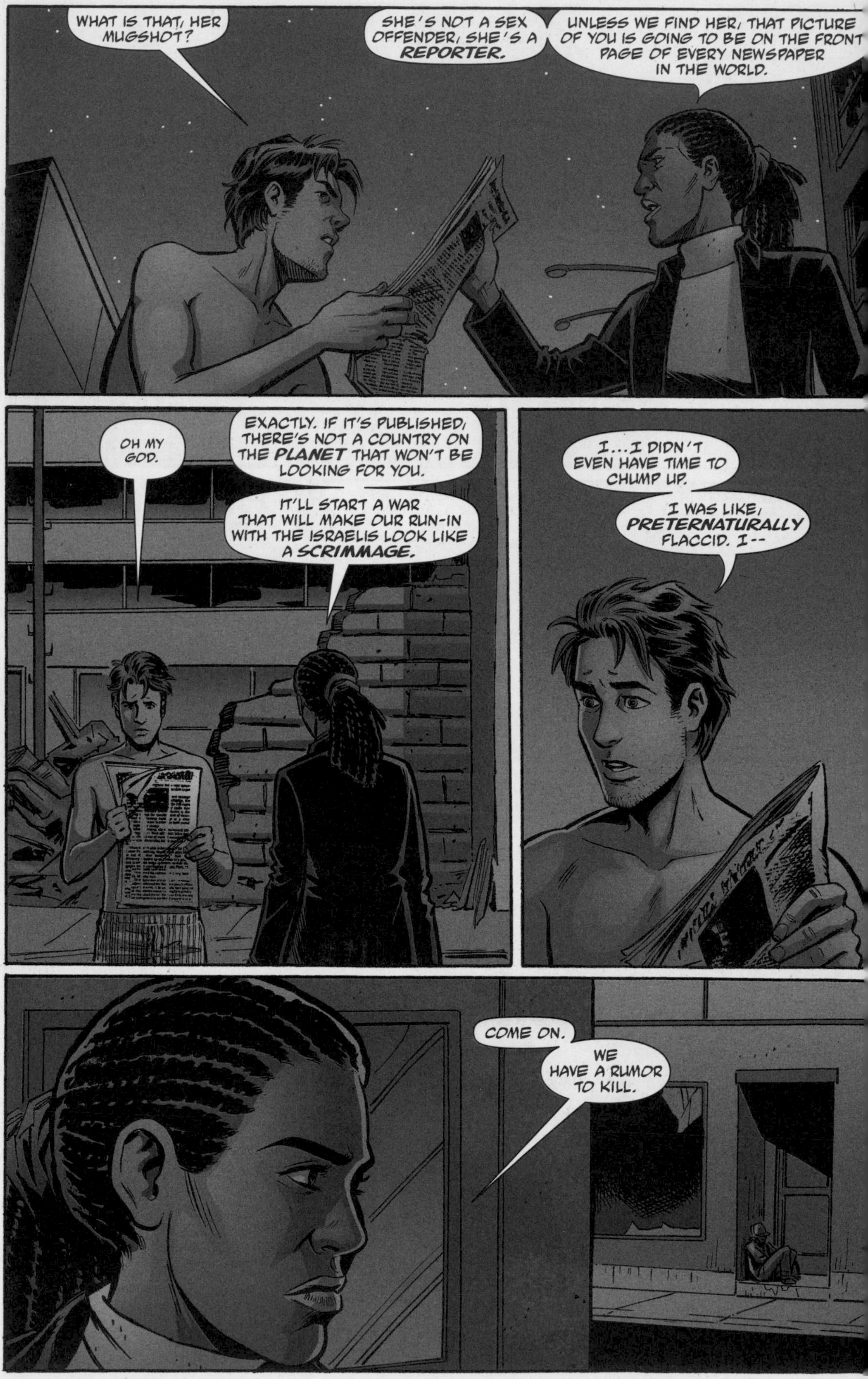
WHAT IS THAT, HER MUGSHOT?
SHE'S NOT A SEX OFFENDER, SHE'S A REPORTER.
UNLESS WE FIND HER, THAT PICTURE OF YOU IS GOING TO BE ON THE FRONT PAGE OF EVERY NEWSPAPER IN THE WORLD.
OH MY GOD.
EXACTLY. IF IT'S PUBLISHED, THERE'S NOT A COUNTRY ON THE PLANET THAT WON'T BE LOOKING FOR YOU.
IT'LL START A WAR THAT WILL MAKE OUR RUN-IN WITH THE ISRAELIS LOOK LIKE A SCRIMMAGE.
I... I DIDN'T EVEN HAVE TIME TO CHUMP UP.
I WAS LIKE, PRETERNATURALLY FLACCID. I--
COME ON.
WE HAVE A RUMOR TO KILL.

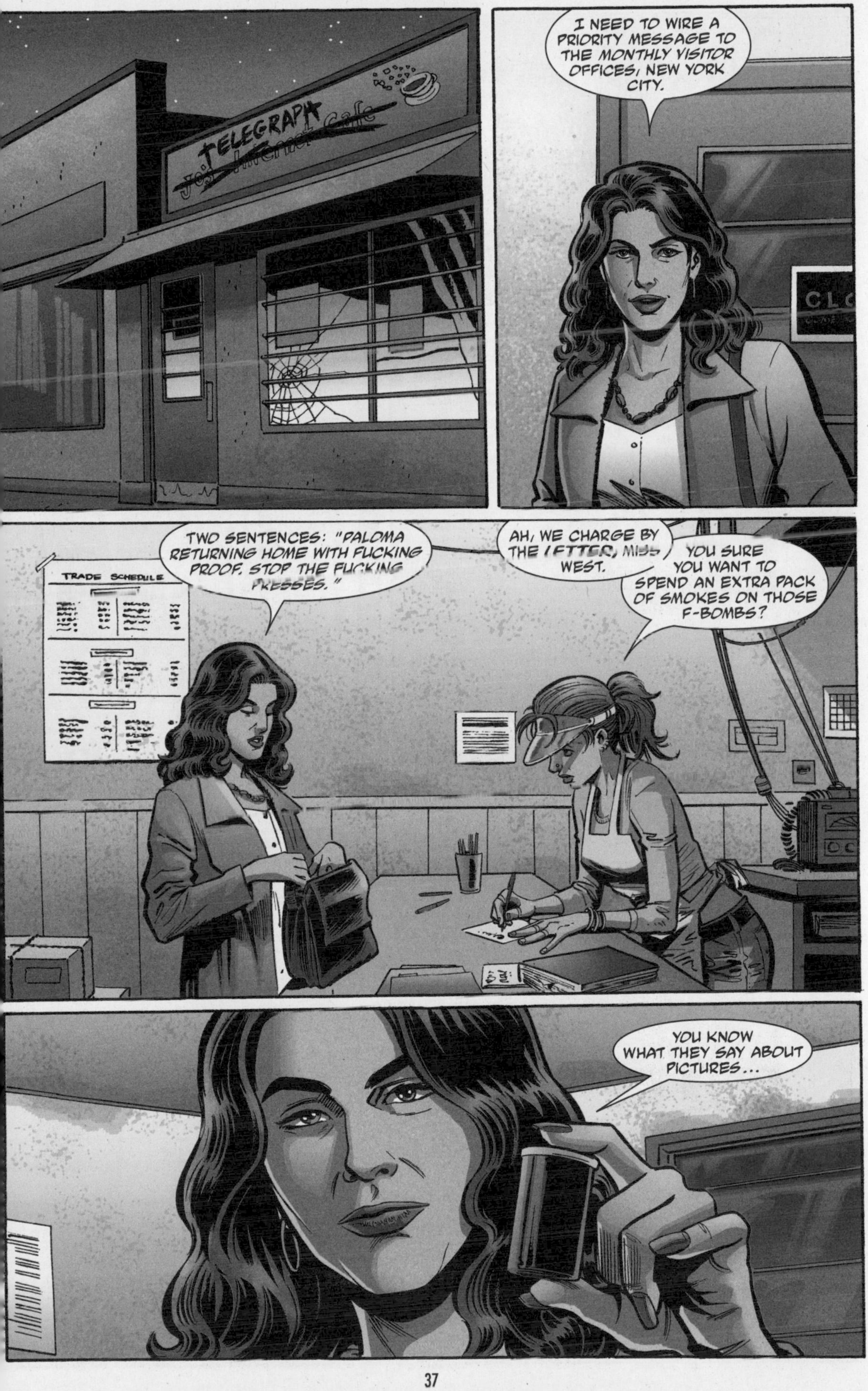

TELEGRAPH
Jo's Internet Cafe
I NEED TO WIRE A PRIORITY MESSAGE TO THE MONTHLY VISITOR OFFICES, NEW YORK CITY.
TRADE SCHEDULE
TWO SENTENCES: "PALOMA RETURNING HOME WITH FUCKING PROOF. STOP THE FUCKING PRESSES."
AH, WE CHARGE BY THE *LETTER,* MISS WEST.
YOU SURE YOU WANT TO SPEND AN EXTRA PACK OF SMOKES ON THOSE F-BOMBS?
YOU KNOW WHAT THEY SAY ABOUT PICTURES...

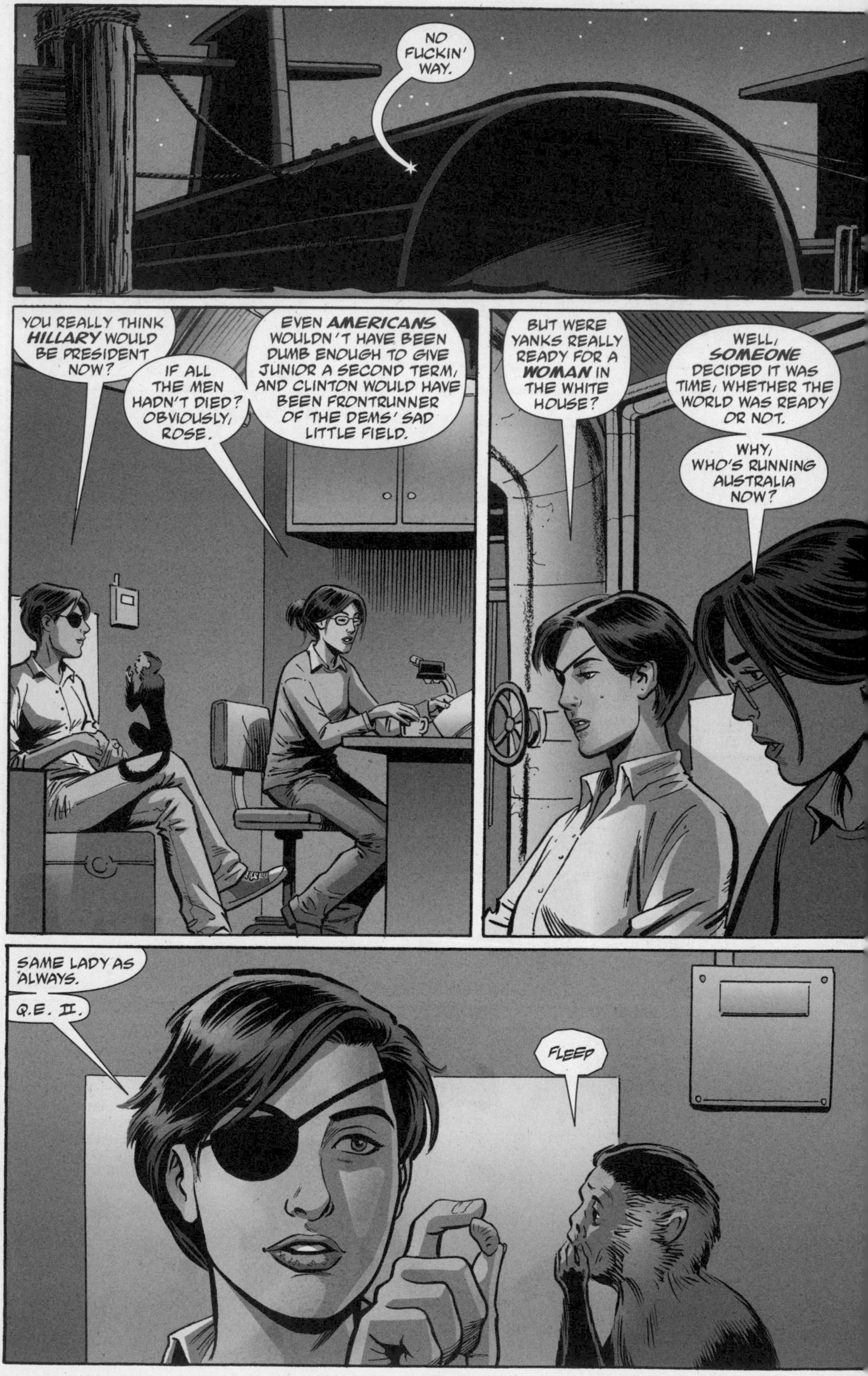
NO FUCKIN' WAY.
YOU REALLY THINK HILLARY WOULD BE PRESIDENT NOW?
IF ALL THE MEN HADN'T DIED? OBVIOUSLY, ROSE.
EVEN AMERICANS WOULDN'T HAVE BEEN DUMB ENOUGH TO GIVE JUNIOR A SECOND TERM, AND CLINTON WOULD HAVE BEEN FRONTRUNNER OF THE DEMS' SAD LITTLE FIELD.
BUT WERE YANKS REALLY READY FOR A WOMAN IN THE WHITE HOUSE?
WELL, SOMEONE DECIDED IT WAS TIME, WHETHER THE WORLD WAS READY OR NOT.
WHY, WHO'S RUNNING AUSTRALIA NOW?
SAME LADY AS ALWAYS.
Q.E. II.
FLEEP

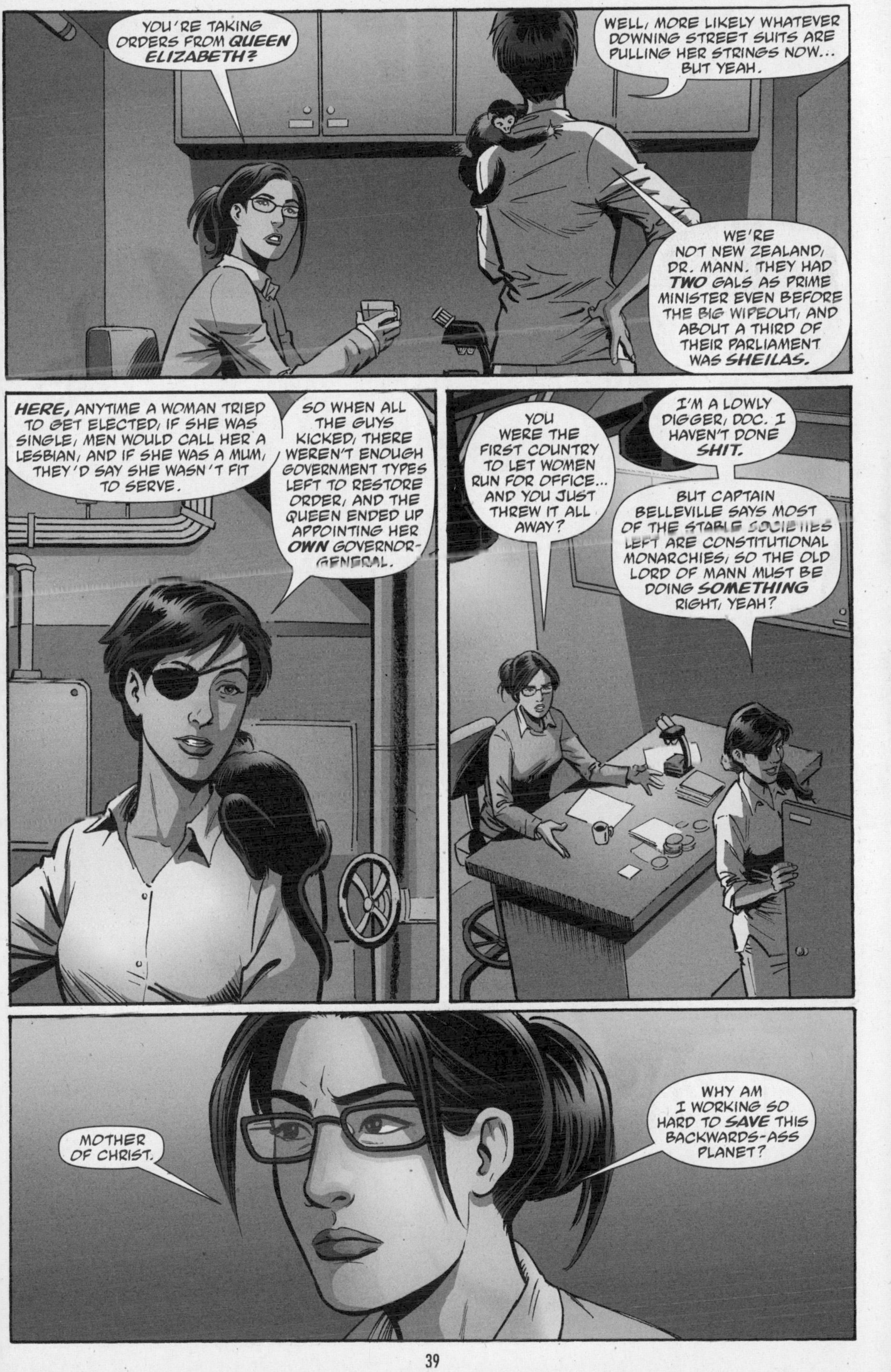
YOU'RE TAKING ORDERS FROM **QUEEN ELIZABETH**?
WELL, MORE LIKELY WHATEVER DOWNING STREET SUITS ARE PULLING HER STRINGS NOW... BUT YEAH.
WE'RE NOT NEW ZEALAND, DR. MANN. THEY HAD **TWO** GALS AS PRIME MINISTER EVEN BEFORE THE BIG WIPEOUT, AND ABOUT A THIRD OF THEIR PARLIAMENT WAS **SHEILAS.**
HERE, ANYTIME A WOMAN TRIED TO GET ELECTED, IF SHE WAS SINGLE, MEN WOULD CALL HER A LESBIAN, AND IF SHE WAS A MUM, THEY'D SAY SHE WASN'T FIT TO SERVE.
SO WHEN ALL THE GUYS KICKED, THERE WEREN'T ENOUGH GOVERNMENT TYPES LEFT TO RESTORE ORDER, AND THE QUEEN ENDED UP APPOINTING HER **OWN** GOVERNOR-GENERAL.
YOU WERE THE FIRST COUNTRY TO LET WOMEN RUN FOR OFFICE... AND YOU JUST THREW IT ALL AWAY?
I'M A LOWLY DIGGER, DOC. I HAVEN'T DONE **SHIT.**
BUT CAPTAIN BELLEVILLE SAYS MOST OF THE STABLE SOCIETIES LEFT ARE CONSTITUTIONAL MONARCHIES, SO THE OLD LORD OF MANN MUST BE DOING **SOMETHING** RIGHT, YEAH?
MOTHER OF CHRIST.
WHY AM I WORKING SO HARD TO **SAVE** THIS BACKWARDS-ASS PLANET?

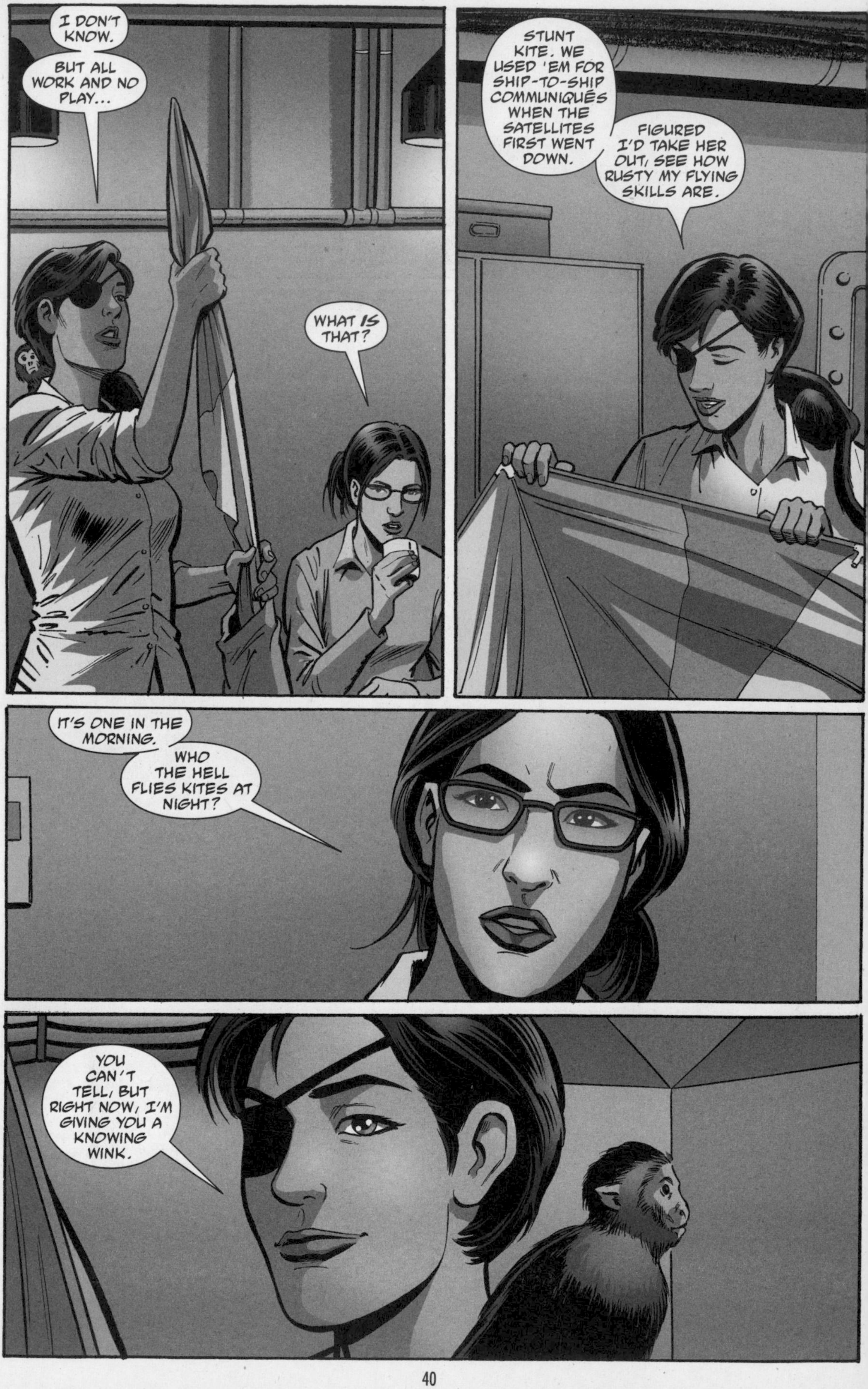
I DON'T KNOW.
BUT ALL WORK AND NO PLAY...
WHAT IS THAT?
STUNT KITE. WE USED 'EM FOR SHIP-TO-SHIP COMMUNIQUÉS WHEN THE SATELLITES FIRST WENT DOWN.
FIGURED I'D TAKE HER OUT, SEE HOW RUSTY MY FLYING SKILLS ARE.
IT'S ONE IN THE MORNING.
WHO THE HELL FLIES KITES AT NIGHT?
YOU CAN'T TELL, BUT RIGHT NOW, I'M GIVING YOU A KNOWING WINK.

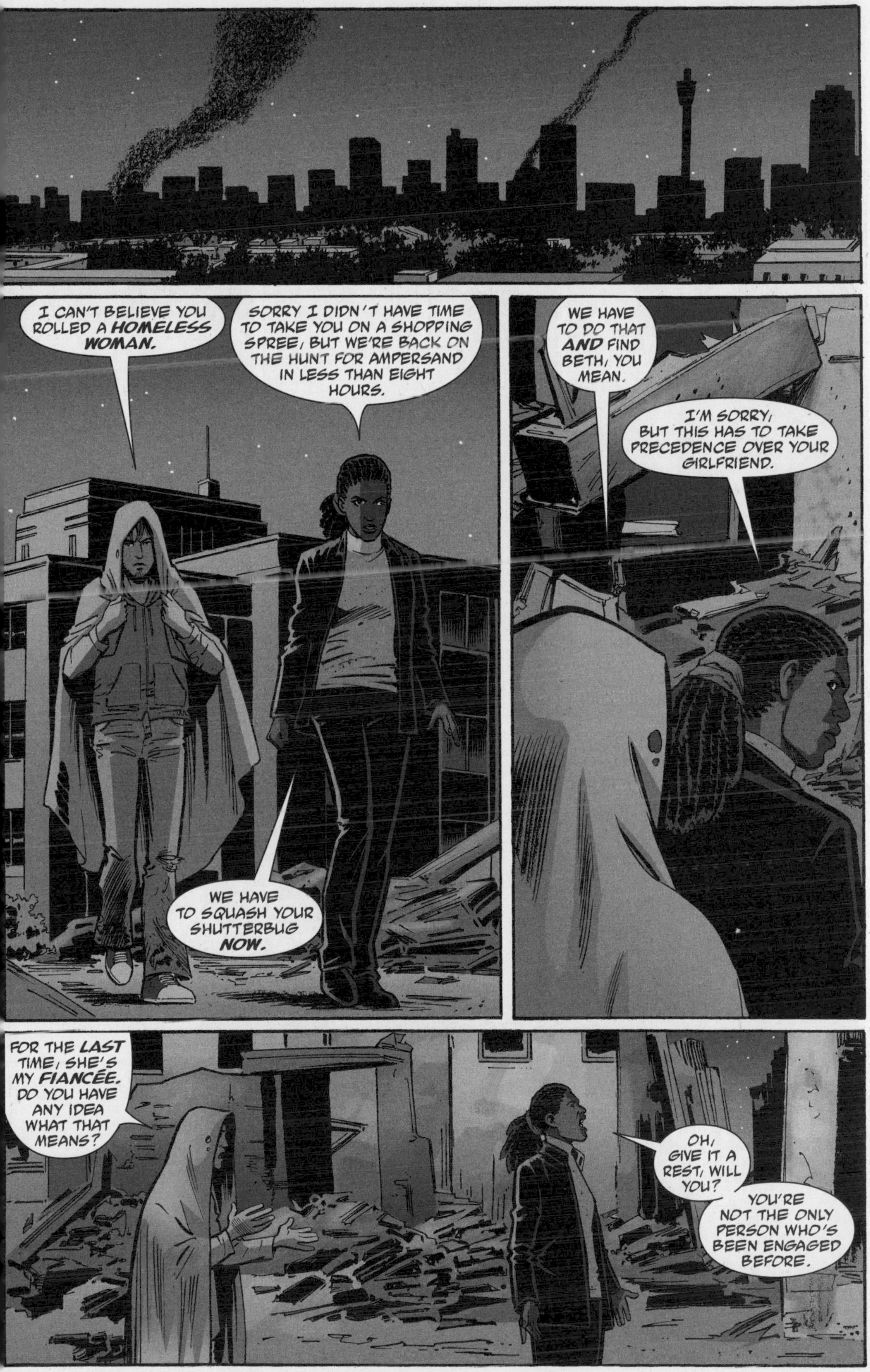
I CAN'T BELIEVE YOU ROLLED A HOMELESS WOMAN.
SORRY I DIDN'T HAVE TIME TO TAKE YOU ON A SHOPPING SPREE, BUT WE'RE BACK ON THE HUNT FOR AMPERSAND IN LESS THAN EIGHT HOURS.
WE HAVE TO SQUASH YOUR SHUTTERBUG NOW.
WE HAVE TO DO THAT AND FIND BETH, YOU MEAN.
I'M SORRY, BUT THIS HAS TO TAKE PRECEDENCE OVER YOUR GIRLFRIEND.
FOR THE LAST TIME, SHE'S MY FIANCÉE. DO YOU HAVE ANY IDEA WHAT THAT MEANS?
OH, GIVE IT A REST, WILL YOU?
YOU'RE NOT THE ONLY PERSON WHO'S BEEN ENGAGED BEFORE.

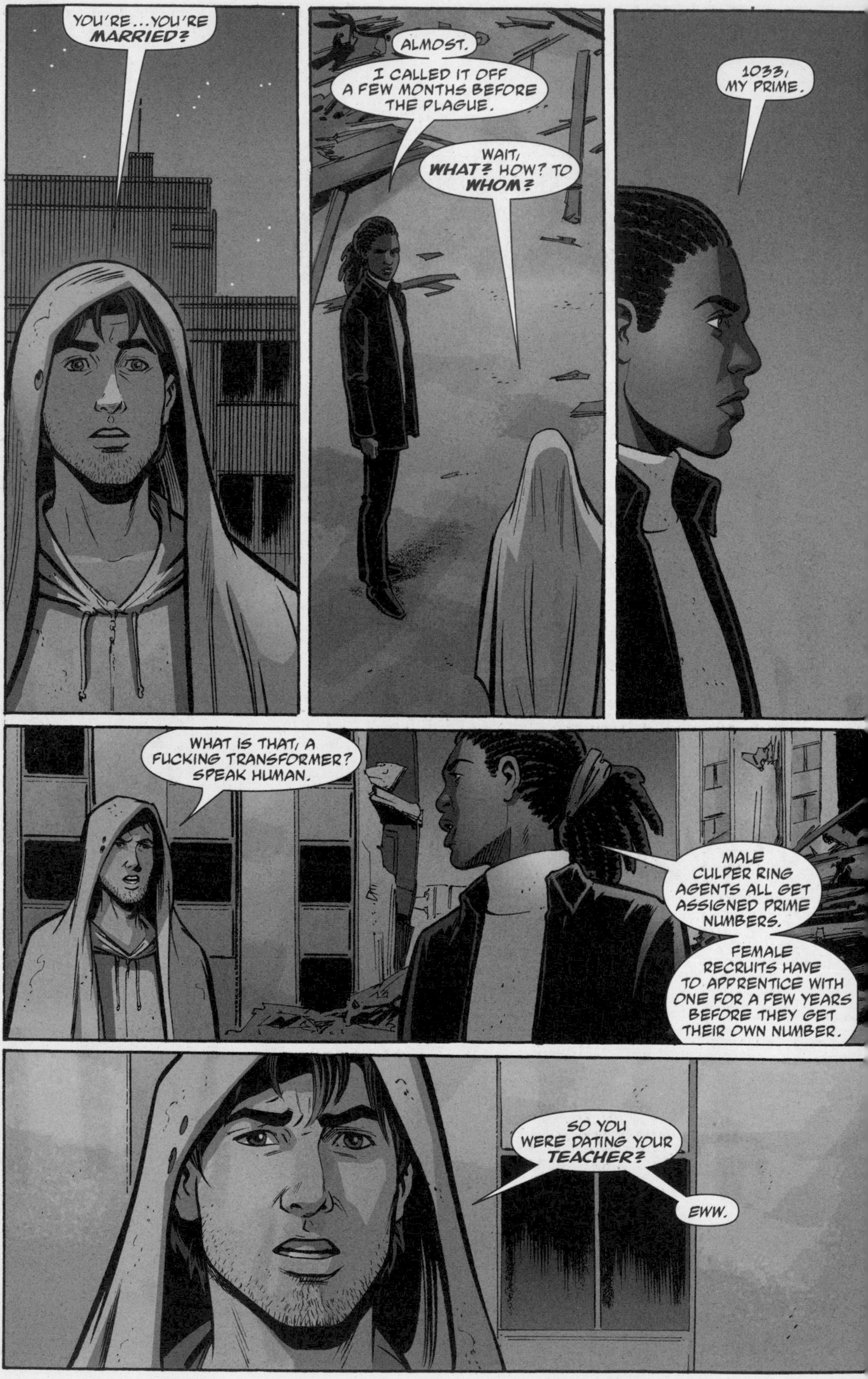
YOU'RE...YOU'RE MARRIED?
ALMOST.
I CALLED IT OFF A FEW MONTHS BEFORE THE PLAGUE.
WAIT, WHAT? HOW? TO WHOM?
1033, MY PRIME.
WHAT IS THAT, A FUCKING TRANSFORMER? SPEAK HUMAN.
MALE CULPER RING AGENTS ALL GET ASSIGNED PRIME NUMBERS.
FEMALE RECRUITS HAVE TO APPRENTICE WITH ONE FOR A FEW YEARS BEFORE THEY GET THEIR OWN NUMBER.
SO YOU WERE DATING YOUR TEACHER?
EWW.

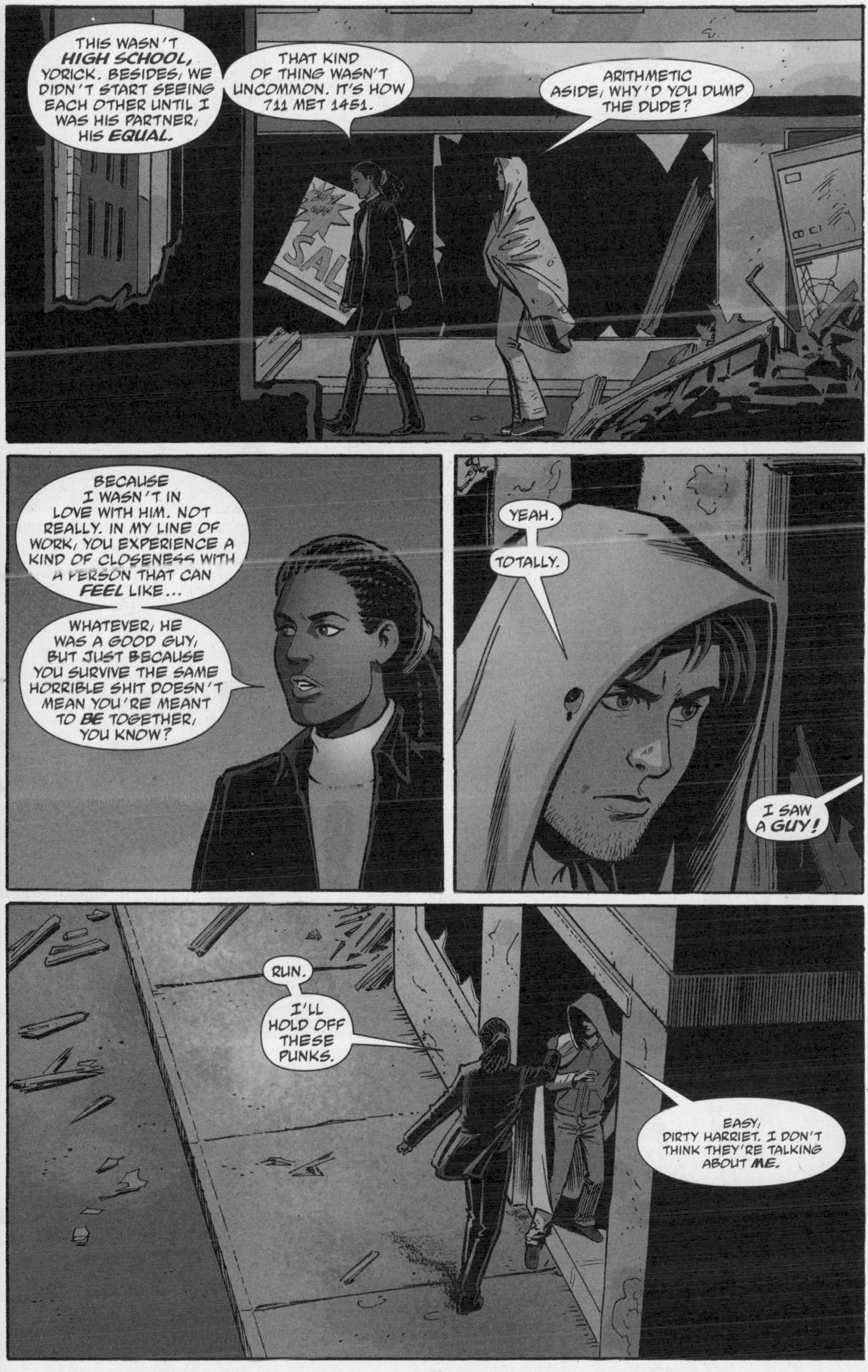

THIS WASN'T HIGH SCHOOL, YORICK. BESIDES, WE DIDN'T START SEEING EACH OTHER UNTIL I WAS HIS PARTNER, HIS EQUAL.
THAT KIND OF THING WASN'T UNCOMMON. IT'S HOW 711 MET 1451.
ARITHMETIC ASIDE, WHY'D YOU DUMP THE DUDE?
SALE
BECAUSE I WASN'T IN LOVE WITH HIM. NOT REALLY. IN MY LINE OF WORK, YOU EXPERIENCE A KIND OF CLOSENESS WITH A PERSON THAT CAN FEEL LIKE...
WHATEVER, HE WAS A GOOD GUY, BUT JUST BECAUSE YOU SURVIVE THE SAME HORRIBLE SHIT DOESN'T MEAN YOU'RE MEANT TO BE TOGETHER, YOU KNOW?
YEAH.
TOTALLY.
I SAW A GUY!
RUN.
I'LL HOLD OFF THESE PUNKS.
EASY, DIRTY HARRIET. I DON'T THINK THEY'RE TALKING ABOUT ME.

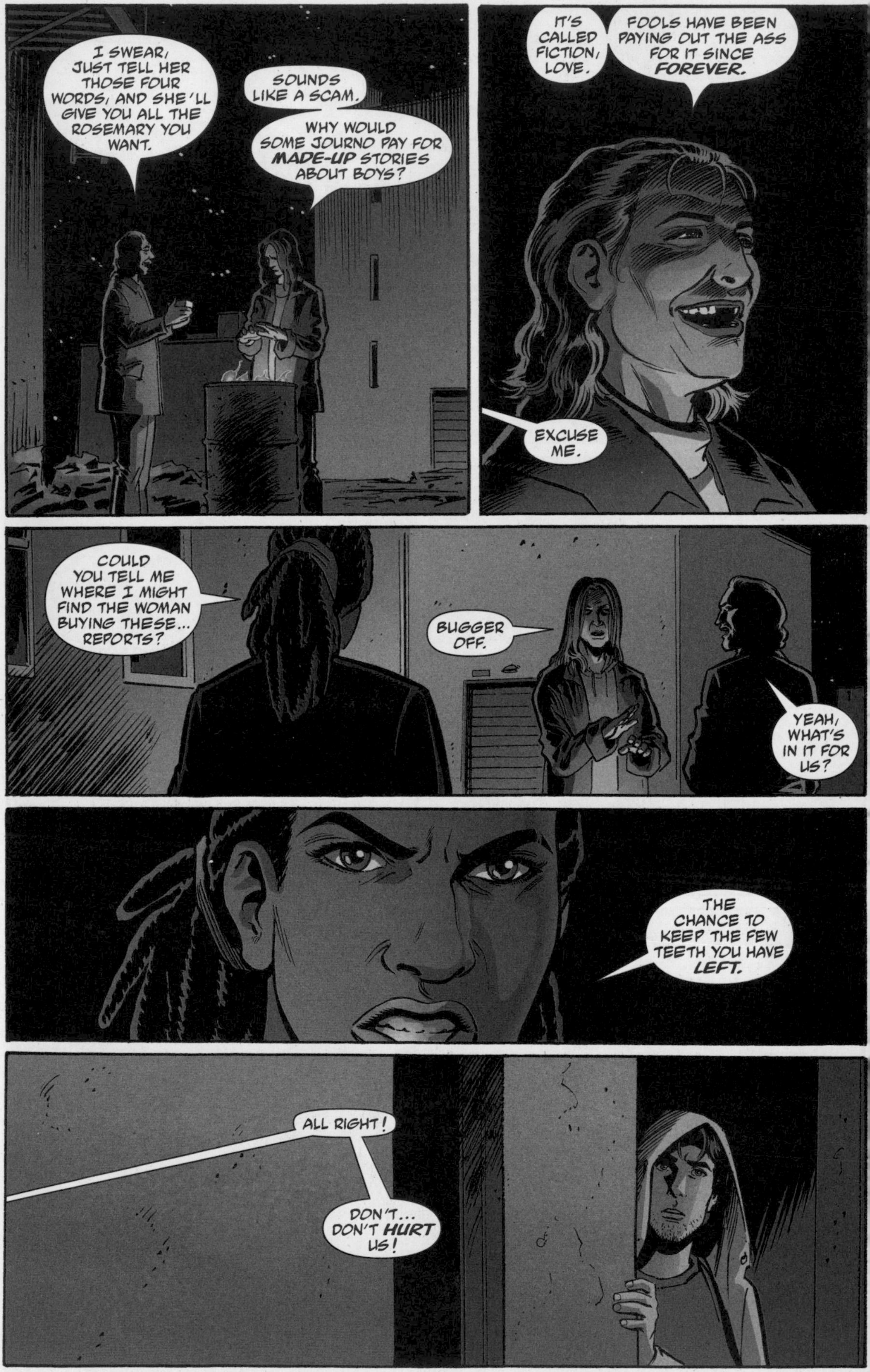
I SWEAR, JUST TELL HER THOSE FOUR WORDS, AND SHE'LL GIVE YOU ALL THE ROSEMARY YOU WANT.
SOUNDS LIKE A SCAM.
WHY WOULD SOME JOURNO PAY FOR MADE-UP STORIES ABOUT BOYS?
IT'S CALLED FICTION, LOVE.
FOOLS HAVE BEEN PAYING OUT THE ASS FOR IT SINCE FOREVER.
EXCUSE ME.
COULD YOU TELL ME WHERE I MIGHT FIND THE WOMAN BUYING THESE... REPORTS?
BUGGER OFF.
YEAH, WHAT'S IN IT FOR US?
THE CHANCE TO KEEP THE FEW TEETH YOU HAVE LEFT.
ALL RIGHT!
DON'T... DON'T HURT US!

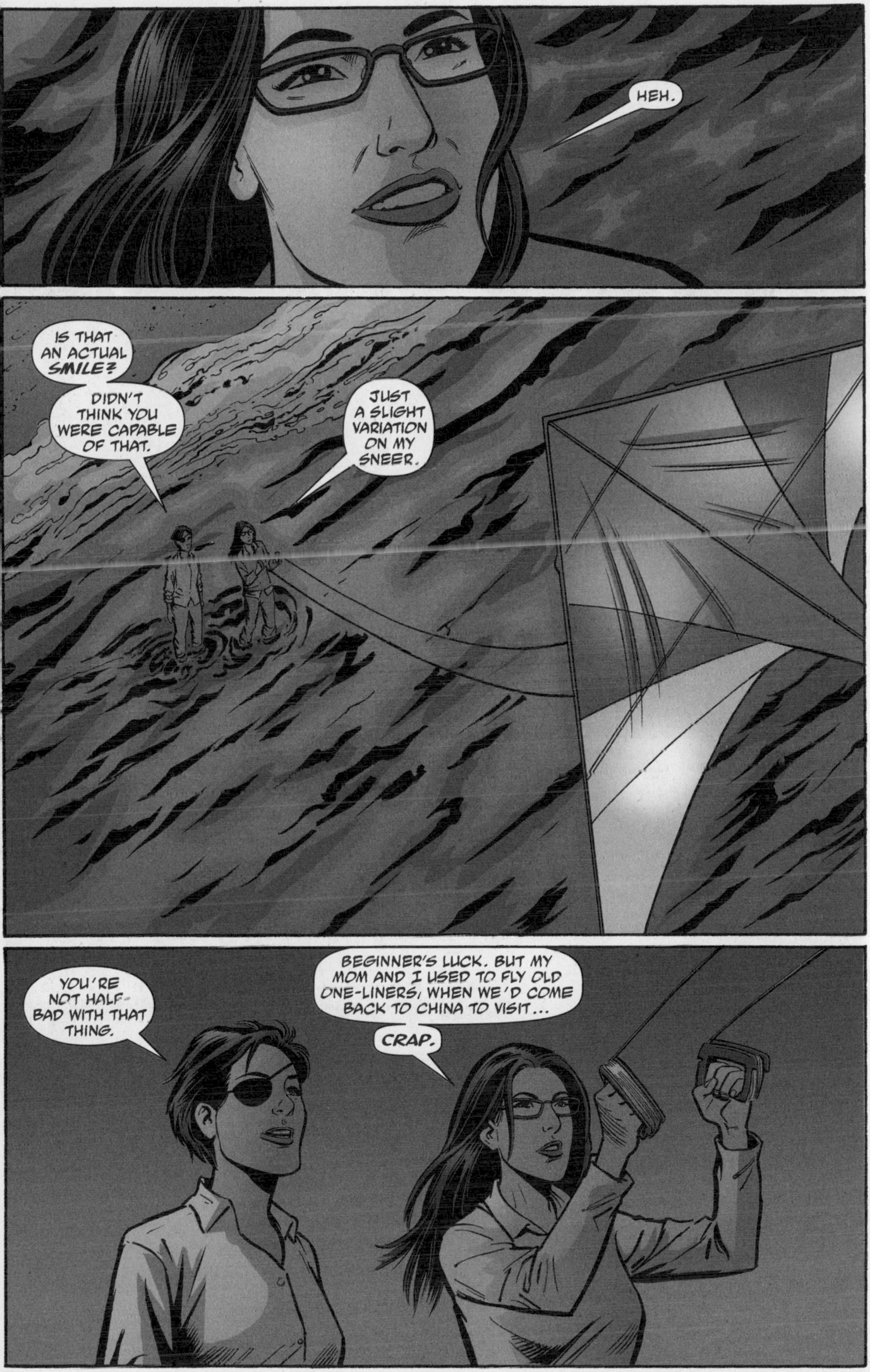
HEH.
IS THAT AN ACTUAL SMILE?
DIDN'T THINK YOU WERE CAPABLE OF THAT.
JUST A SLIGHT VARIATION ON MY SNEER.
YOU'RE NOT HALF-BAD WITH THAT THING.
BEGINNER'S LUCK. BUT MY MOM AND I USED TO FLY OLD ONE-LINERS, WHEN WE'D COME BACK TO CHINA TO VISIT...
CRAP.

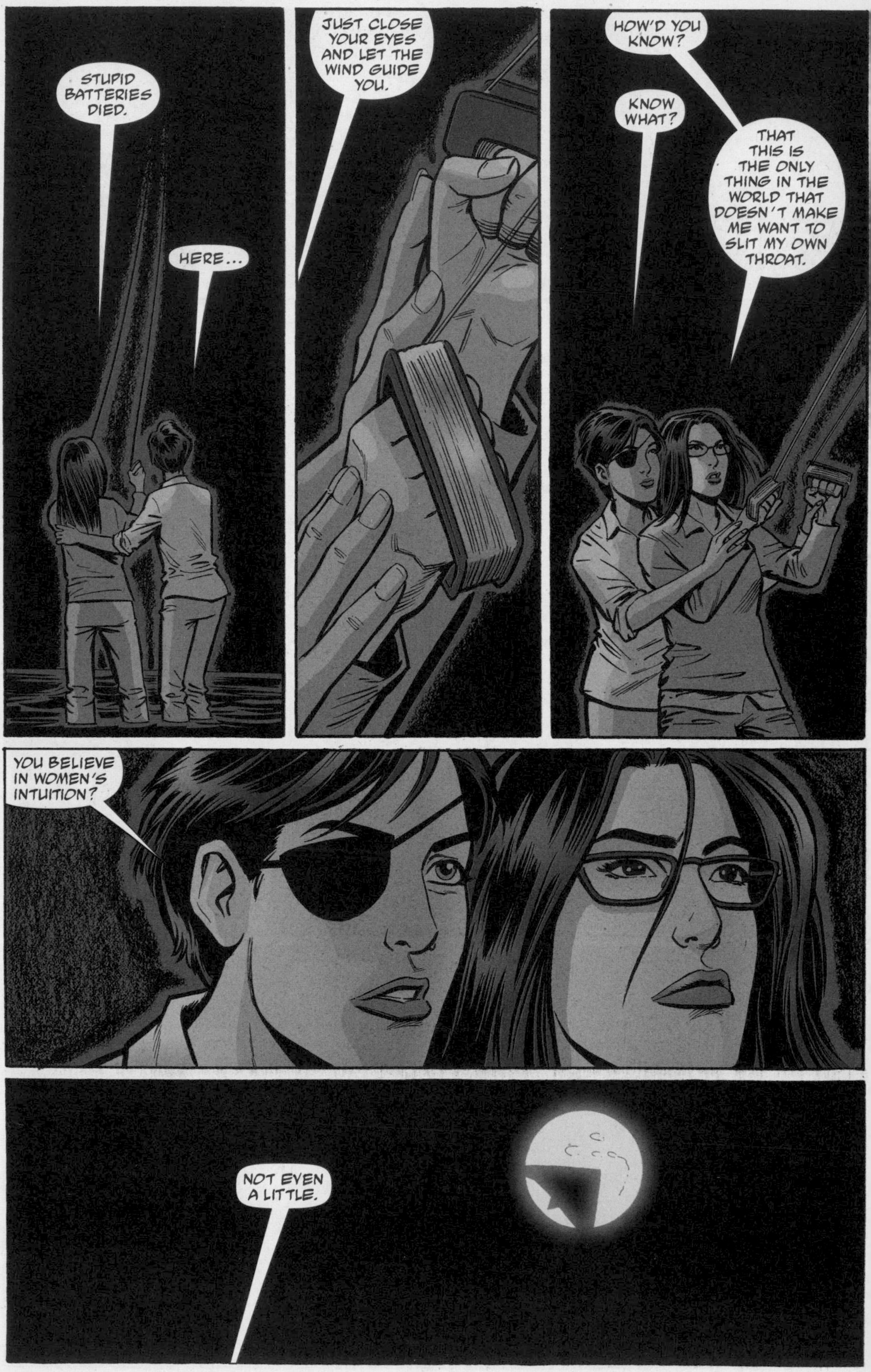
STUPID BATTERIES DIED.
HERE...
JUST CLOSE YOUR EYES AND LET THE WIND GUIDE YOU.
HOW'D YOU KNOW?
KNOW WHAT?
THAT THIS IS THE ONLY THING IN THE WORLD THAT DOESN'T MAKE ME WANT TO SLIT MY OWN THROAT.
YOU BELIEVE IN WOMEN'S INTUITION?
NOT EVEN A LITTLE.

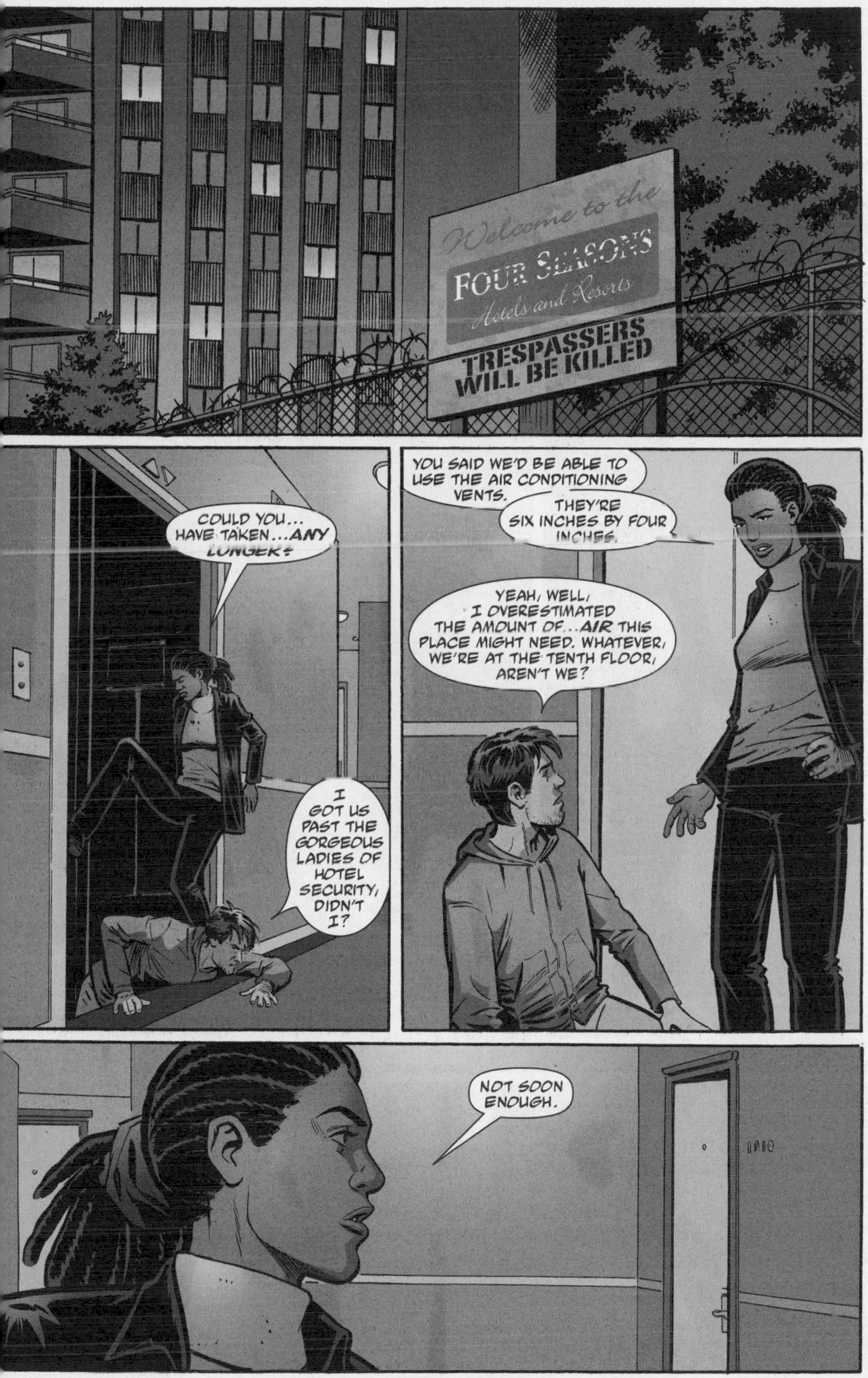
Welcome to the
FOUR SEASONS
Hotels and Resorts
TRESPASSERS WILL BE KILLED
COULD YOU... HAVE TAKEN... ANY LONGER?
I GOT US PAST THE GORGEOUS LADIES OF HOTEL SECURITY, DIDN'T I?
YOU SAID WE'D BE ABLE TO USE THE AIR CONDITIONING VENTS.
THEY'RE SIX INCHES BY FOUR INCHES.
YEAH, WELL, I OVERESTIMATED THE AMOUNT OF...AIR THIS PLACE MIGHT NEED. WHATEVER, WE'RE AT THE TENTH FLOOR, AREN'T WE?
NOT SOON ENOUGH.

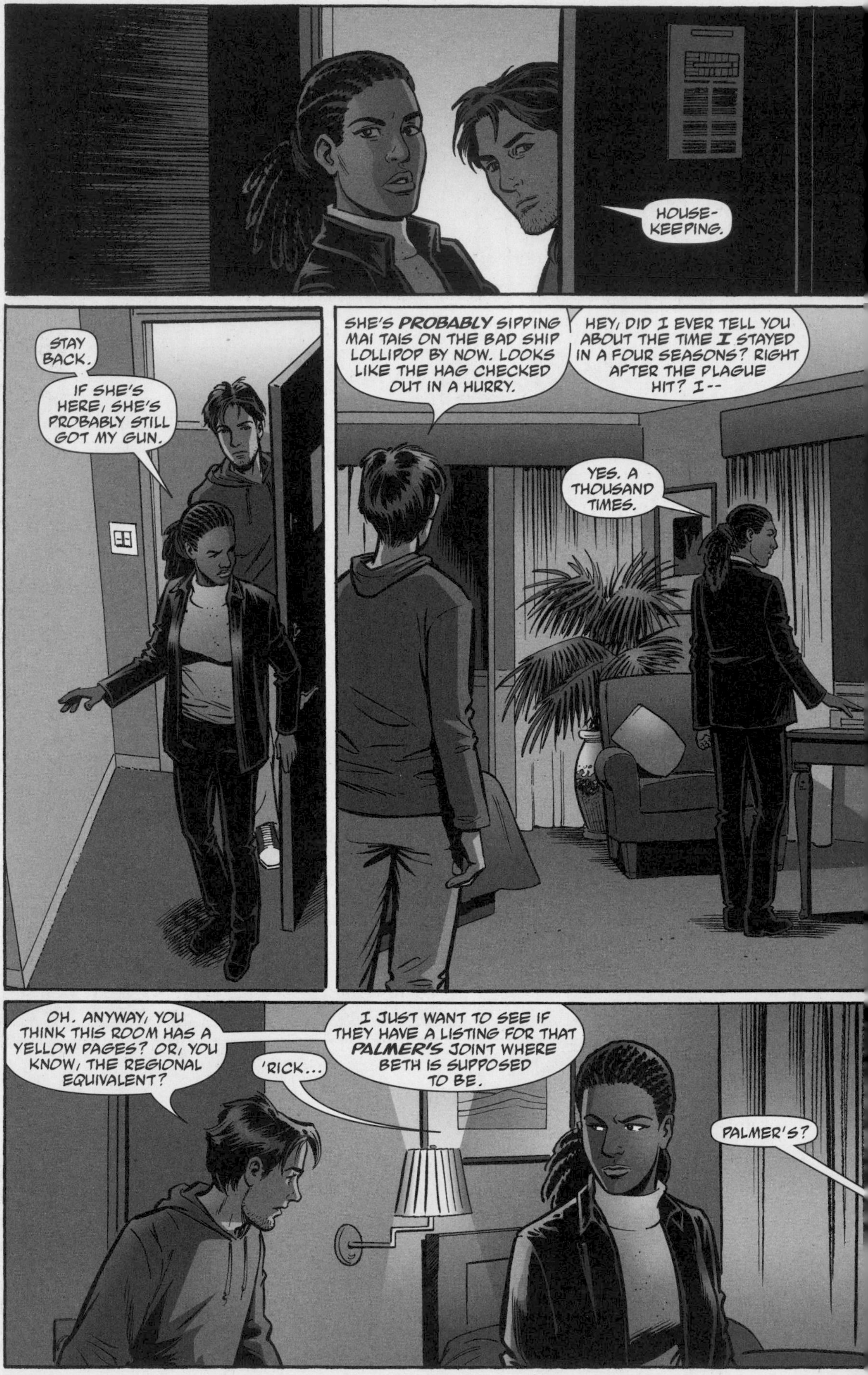
HOUSE-KEEPING.
STAY BACK.
IF SHE'S HERE, SHE'S PROBABLY STILL GOT MY GUN.
SHE'S PROBABLY SIPPING MAI TAIS ON THE BAD SHIP LOLLIPOP BY NOW. LOOKS LIKE THE HAG CHECKED OUT IN A HURRY.
HEY, DID I EVER TELL YOU ABOUT THE TIME I STAYED IN A FOUR SEASONS? RIGHT AFTER THE PLAGUE HIT? I--
YES. A THOUSAND TIMES.
OH. ANYWAY, YOU THINK THIS ROOM HAS A YELLOW PAGES? OR, YOU KNOW, THE REGIONAL EQUIVALENT?
I JUST WANT TO SEE IF THEY HAVE A LISTING FOR THAT PALMER'S JOINT WHERE BETH IS SUPPOSED TO BE.
'RICK...
PALMER'S?

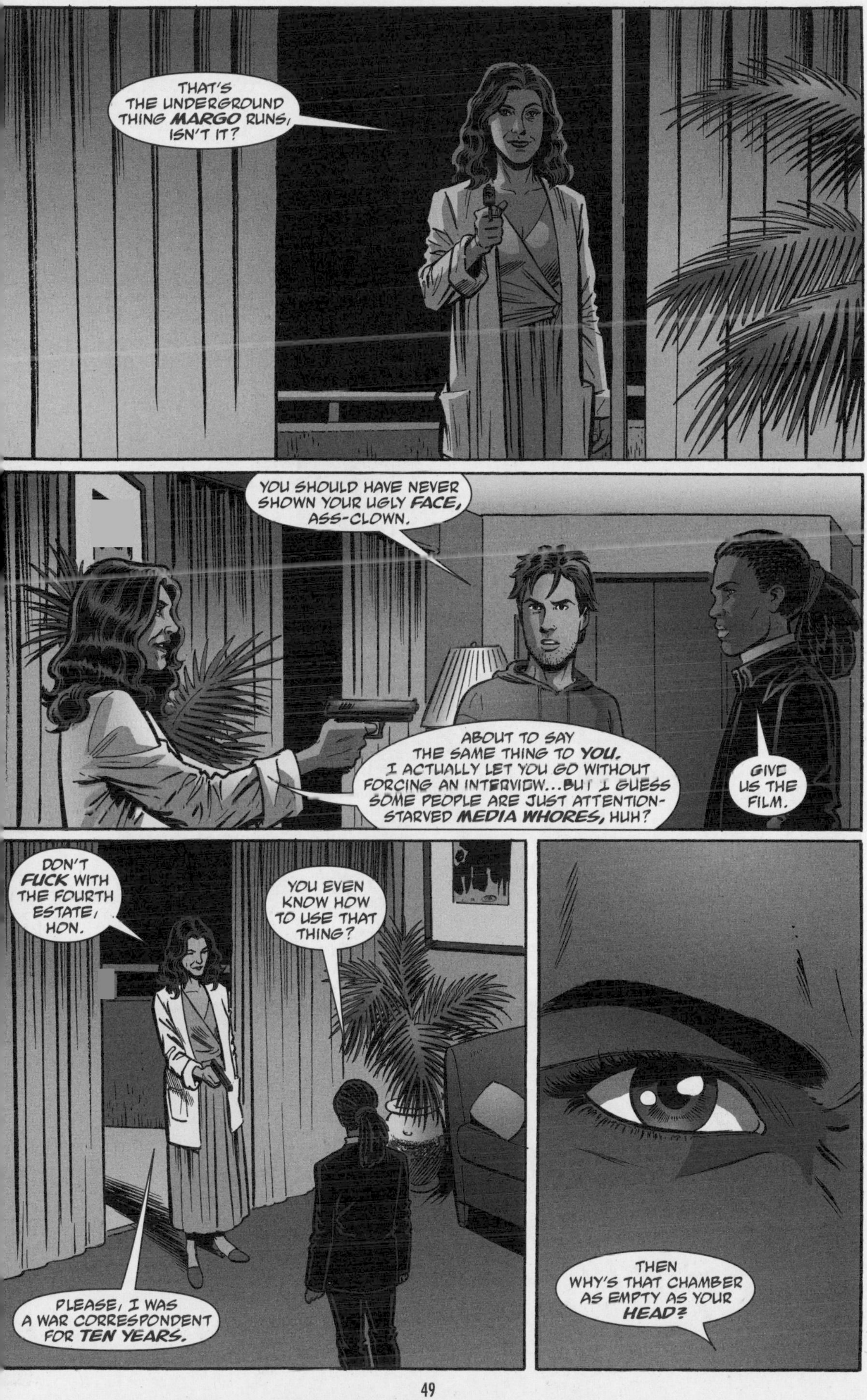
THAT'S THE UNDERGROUND THING MARGO RUNS, ISN'T IT?
YOU SHOULD HAVE NEVER SHOWN YOUR UGLY FACE, ASS-CLOWN.
ABOUT TO SAY THE SAME THING TO YOU. I ACTUALLY LET YOU GO WITHOUT FORCING AN INTERVIEW... BUT I GUESS SOME PEOPLE ARE JUST ATTENTION-STARVED MEDIA WHORES, HUH?
GIVE US THE FILM.
DON'T FUCK WITH THE FOURTH ESTATE, HON.
YOU EVEN KNOW HOW TO USE THAT THING?
PLEASE, I WAS A WAR CORRESPONDENT FOR TEN YEARS.
THEN WHY'S THAT CHAMBER AS EMPTY AS YOUR HEAD?

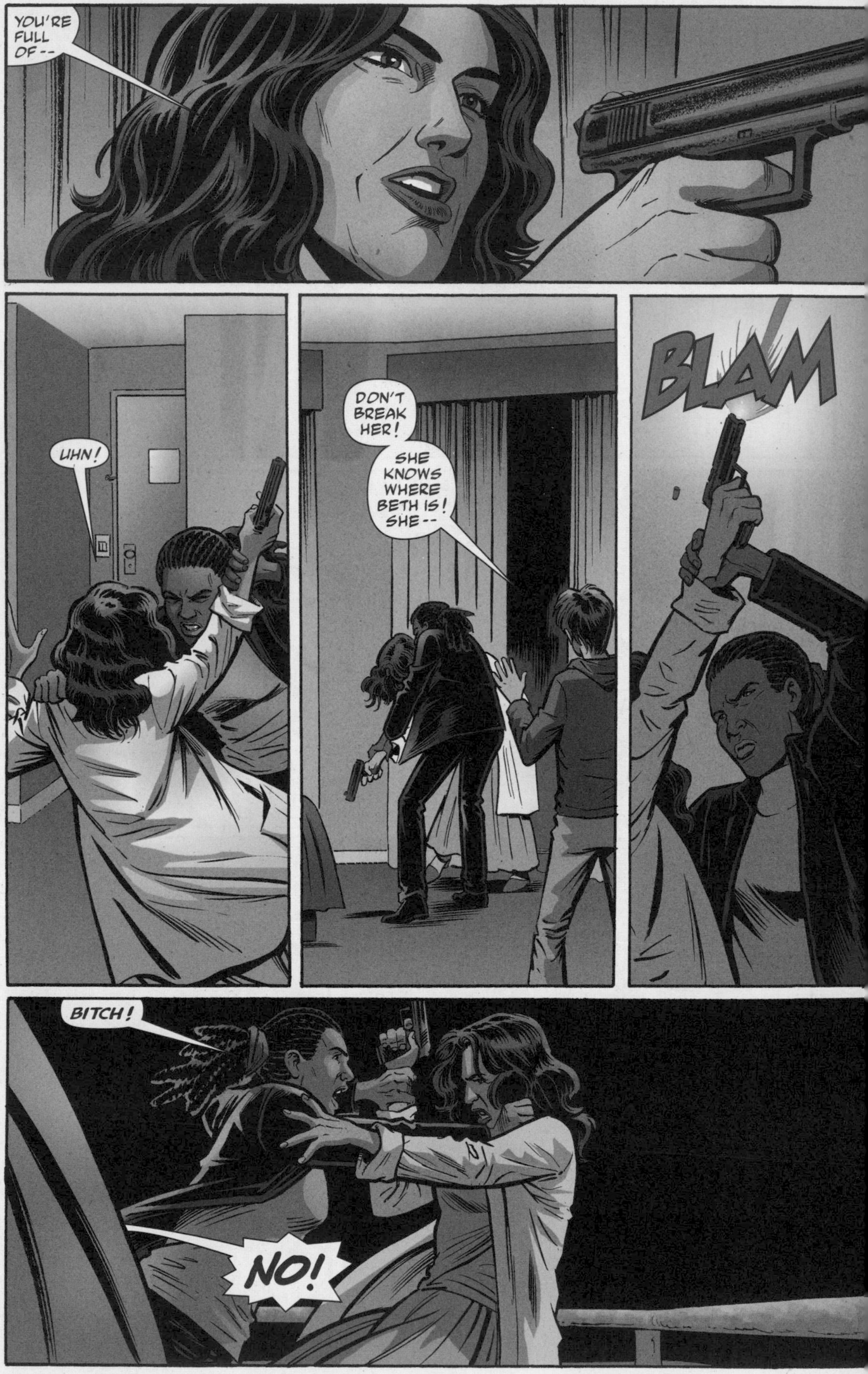
YOU'RE FULL OF --
UHN!
DON'T BREAK HER!
SHE KNOWS WHERE BETH IS! SHE --
BLAM
BITCH!
NO!

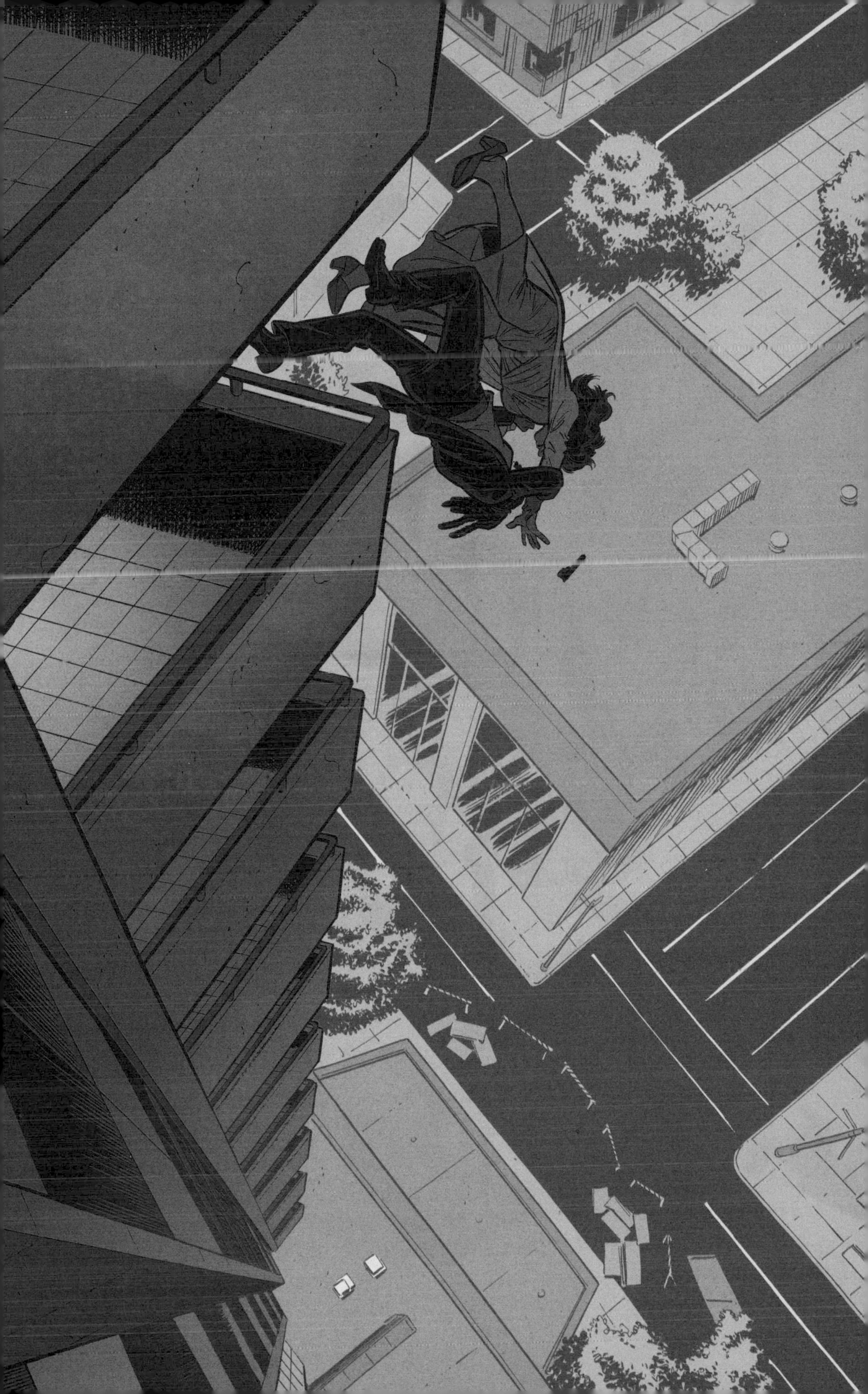

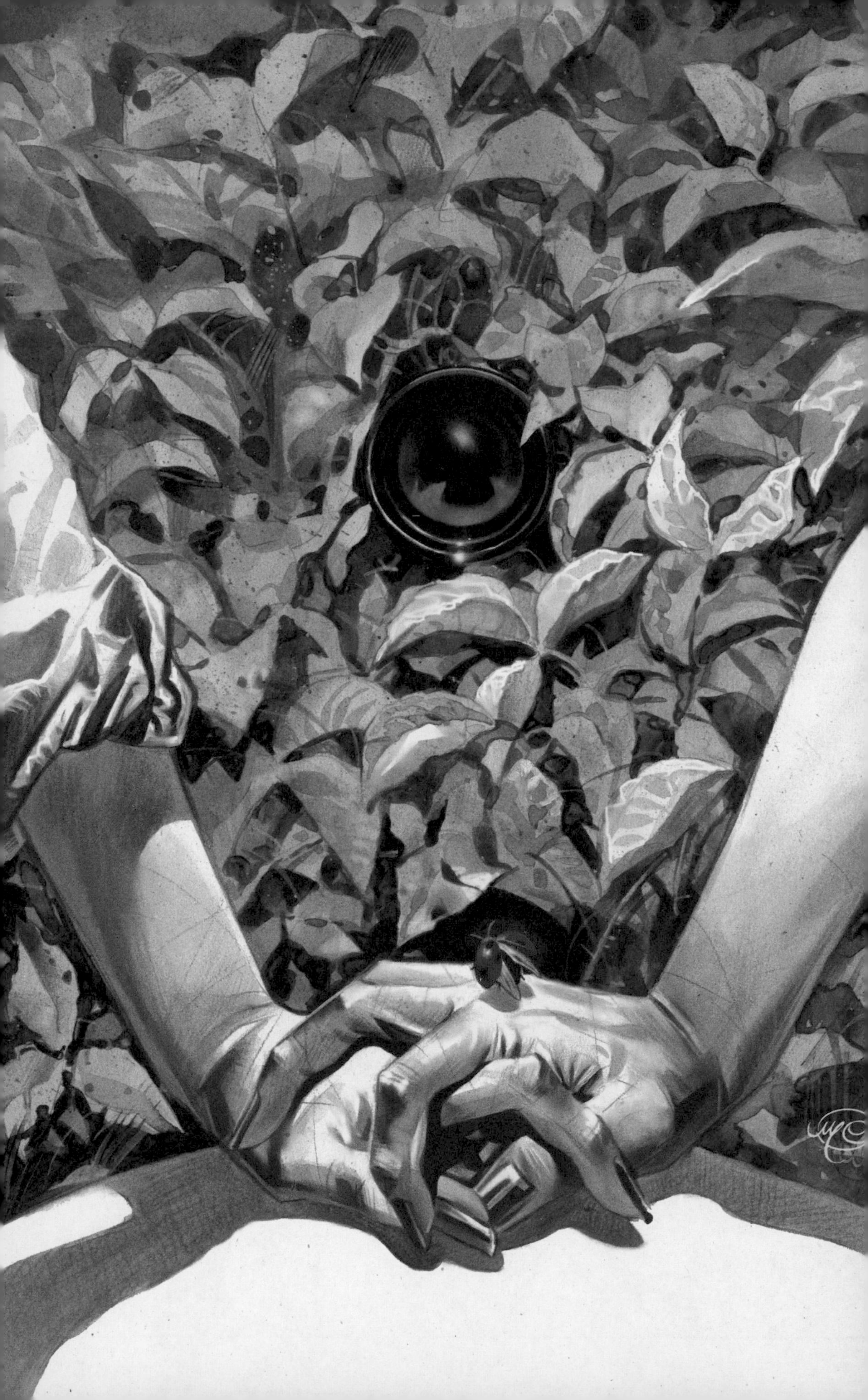

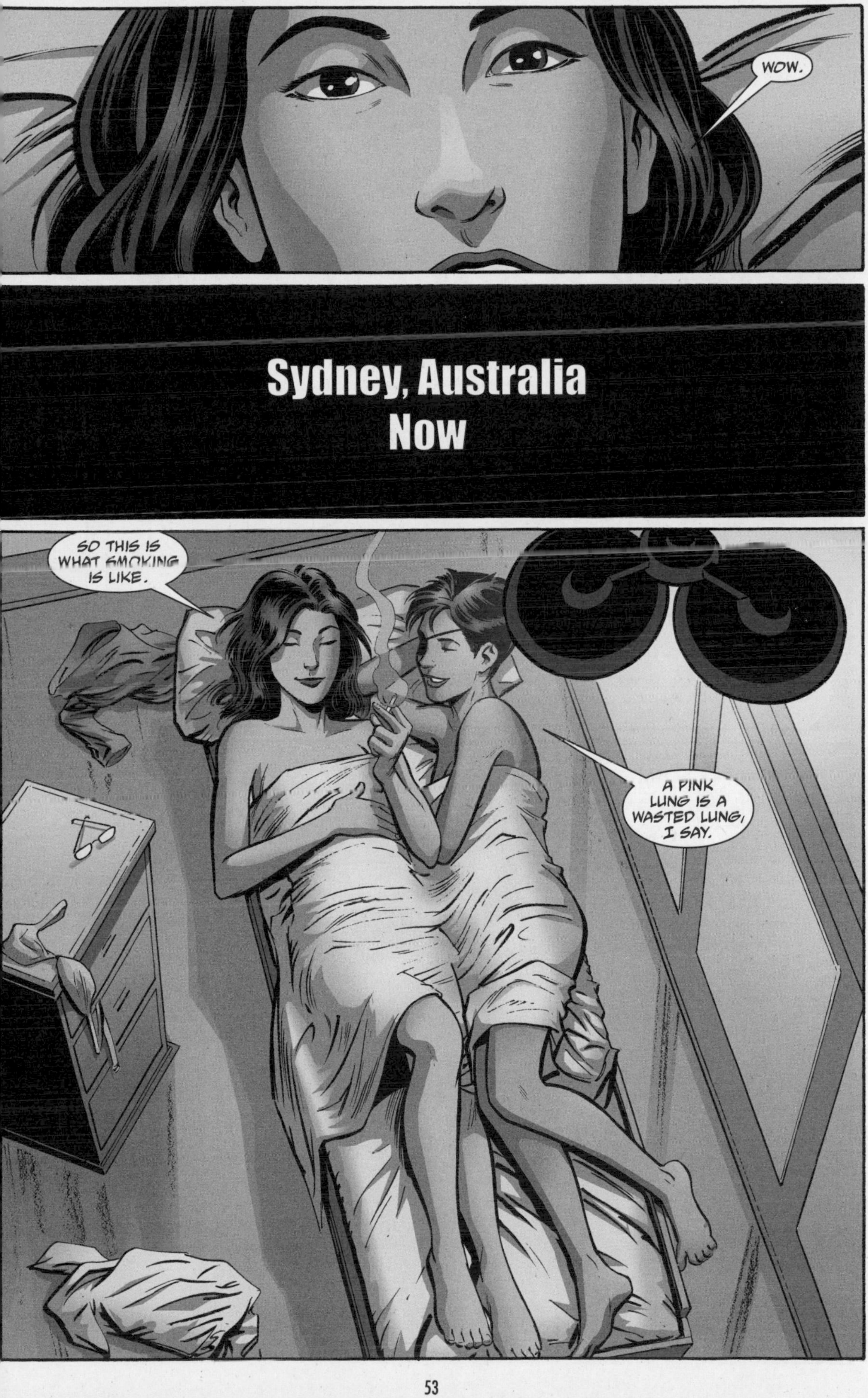
WOW.
Sydney, Australia
Now
SO THIS IS WHAT SMOKING IS LIKE.
A PINK LUNG IS A WASTED LUNG, I SAY.

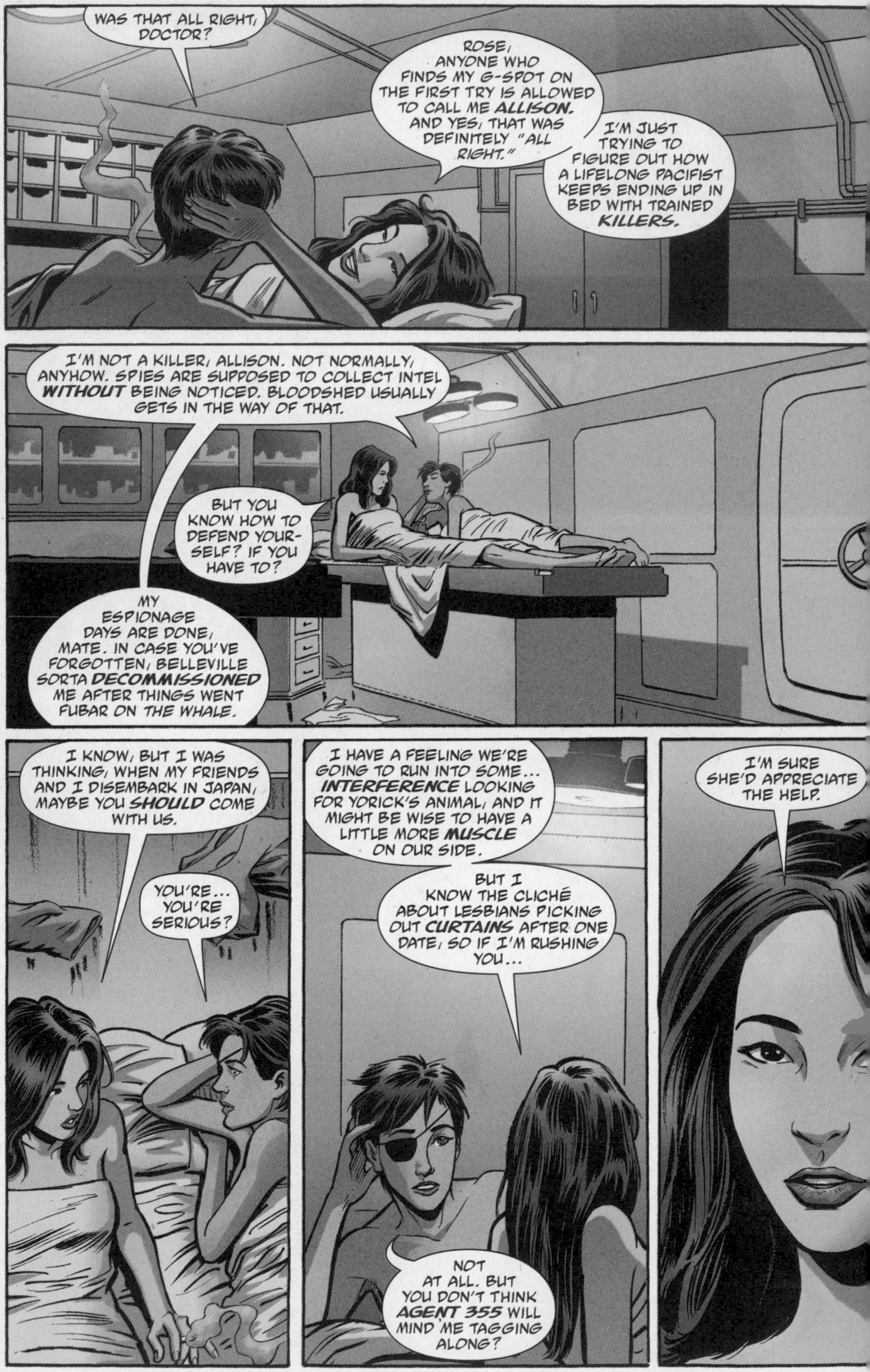
WAS THAT ALL RIGHT, DOCTOR?
ROSE, ANYONE WHO FINDS MY G-SPOT ON THE FIRST TRY IS ALLOWED TO CALL ME ALLISON. AND YES, THAT WAS DEFINITELY "ALL RIGHT."
I'M JUST TRYING TO FIGURE OUT HOW A LIFELONG PACIFIST KEEPS ENDING UP IN BED WITH TRAINED KILLERS.
I'M NOT A KILLER, ALLISON. NOT NORMALLY, ANYHOW. SPIES ARE SUPPOSED TO COLLECT INTEL WITHOUT BEING NOTICED. BLOODSHED USUALLY GETS IN THE WAY OF THAT.
BUT YOU KNOW HOW TO DEFEND YOURSELF? IF YOU HAVE TO?
MY ESPIONAGE DAYS ARE DONE, MATE. IN CASE YOU'VE FORGOTTEN, BELLEVILLE SORTA DECOMMISSIONED ME AFTER THINGS WENT FUBAR ON THE WHALE.
I KNOW, BUT I WAS THINKING, WHEN MY FRIENDS AND I DISEMBARK IN JAPAN, MAYBE YOU SHOULD COME WITH US.
YOU'RE... YOU'RE SERIOUS?
I HAVE A FEELING WE'RE GOING TO RUN INTO SOME... INTERFERENCE LOOKING FOR YORICK'S ANIMAL, AND IT MIGHT BE WISE TO HAVE A LITTLE MORE MUSCLE ON OUR SIDE.
BUT I KNOW THE CLICHÉ ABOUT LESBIANS PICKING OUT CURTAINS AFTER ONE DATE, SO IF I'M RUSHING YOU...
NOT AT ALL. BUT YOU DON'T THINK AGENT 355 WILL MIND ME TAGGING ALONG?
I'M SURE SHE'D APPRECIATE THE HELP.

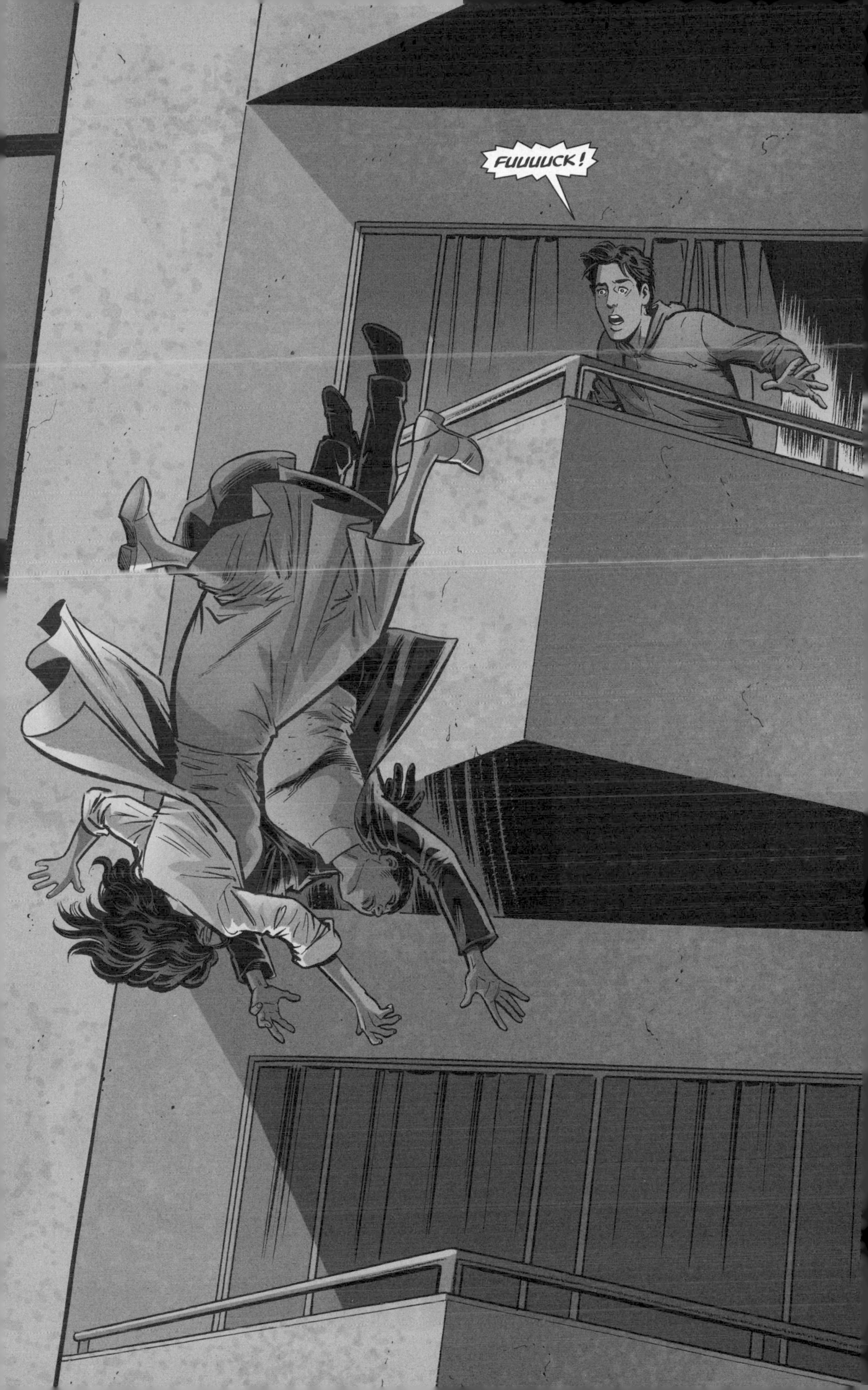
FUUUUCK!

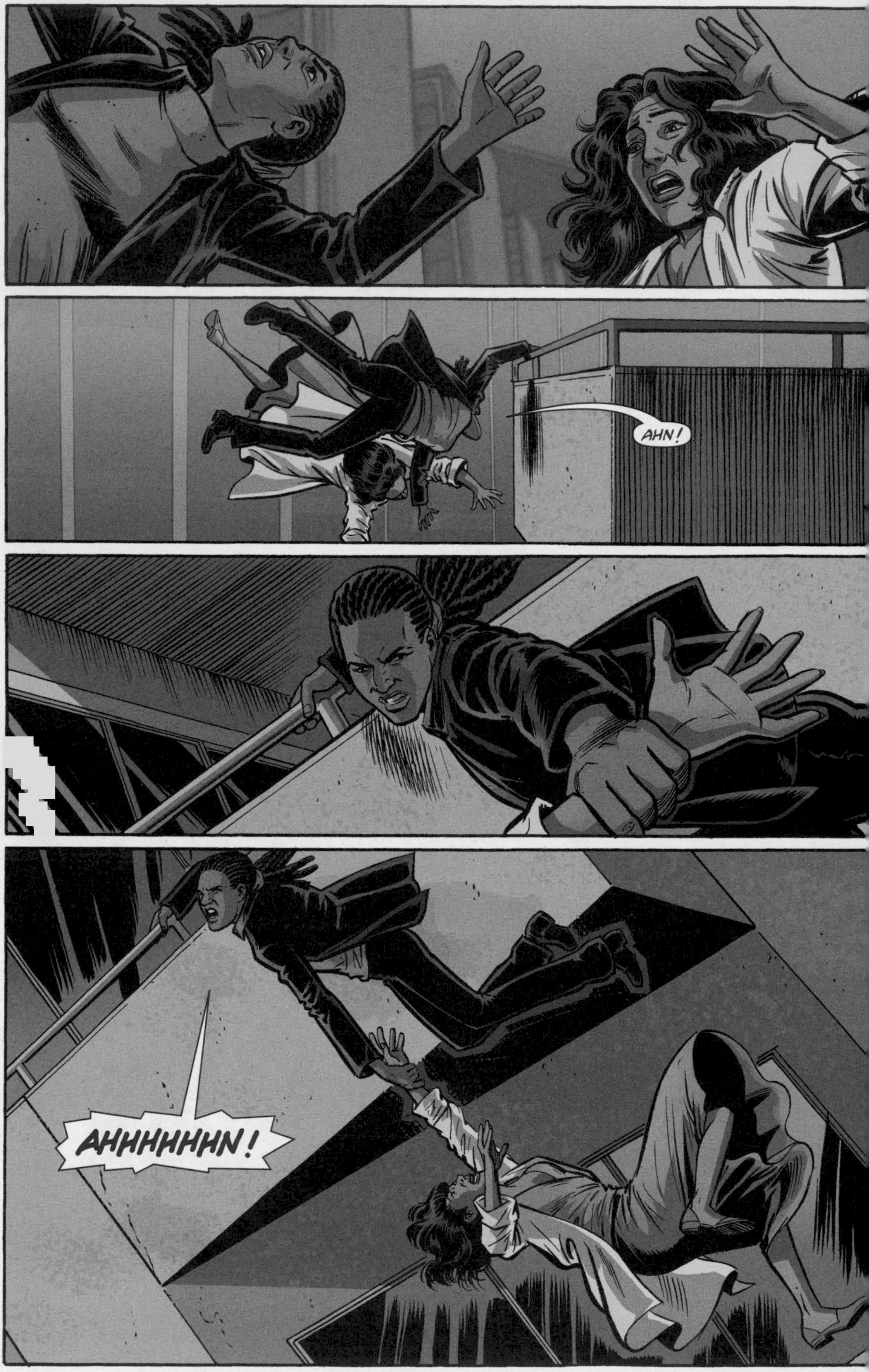
AHN!
AHHHHHHN!

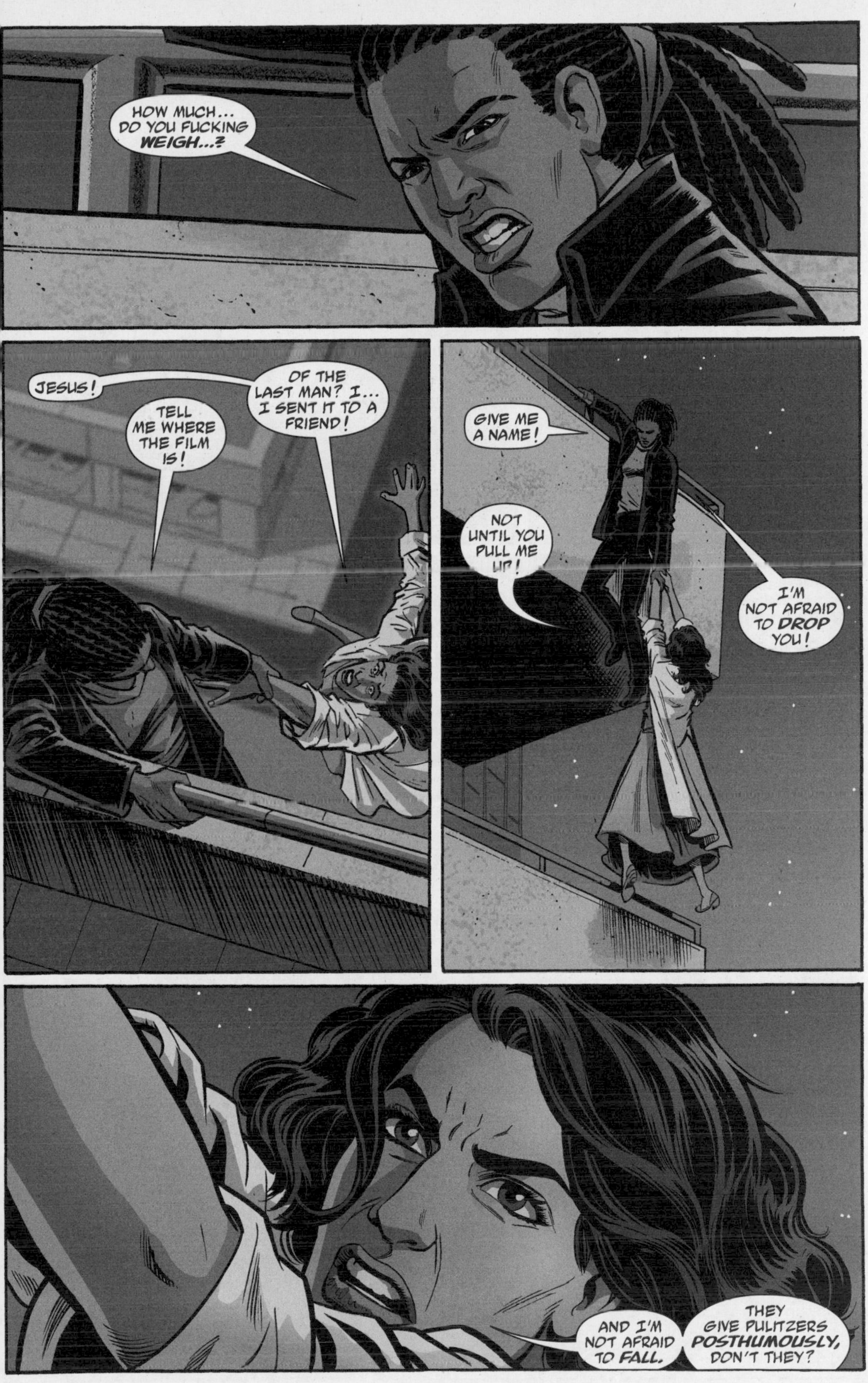
HOW MUCH... DO YOU FUCKING WEIGH...?
JESUS!
TELL ME WHERE THE FILM IS!
OF THE LAST MAN? I... I SENT IT TO A FRIEND!
GIVE ME A NAME!
NOT UNTIL YOU PULL ME UP!
I'M NOT AFRAID TO DROP YOU!
AND I'M NOT AFRAID TO FALL.
THEY GIVE PULITZERS POSTHUMOUSLY, DON'T THEY?

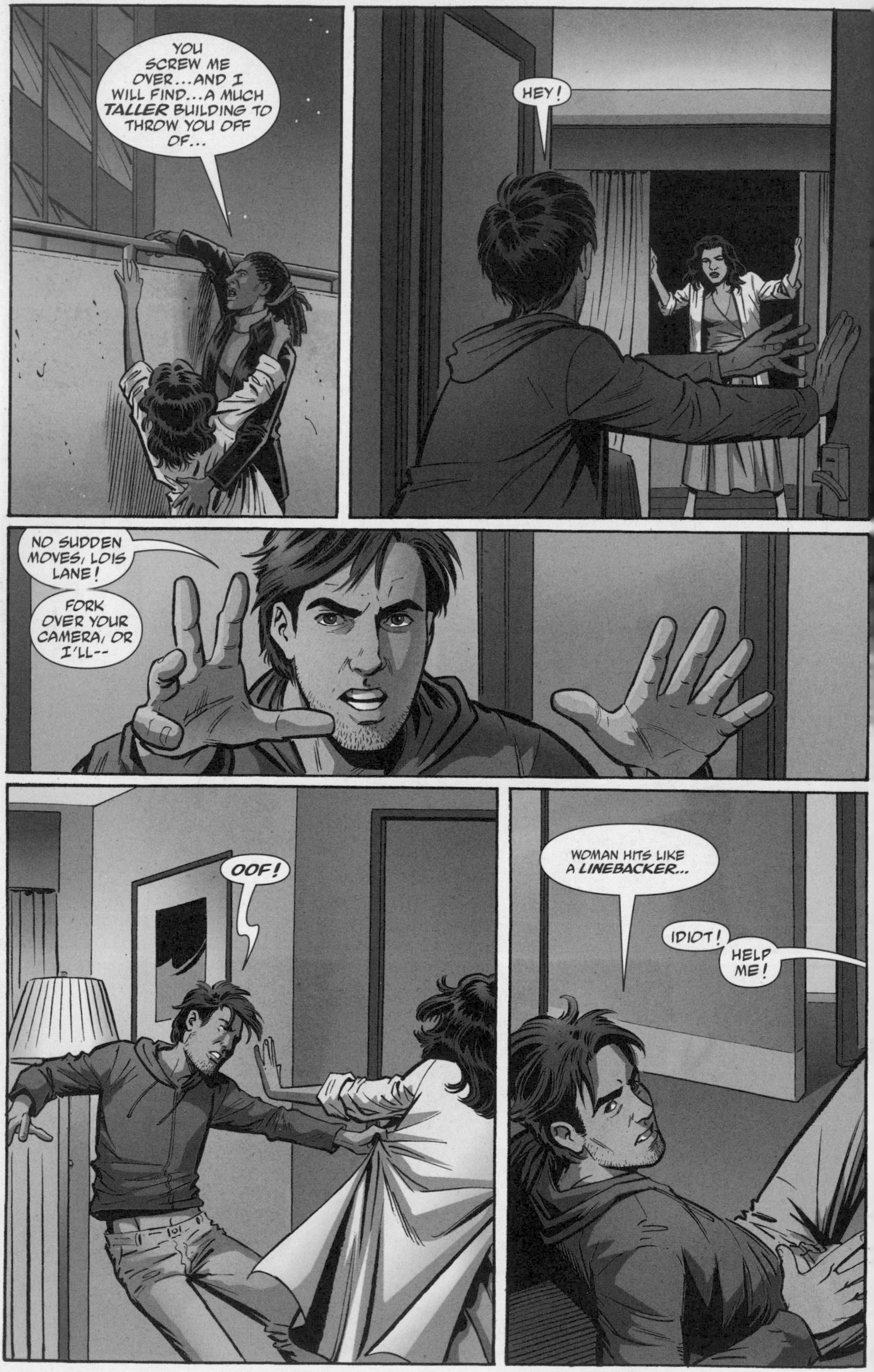
YOU SCREW ME OVER...AND I WILL FIND...A MUCH TALLER BUILDING TO THROW YOU OFF OF...
HEY!
NO SUDDEN MOVES, LOIS LANE!
FORK OVER YOUR CAMERA, OR I'LL--
OOF!
WOMAN HITS LIKE A LINEBACKER...
IDIOT!
HELP ME!

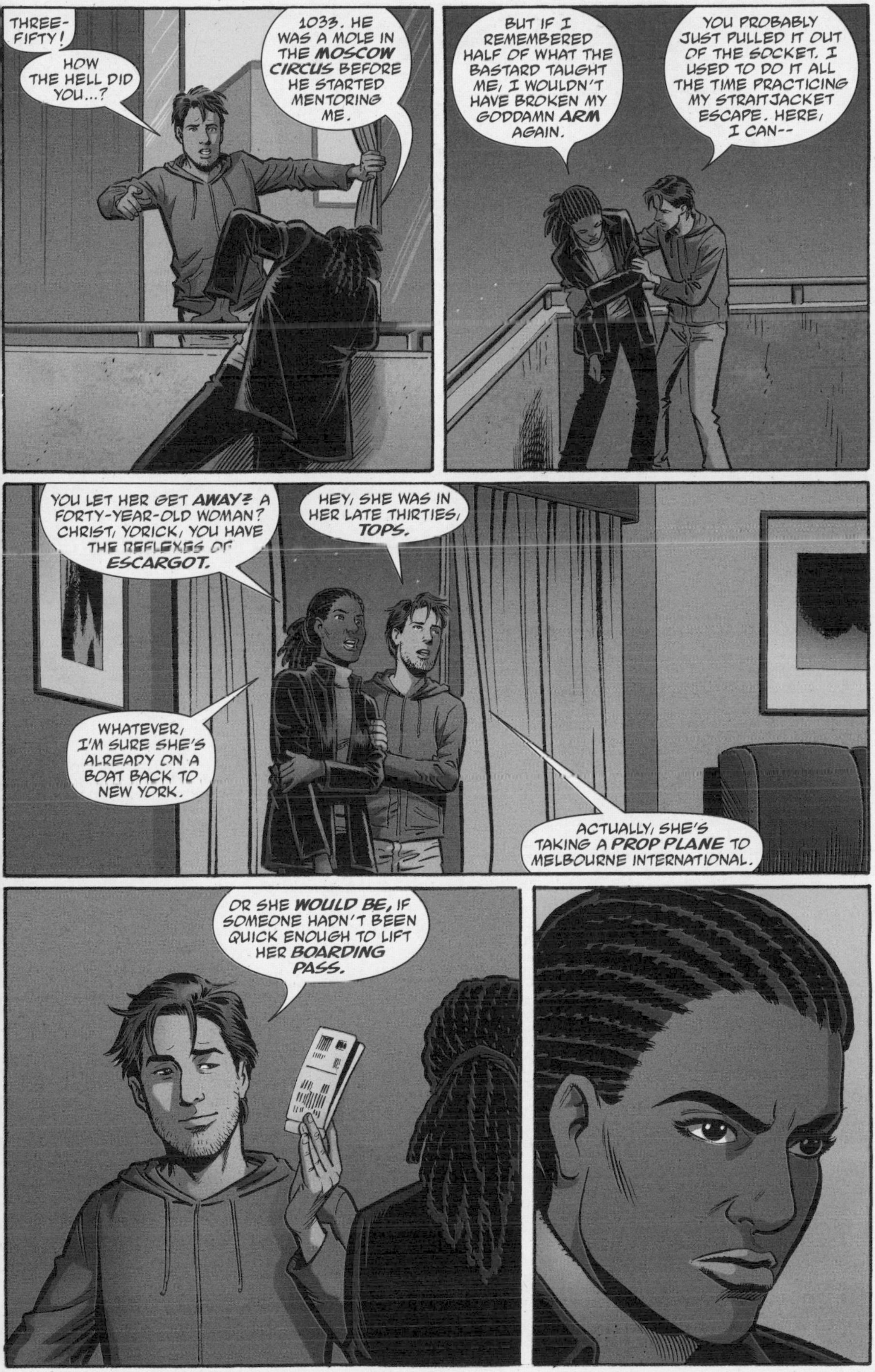
THREE-FIFTY! HOW THE HELL DID YOU...?
1033. HE WAS A MOLE IN THE MOSCOW CIRCUS BEFORE HE STARTED MENTORING ME.
BUT IF I REMEMBERED HALF OF WHAT THE BASTARD TAUGHT ME, I WOULDN'T HAVE BROKEN MY GODDAMN ARM AGAIN.
YOU PROBABLY JUST PULLED IT OUT OF THE SOCKET. I USED TO DO IT ALL THE TIME PRACTICING MY STRAITJACKET ESCAPE. HERE, I CAN--
YOU LET HER GET AWAY? A FORTY-YEAR-OLD WOMAN? CHRIST, YORICK, YOU HAVE THE REFLEXES OF ESCARGOT.
HEY, SHE WAS IN HER LATE THIRTIES, TOPS.
WHATEVER, I'M SURE SHE'S ALREADY ON A BOAT BACK TO NEW YORK.
ACTUALLY, SHE'S TAKING A PROP PLANE TO MELBOURNE INTERNATIONAL.
OR SHE WOULD BE, IF SOMEONE HADN'T BEEN QUICK ENOUGH TO LIFT HER BOARDING PASS.

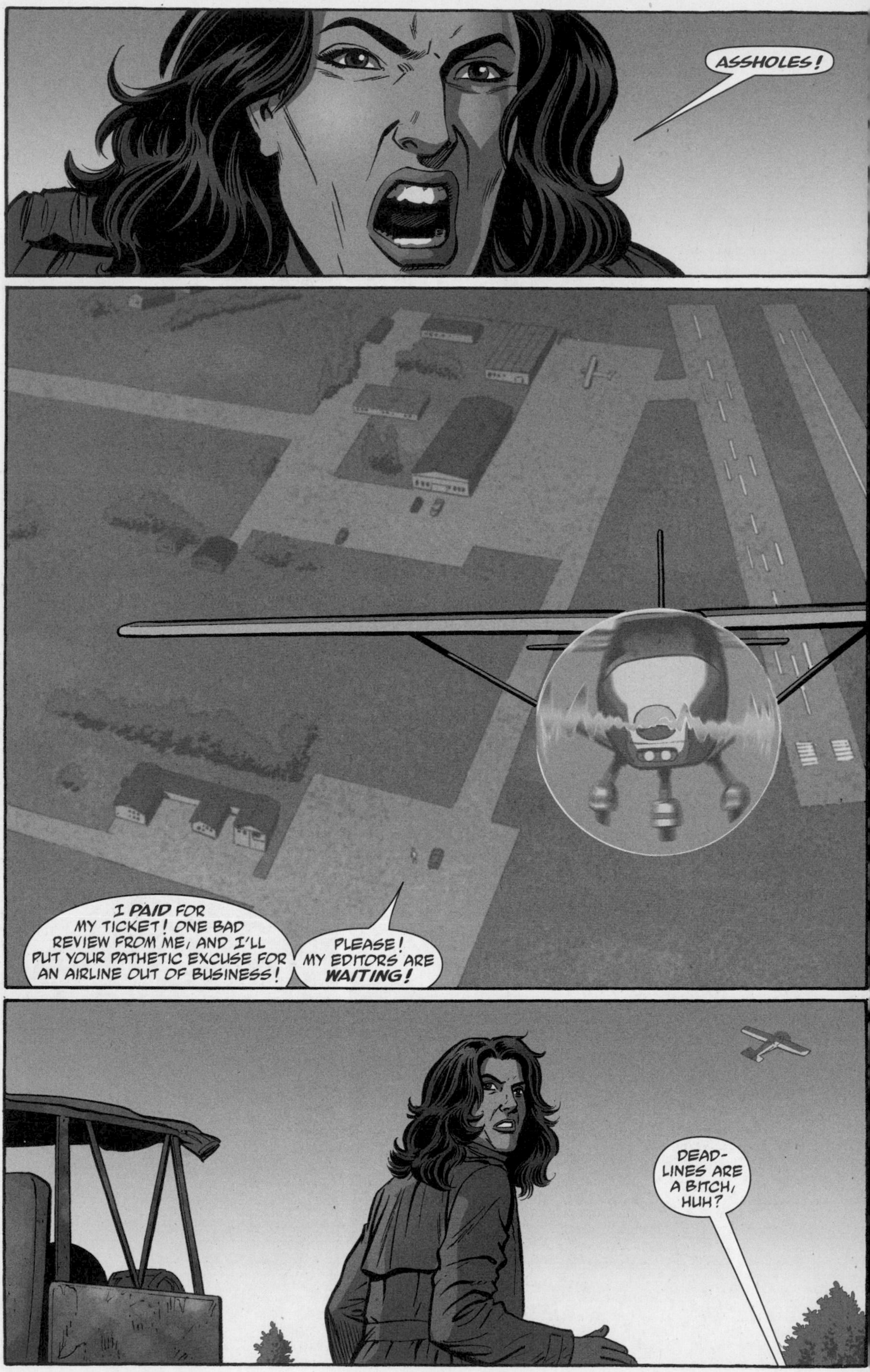
ASSHOLES!
I PAID FOR MY TICKET! ONE BAD REVIEW FROM ME, AND I'LL PUT YOUR PATHETIC EXCUSE FOR AN AIRLINE OUT OF BUSINESS!
PLEASE! MY EDITORS ARE WAITING!
DEAD-LINES ARE A BITCH, HUH?

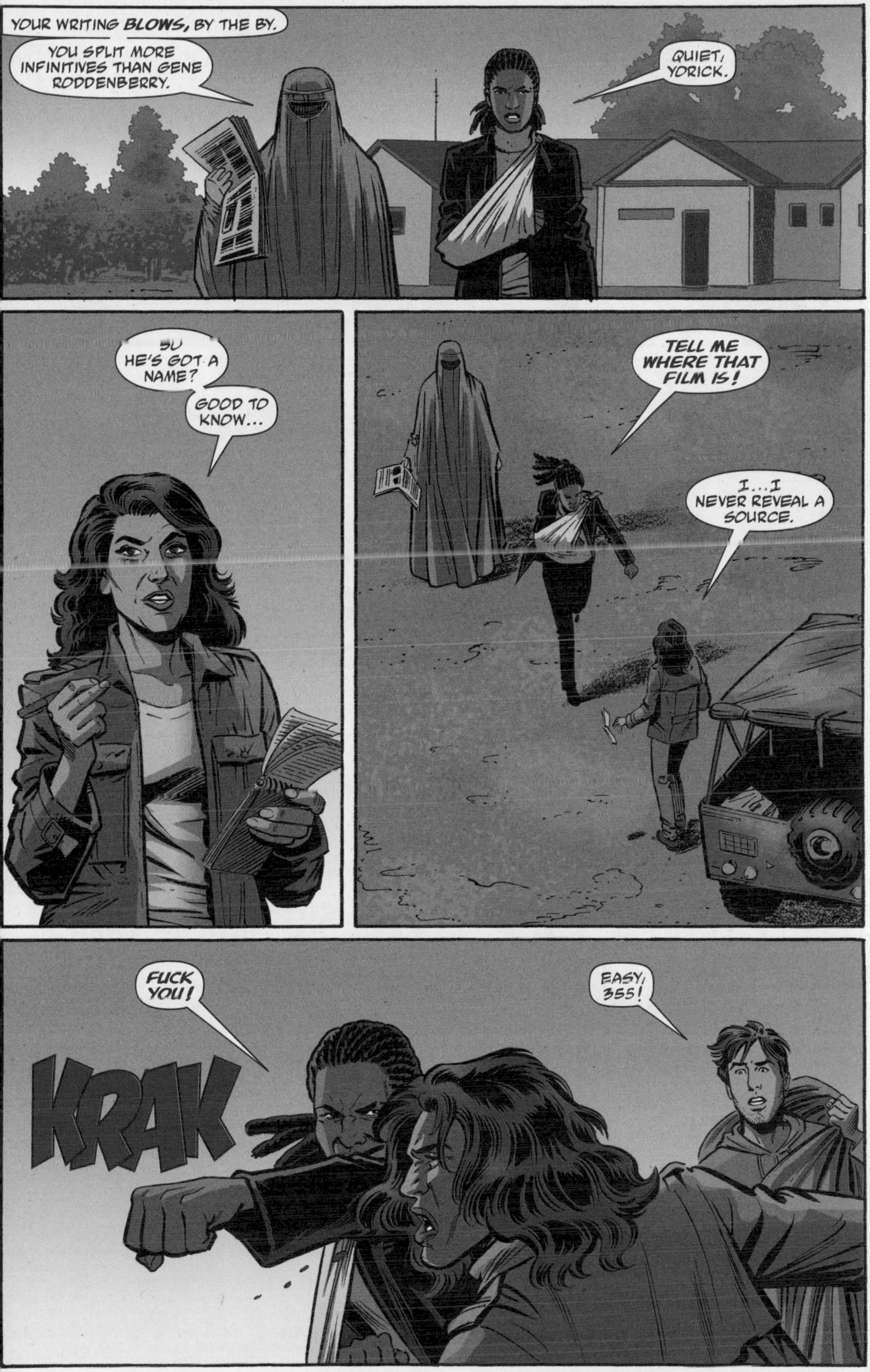
YOUR WRITING BLOWS, BY THE BY.
YOU SPLIT MORE INFINITIVES THAN GENE RODDENBERRY.
QUIET, YORICK.
SO HE'S GOT A NAME?
GOOD TO KNOW...
TELL ME WHERE THAT FILM IS!
I...I NEVER REVEAL A SOURCE.
FUCK YOU!
KRAK
EASY, 355!

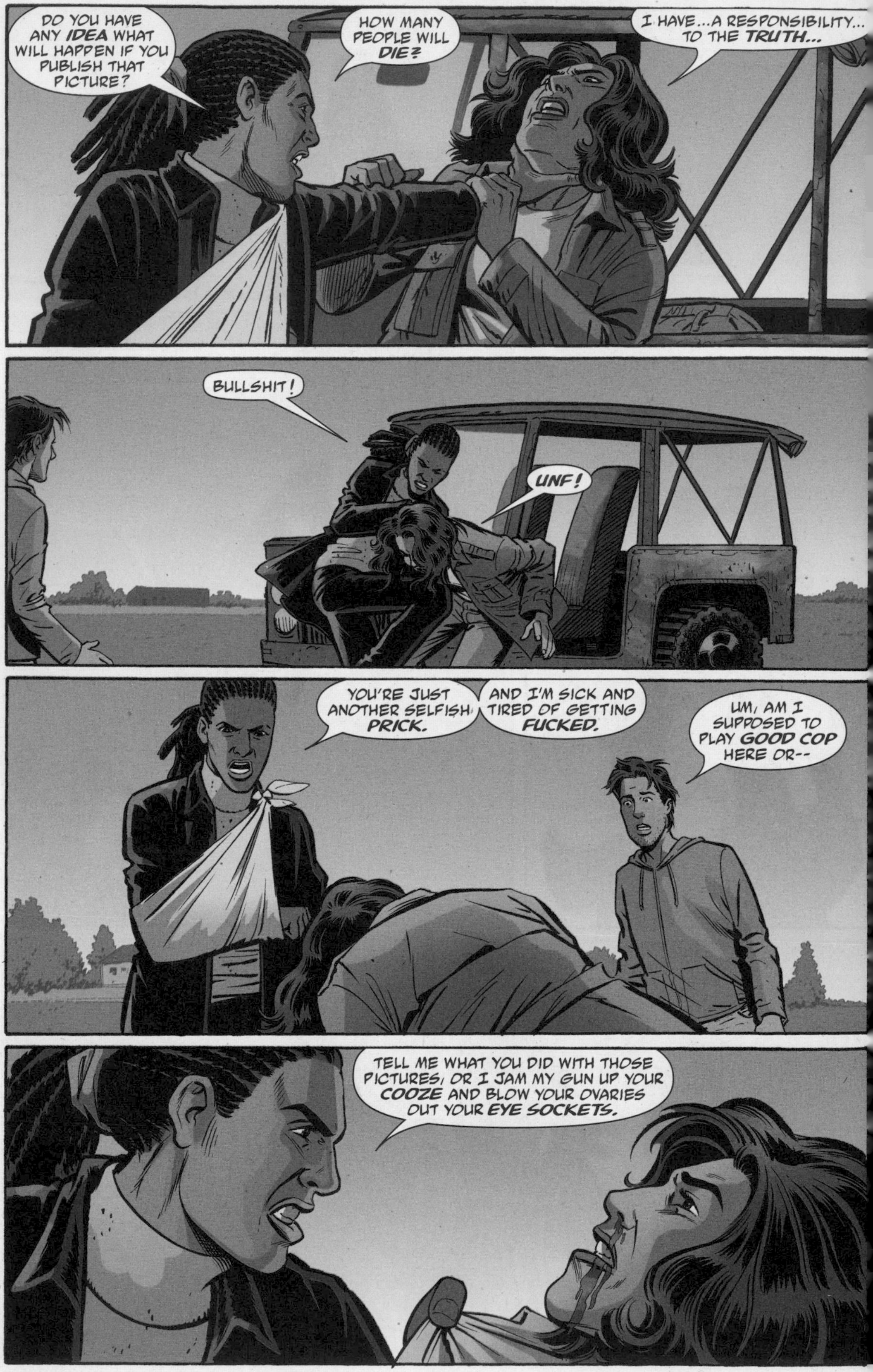
DO YOU HAVE ANY IDEA WHAT WILL HAPPEN IF YOU PUBLISH THAT PICTURE?
HOW MANY PEOPLE WILL DIE?
I HAVE...A RESPONSIBILITY... TO THE TRUTH...
BULLSHIT!
UNF!
YOU'RE JUST ANOTHER SELFISH PRICK.
AND I'M SICK AND TIRED OF GETTING FUCKED.
UM, AM I SUPPOSED TO PLAY GOOD COP HERE OR--
TELL ME WHAT YOU DID WITH THOSE PICTURES, OR I JAM MY GUN UP YOUR COOZE AND BLOW YOUR OVARIES OUT YOUR EYE SOCKETS.

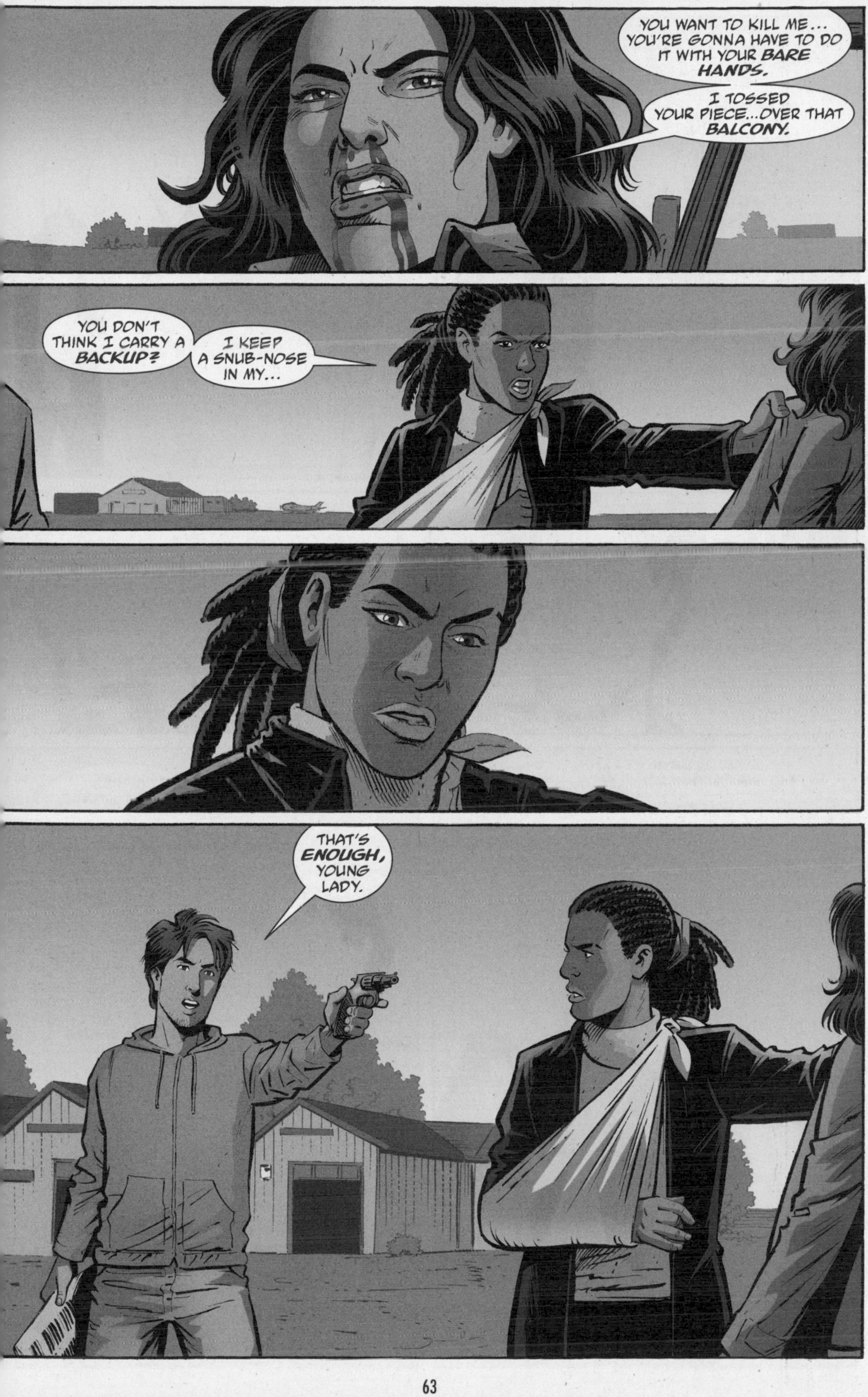
YOU WANT TO KILL ME... YOU'RE GONNA HAVE TO DO IT WITH YOUR BARE HANDS.
I TOSSED YOUR PIECE...OVER THAT BALCONY.
YOU DON'T THINK I CARRY A BACKUP?
I KEEP A SNUB-NOSE IN MY...
THAT'S ENOUGH, YOUNG LADY.

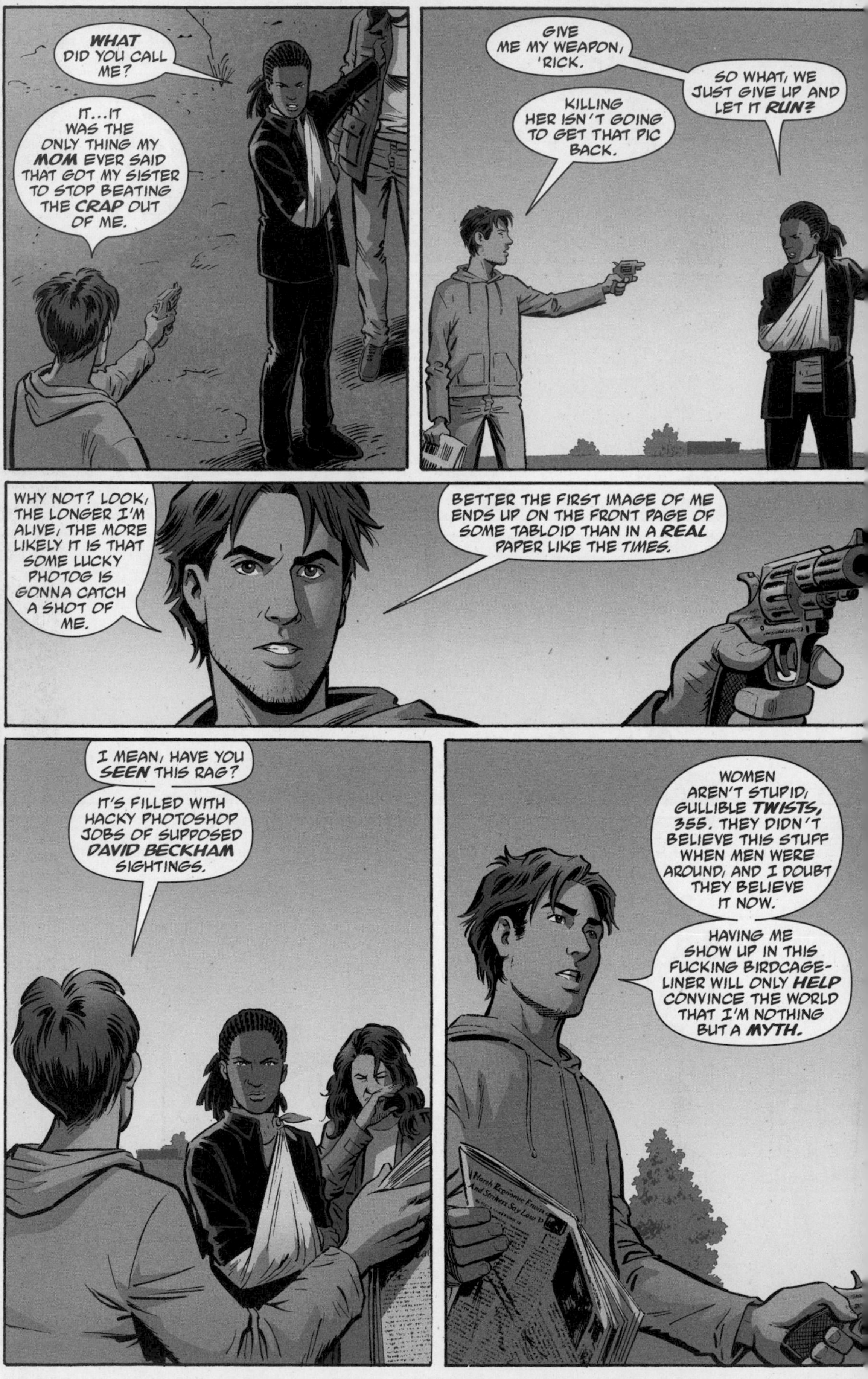
WHAT DID YOU CALL ME?
IT...IT WAS THE ONLY THING MY MOM EVER SAID THAT GOT MY SISTER TO STOP BEATING THE CRAP OUT OF ME.
GIVE ME MY WEAPON, 'RICK.
KILLING HER ISN'T GOING TO GET THAT PIC BACK.
SO WHAT, WE JUST GIVE UP AND LET IT RUN?
WHY NOT? LOOK, THE LONGER I'M ALIVE, THE MORE LIKELY IT IS THAT SOME LUCKY PHOTOG IS GONNA CATCH A SHOT OF ME.
BETTER THE FIRST IMAGE OF ME ENDS UP ON THE FRONT PAGE OF SOME TABLOID THAN IN A REAL PAPER LIKE THE TIMES.
I MEAN, HAVE YOU SEEN THIS RAG?
IT'S FILLED WITH HACKY PHOTOSHOP JOBS OF SUPPOSED DAVID BECKHAM SIGHTINGS.
WOMEN AREN'T STUPID, GULLIBLE TWISTS, 355. THEY DIDN'T BELIEVE THIS STUFF WHEN MEN WERE AROUND, AND I DOUBT THEY BELIEVE IT NOW.
HAVING ME SHOW UP IN THIS FUCKING BIRDCAGE-LINER WILL ONLY HELP CONVINCE THE WORLD THAT I'M NOTHING BUT A MYTH.

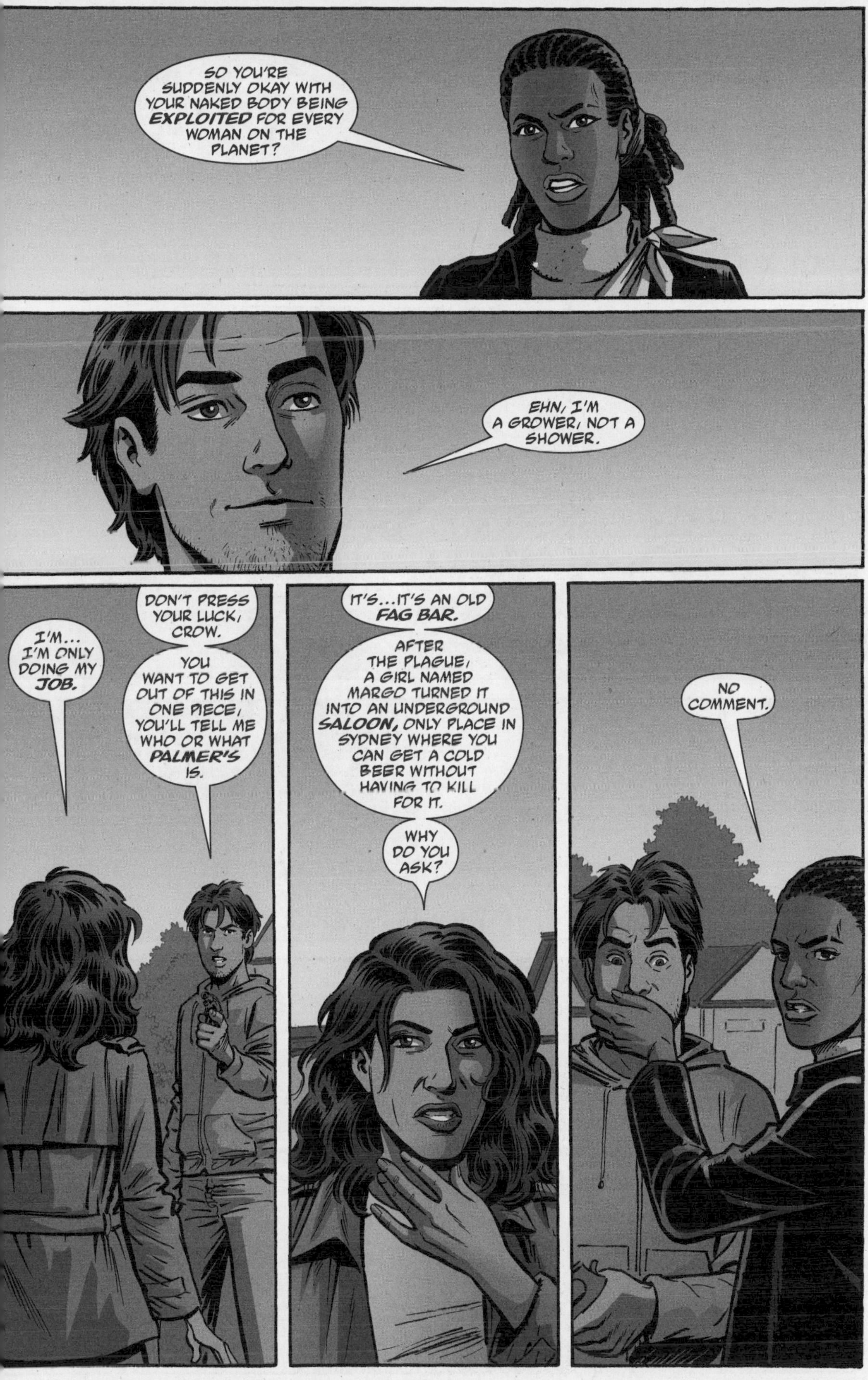
SO YOU'RE SUDDENLY OKAY WITH YOUR NAKED BODY BEING EXPLOITED FOR EVERY WOMAN ON THE PLANET?
EHN, I'M A GROWER, NOT A SHOWER.
DON'T PRESS YOUR LUCK, CROW.
I'M... I'M ONLY DOING MY JOB.
YOU WANT TO GET OUT OF THIS IN ONE PIECE, YOU'LL TELL ME WHO OR WHAT PALMER'S IS.
IT'S...IT'S AN OLD FAG BAR.
AFTER THE PLAGUE, A GIRL NAMED MARGO TURNED IT INTO AN UNDERGROUND SALOON, ONLY PLACE IN SYDNEY WHERE YOU CAN GET A COLD BEER WITHOUT HAVING TO KILL FOR IT.
WHY DO YOU ASK?
NO COMMENT.

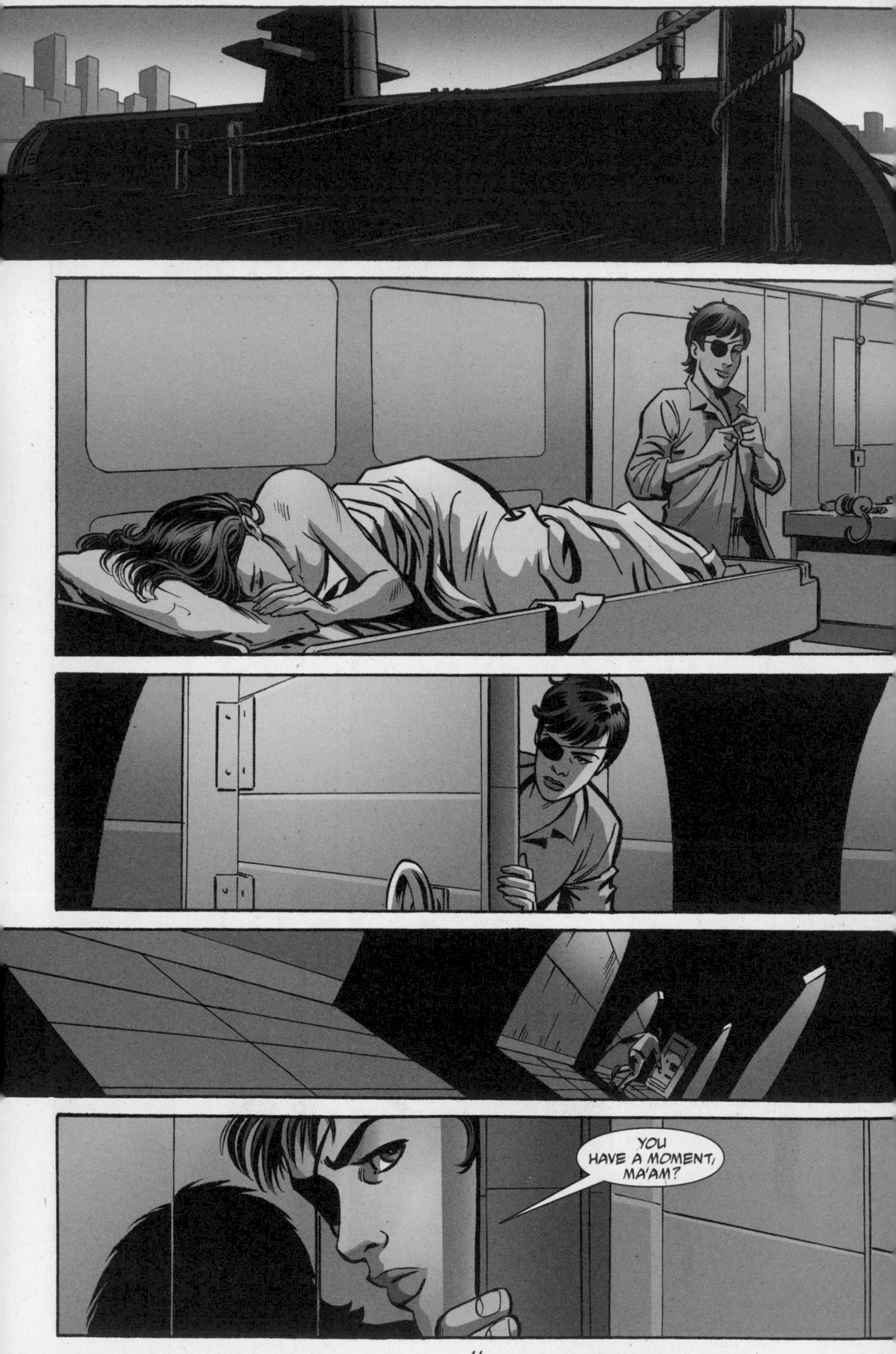
YOU HAVE A MOMENT, MA'AM?

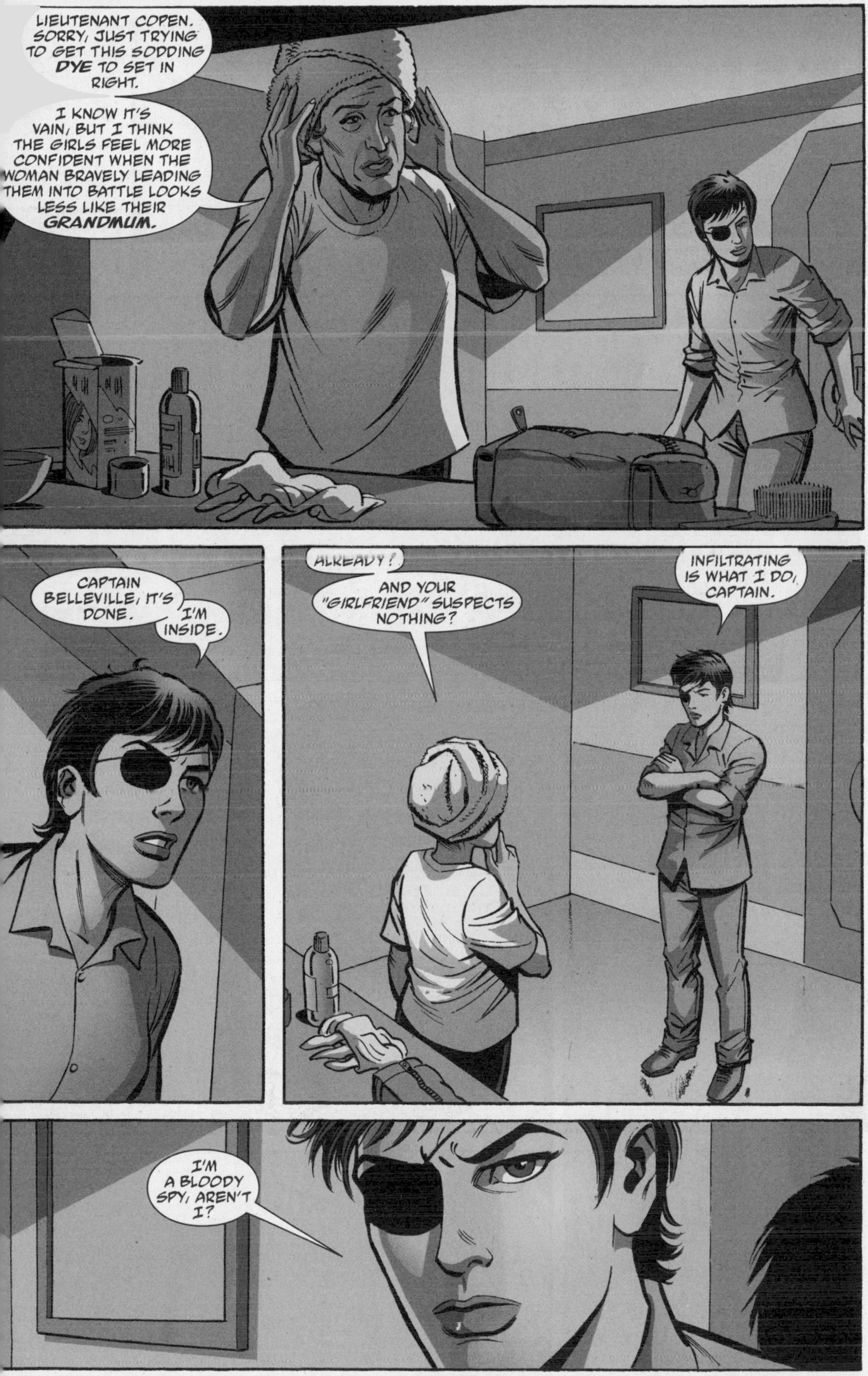
LIEUTENANT COPEN. SORRY, JUST TRYING TO GET THIS SODDING DYE TO SET IN RIGHT.
I KNOW IT'S VAIN, BUT I THINK THE GIRLS FEEL MORE CONFIDENT WHEN THE WOMAN BRAVELY LEADING THEM INTO BATTLE LOOKS LESS LIKE THEIR GRANDMUM.
CAPTAIN BELLEVILLE, IT'S DONE.
I'M INSIDE.
ALREADY?
AND YOUR "GIRLFRIEND" SUSPECTS NOTHING?
INFILTRATING IS WHAT I DO, CAPTAIN.
I'M A BLOODY SPY, AREN'T I?

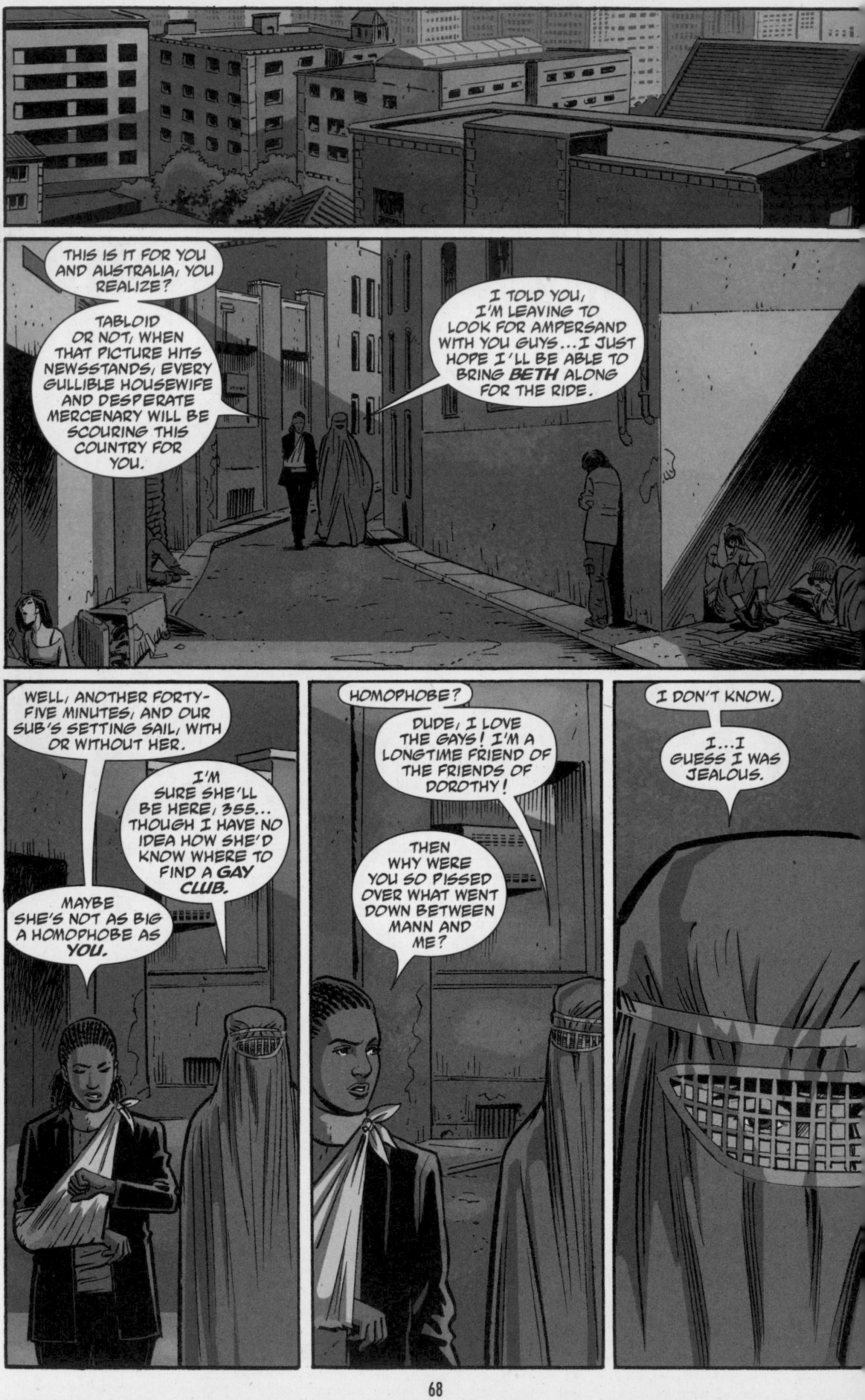

THIS IS IT FOR YOU AND AUSTRALIA, YOU REALIZE?
TABLOID OR NOT, WHEN THAT PICTURE HITS NEWSSTANDS, EVERY GULLIBLE HOUSEWIFE AND DESPERATE MERCENARY WILL BE SCOURING THIS COUNTRY FOR YOU.
I TOLD YOU, I'M LEAVING TO LOOK FOR AMPERSAND WITH YOU GUYS... I JUST HOPE I'LL BE ABLE TO BRING BETH ALONG FOR THE RIDE.
WELL, ANOTHER FORTY-FIVE MINUTES, AND OUR SUB'S SETTING SAIL, WITH OR WITHOUT HER.
I'M SURE SHE'LL BE HERE, 355... THOUGH I HAVE NO IDEA HOW SHE'D KNOW WHERE TO FIND A GAY CLUB.
MAYBE SHE'S NOT AS BIG A HOMOPHOBE AS YOU.
HOMOPHOBE?
DUDE, I LOVE THE GAYS! I'M A LONGTIME FRIEND OF THE FRIENDS OF DOROTHY!
THEN WHY WERE YOU SO PISSED OVER WHAT WENT DOWN BETWEEN MANN AND ME?
I DON'T KNOW.
I...I GUESS I WAS JEALOUS.

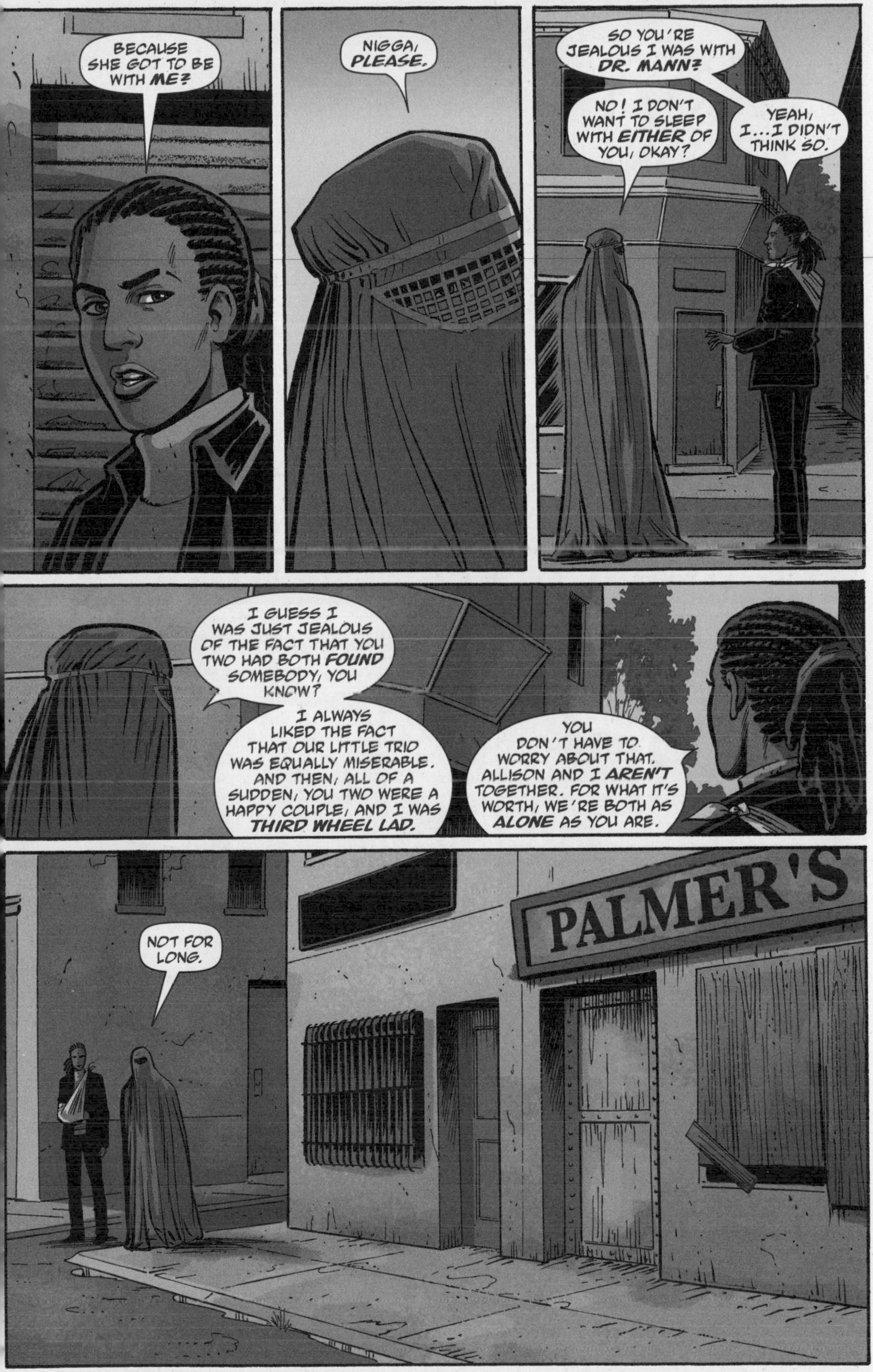
BECAUSE SHE GOT TO BE WITH ME?
NIGGA, PLEASE.
SO YOU'RE JEALOUS I WAS WITH DR. MANN?
YEAH, I...I DIDN'T THINK SO.
NO! I DON'T WANT TO SLEEP WITH EITHER OF YOU, OKAY?
I GUESS I WAS JUST JEALOUS OF THE FACT THAT YOU TWO HAD BOTH FOUND SOMEBODY, YOU KNOW?
I ALWAYS LIKED THE FACT THAT OUR LITTLE TRIO WAS EQUALLY MISERABLE. AND THEN, ALL OF A SUDDEN, YOU TWO WERE A HAPPY COUPLE, AND I WAS THIRD WHEEL LAD.
YOU DON'T HAVE TO WORRY ABOUT THAT. ALLISON AND I AREN'T TOGETHER. FOR WHAT IT'S WORTH, WE'RE BOTH AS ALONE AS YOU ARE.
PALMER'S
NOT FOR LONG.

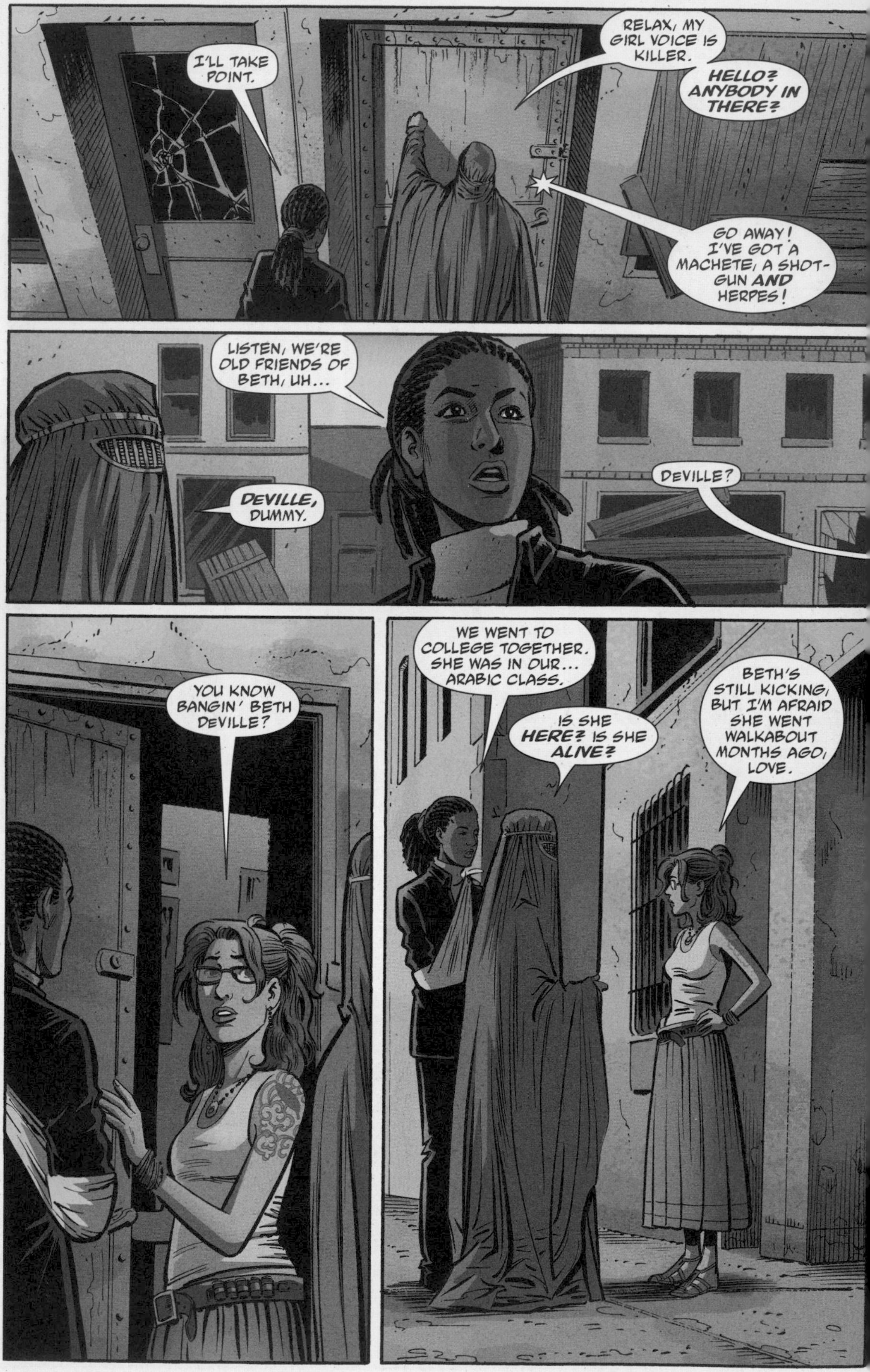
I'LL TAKE POINT.
RELAX, MY GIRL VOICE IS KILLER.
HELLO? ANYBODY IN THERE?
GO AWAY! I'VE GOT A MACHETE, A SHOT-GUN AND HERPES!
LISTEN, WE'RE OLD FRIENDS OF BETH, UH...
DEVILLE, DUMMY.
DEVILLE?
YOU KNOW BANGIN' BETH DEVILLE?
WE WENT TO COLLEGE TOGETHER. SHE WAS IN OUR... ARABIC CLASS.
IS SHE HERE? IS SHE ALIVE?
BETH'S STILL KICKING, BUT I'M AFRAID SHE WENT WALKABOUT MONTHS AGO, LOVE.

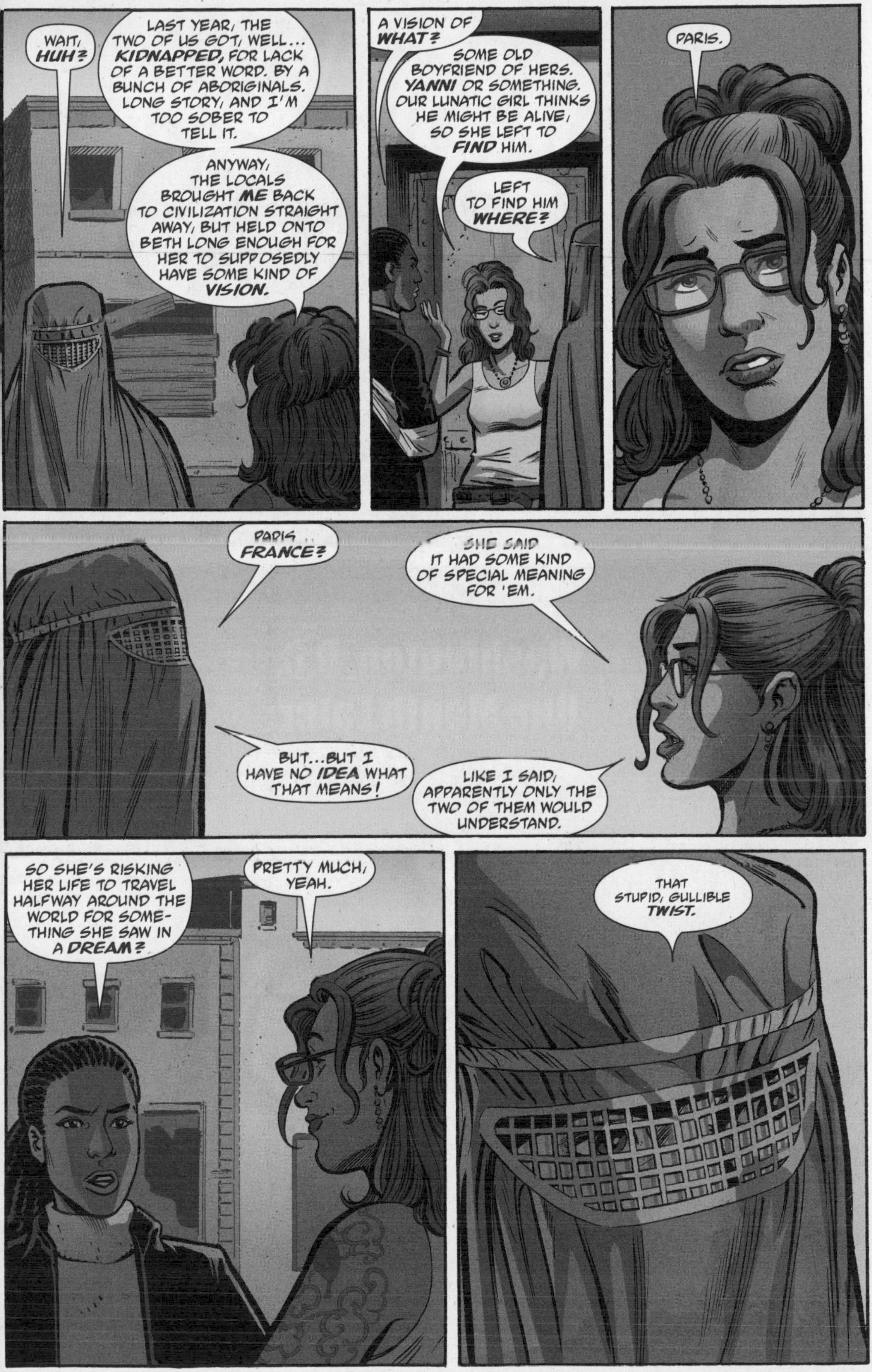
WAIT, HUH?
LAST YEAR, THE TWO OF US GOT, WELL... KIDNAPPED, FOR LACK OF A BETTER WORD. BY A BUNCH OF ABORIGINALS. LONG STORY, AND I'M TOO SOBER TO TELL IT.
ANYWAY, THE LOCALS BROUGHT ME BACK TO CIVILIZATION STRAIGHT AWAY, BUT HELD ONTO BETH LONG ENOUGH FOR HER TO SUPPOSEDLY HAVE SOME KIND OF VISION.
A VISION OF WHAT?
SOME OLD BOYFRIEND OF HERS. YANNI OR SOMETHING. OUR LUNATIC GIRL THINKS HE MIGHT BE ALIVE, SO SHE LEFT TO FIND HIM.
LEFT TO FIND HIM WHERE?
PARIS.
PARIS... FRANCE?
SHE SAID IT HAD SOME KIND OF SPECIAL MEANING FOR 'EM.
BUT...BUT I HAVE NO IDEA WHAT THAT MEANS!
LIKE I SAID, APPARENTLY ONLY THE TWO OF THEM WOULD UNDERSTAND.
SO SHE'S RISKING HER LIFE TO TRAVEL HALFWAY AROUND THE WORLD FOR SOMETHING SHE SAW IN A DREAM?
PRETTY MUCH, YEAH.
THAT STUPID, GULLIBLE TWIST.

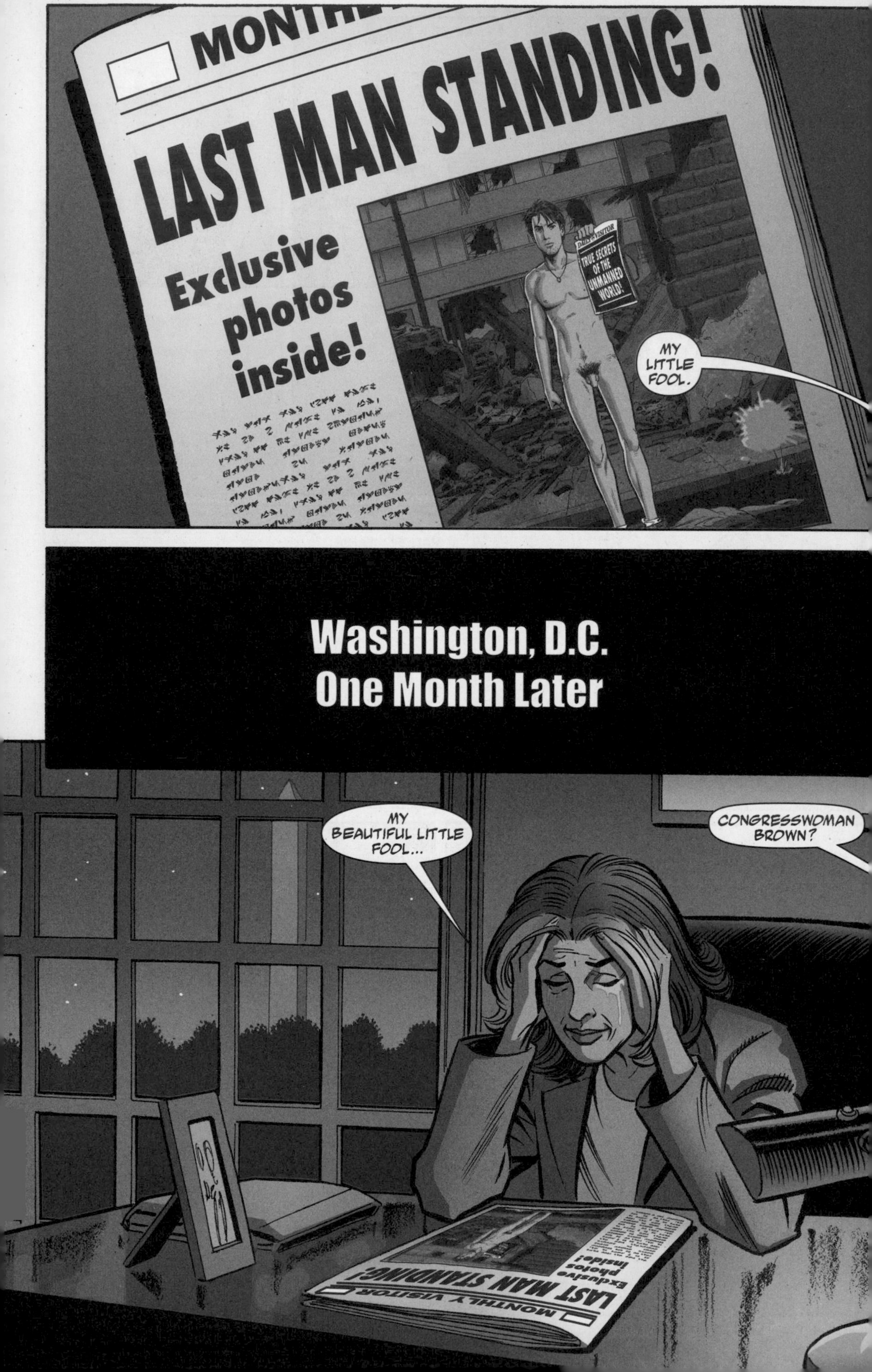
LAST MAN STANDING!
Exclusive photos inside!
TRUE SECRETS OF THE UNMANNED WORLD!
MY LITTLE FOOL.
Washington, D.C.
One Month Later
MY BEAUTIFUL LITTLE FOOL...
CONGRESSWOMAN BROWN?
MONTHLY VISITOR
LAST MAN STANDING!
Exclusive photos inside!

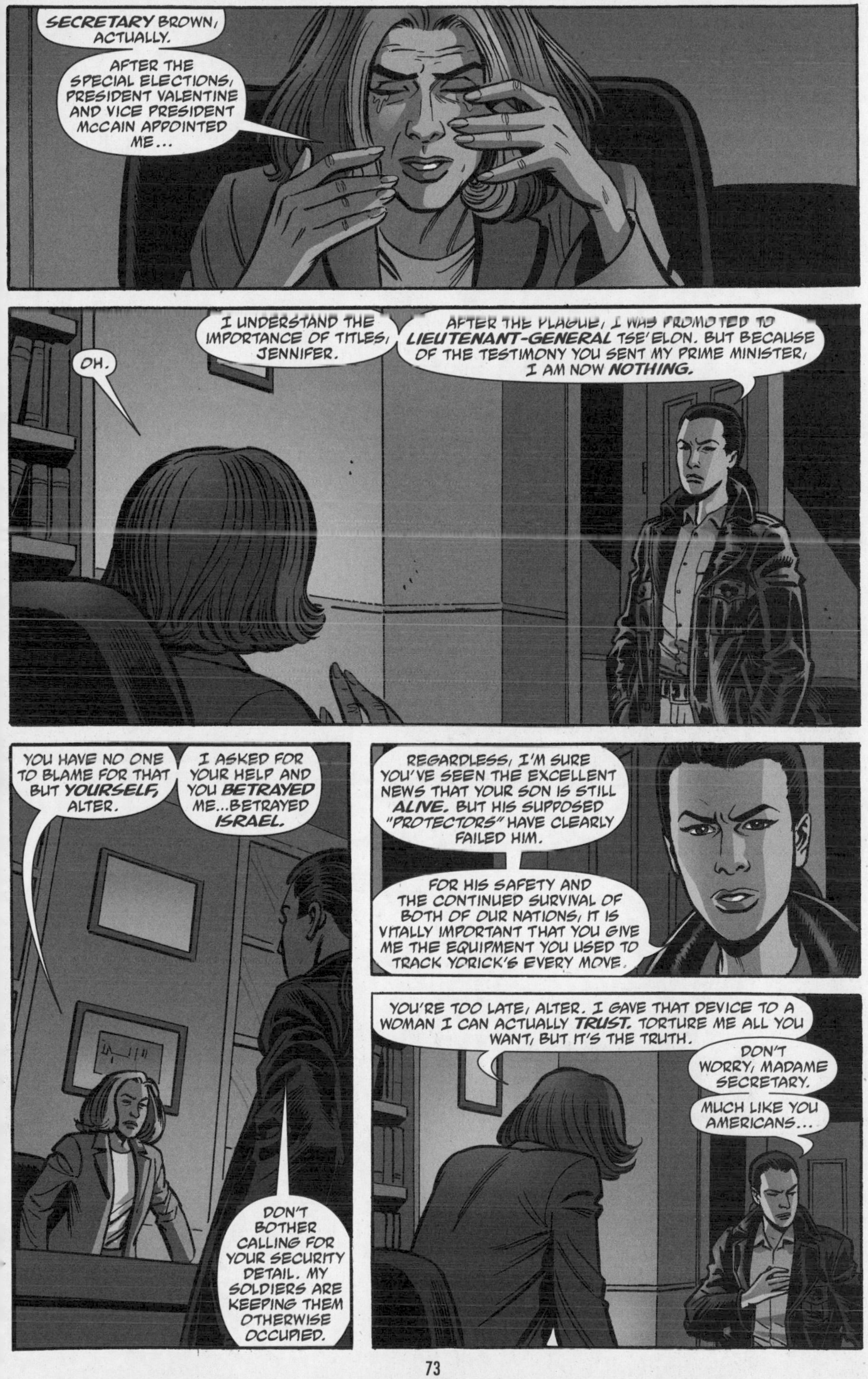
SECRETARY BROWN, ACTUALLY.
AFTER THE SPECIAL ELECTIONS, PRESIDENT VALENTINE AND VICE PRESIDENT McCAIN APPOINTED ME...
OH.
I UNDERSTAND THE IMPORTANCE OF TITLES, JENNIFER.
AFTER THE PLAGUE, I WAS PROMOTED TO LIEUTENANT-GENERAL TSE'ELON. BUT BECAUSE OF THE TESTIMONY YOU SENT MY PRIME MINISTER, I AM NOW NOTHING.
YOU HAVE NO ONE TO BLAME FOR THAT BUT YOURSELF, ALTER.
I ASKED FOR YOUR HELP AND YOU BETRAYED ME...BETRAYED ISRAEL.
DON'T BOTHER CALLING FOR YOUR SECURITY DETAIL. MY SOLDIERS ARE KEEPING THEM OTHERWISE OCCUPIED.
REGARDLESS, I'M SURE YOU'VE SEEN THE EXCELLENT NEWS THAT YOUR SON IS STILL ALIVE. BUT HIS SUPPOSED "PROTECTORS" HAVE CLEARLY FAILED HIM.
FOR HIS SAFETY AND THE CONTINUED SURVIVAL OF BOTH OF OUR NATIONS, IT IS VITALLY IMPORTANT THAT YOU GIVE ME THE EQUIPMENT YOU USED TO TRACK YORICK'S EVERY MOVE.
YOU'RE TOO LATE, ALTER. I GAVE THAT DEVICE TO A WOMAN I CAN ACTUALLY TRUST. TORTURE ME ALL YOU WANT, BUT IT'S THE TRUTH.
DON'T WORRY, MADAME SECRETARY.
MUCH LIKE YOU AMERICANS...

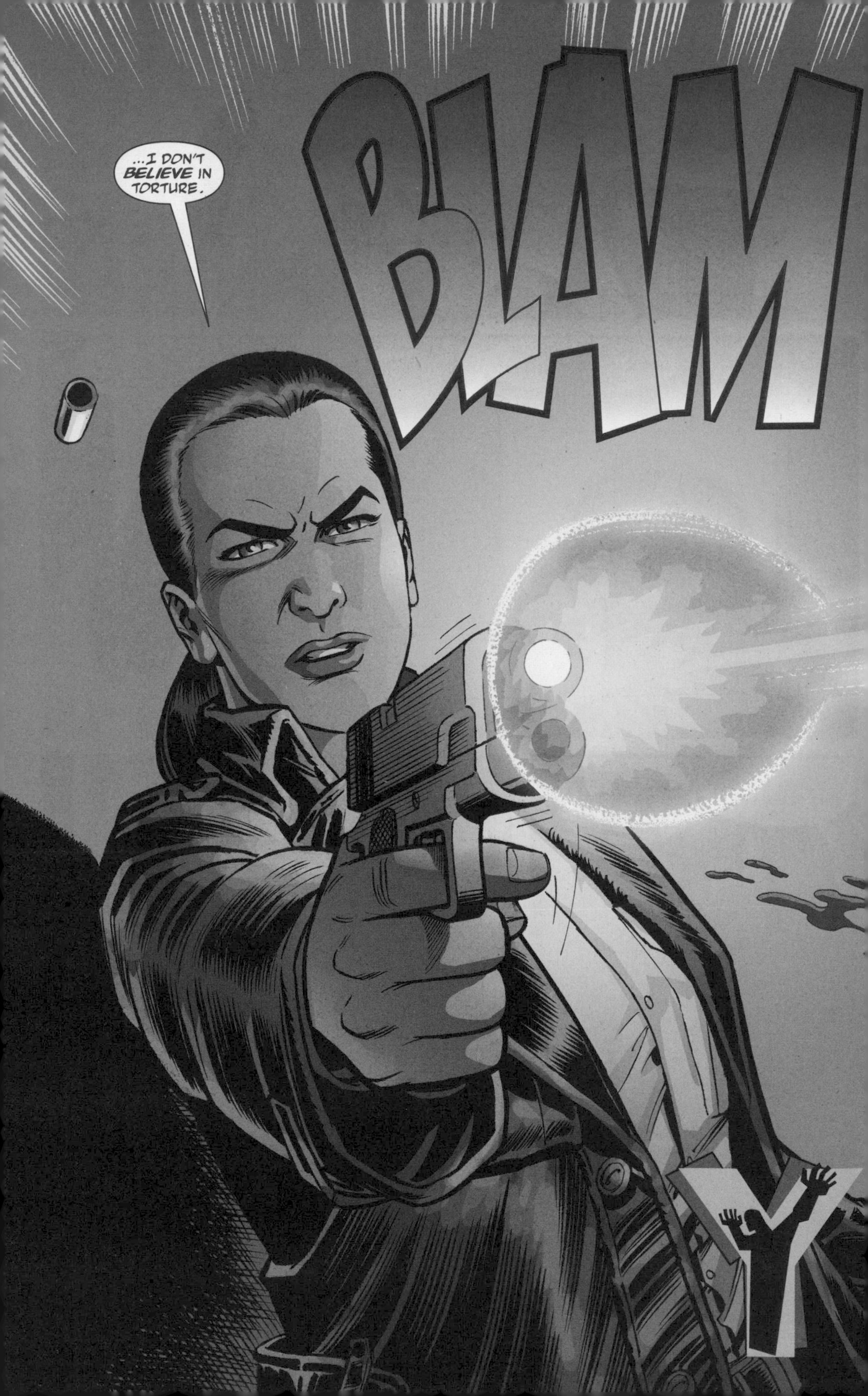
...I DON'T BELIEVE IN TORTURE.
BLAM

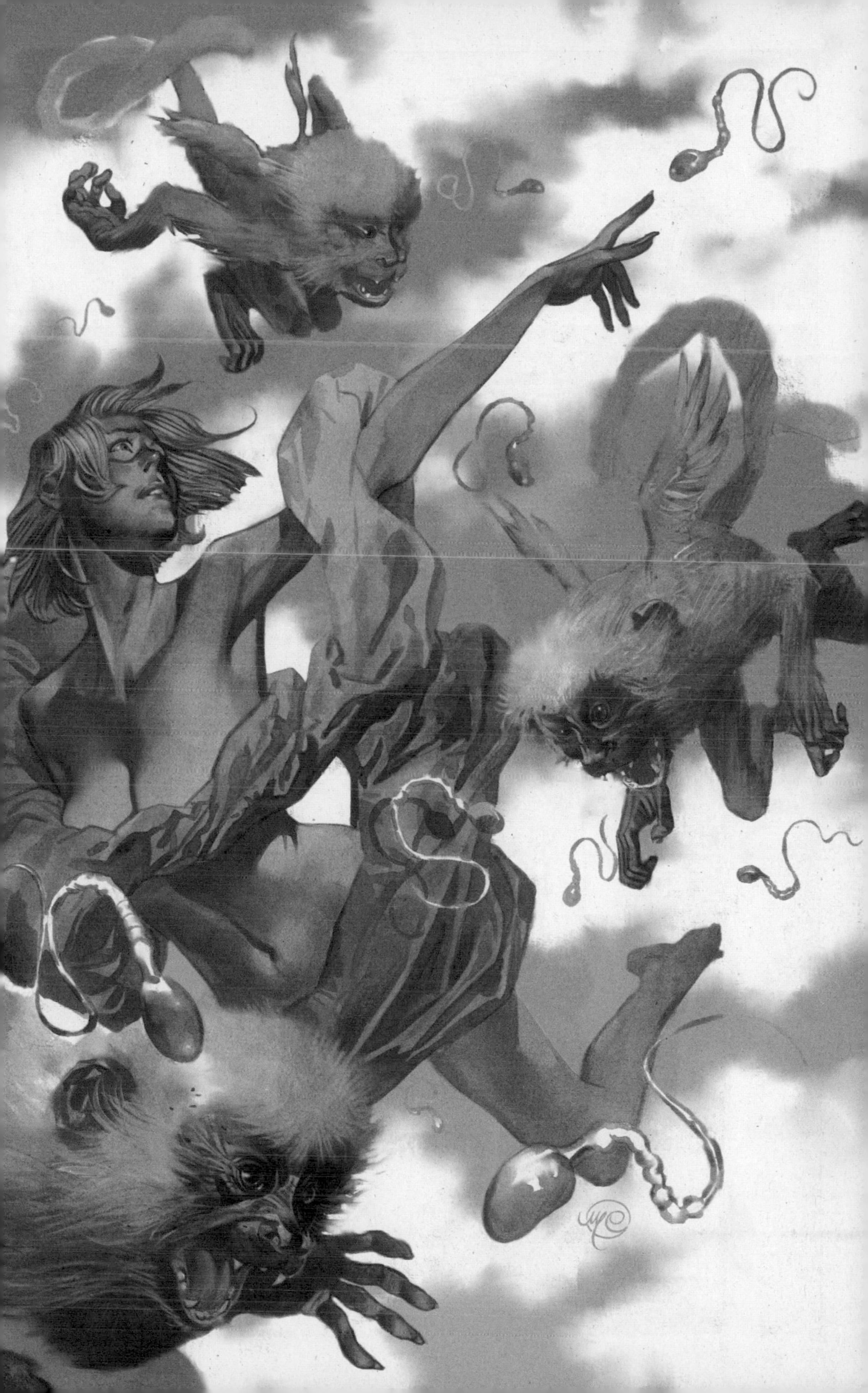

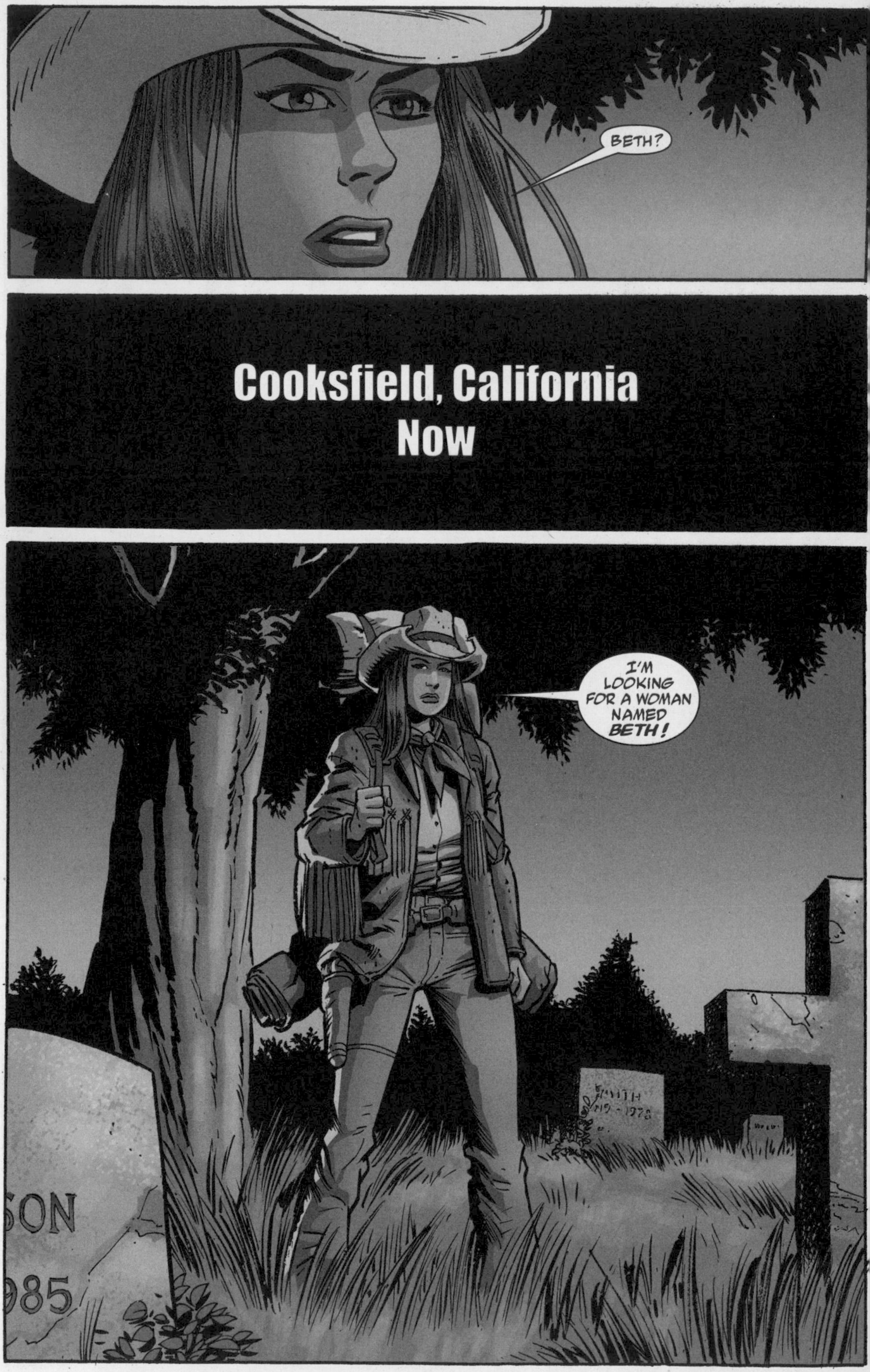
BETH?
Cooksfield, California
Now
I'M LOOKING FOR A WOMAN NAMED BETH!
SON
985

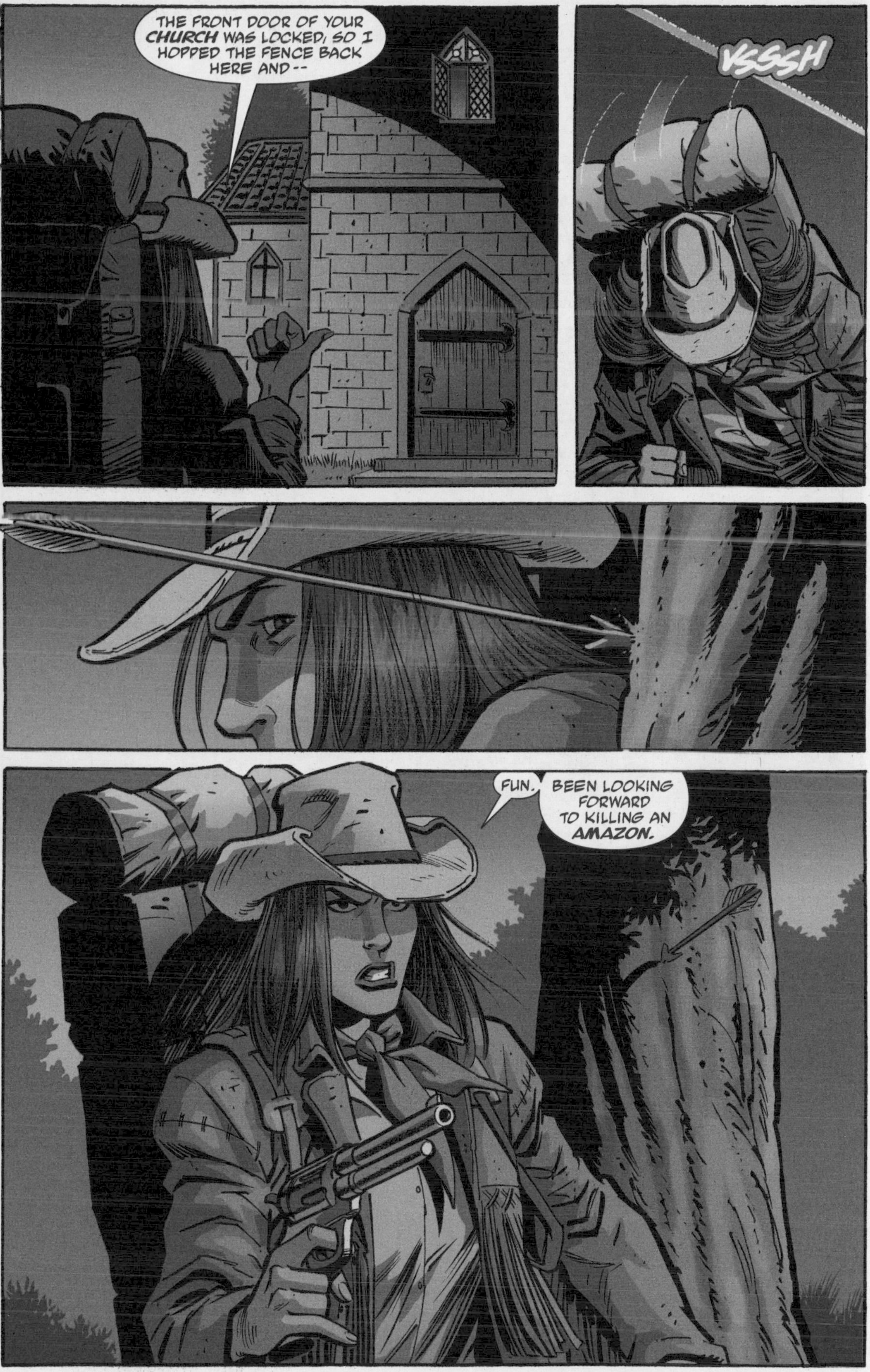
THE FRONT DOOR OF YOUR CHURCH WAS LOCKED, SO I HOPPED THE FENCE BACK HERE AND --
VSSSH
FUN.
BEEN LOOKING FORWARD TO KILLING AN AMAZON.

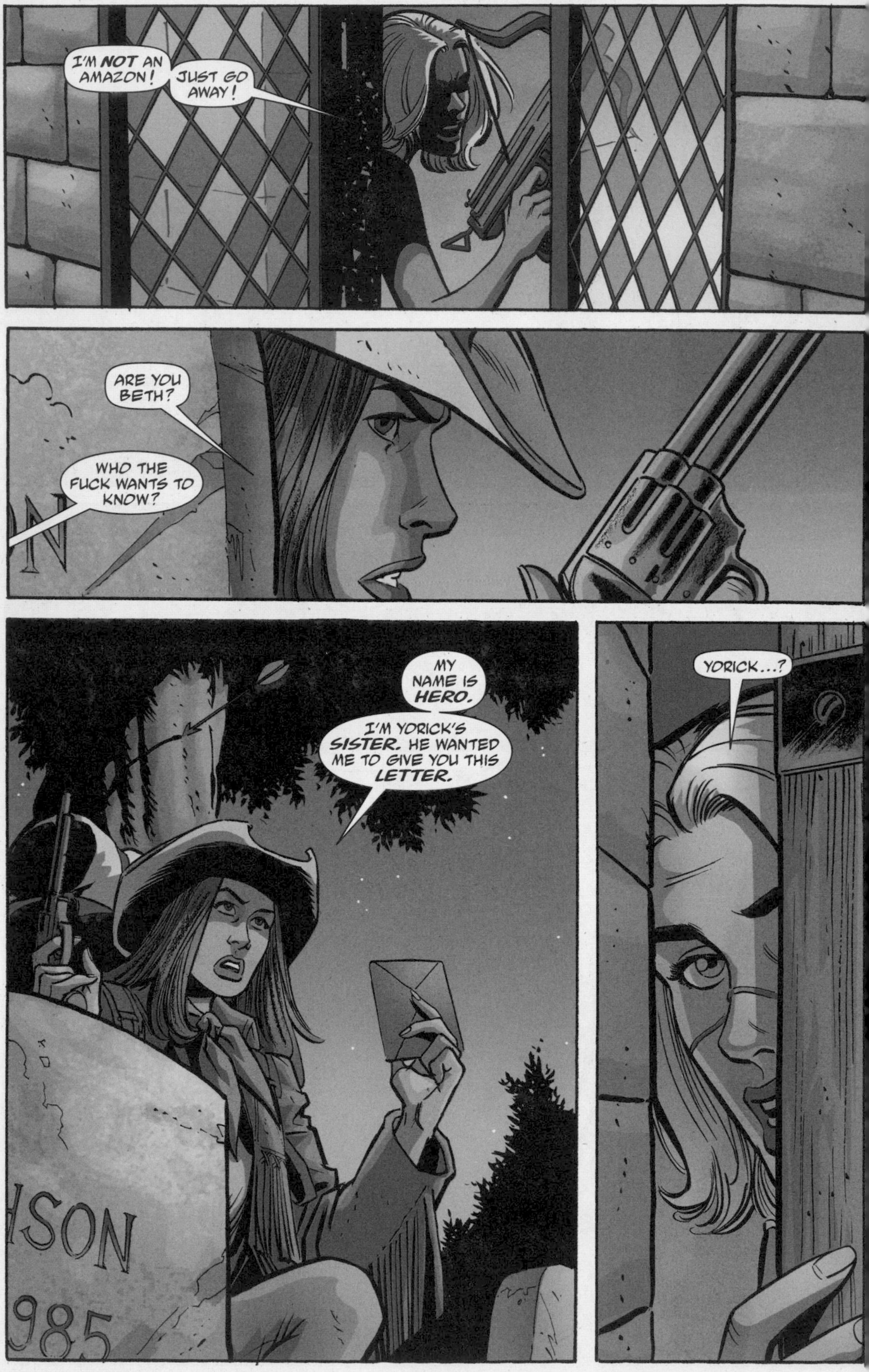
I'M NOT AN AMAZON!
JUST GO AWAY!
ARE YOU BETH?
WHO THE FUCK WANTS TO KNOW?
MY NAME IS HERO.
I'M YORICK'S SISTER. HE WANTED ME TO GIVE YOU THIS LETTER.
YORICK...?

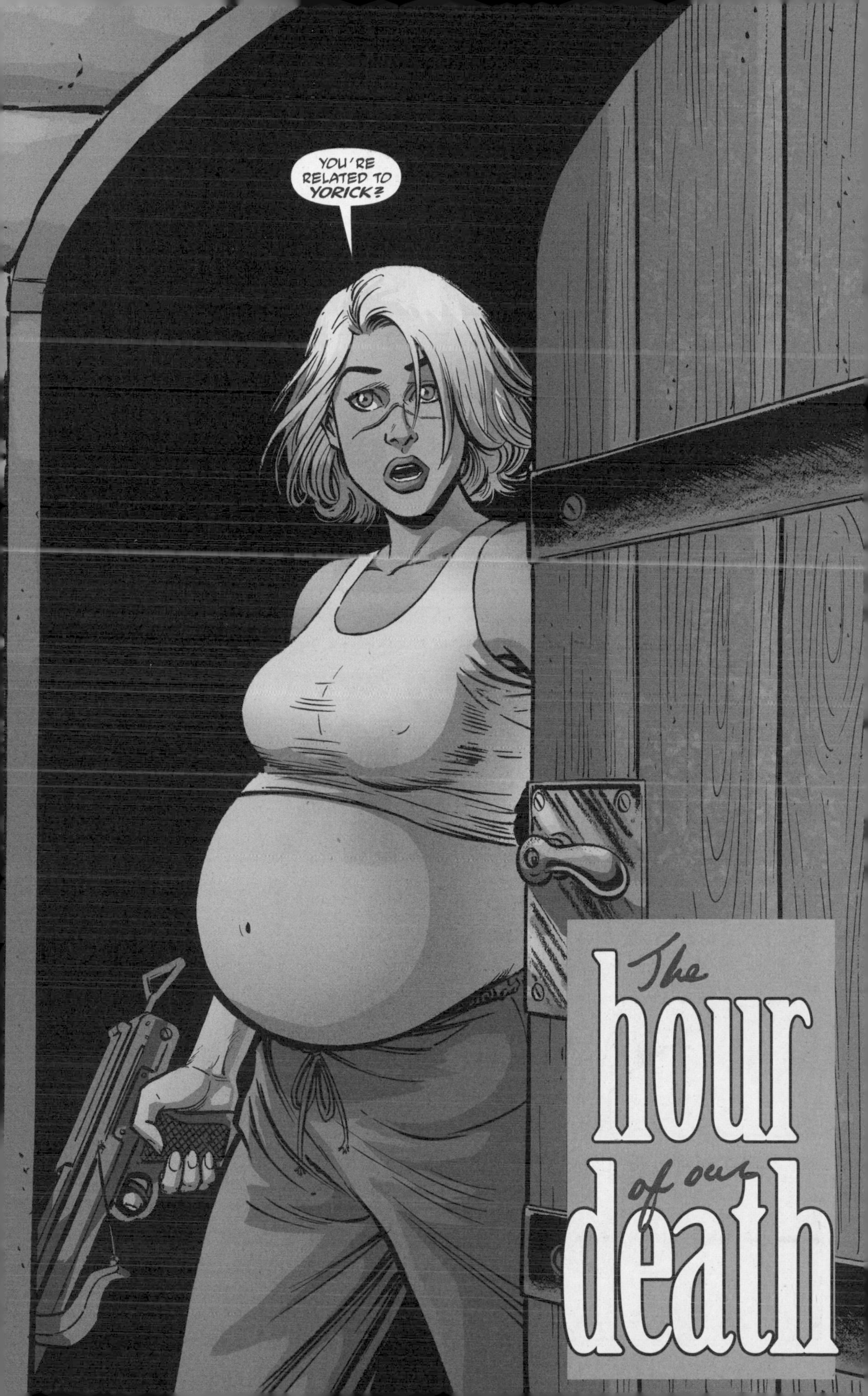
YOU'RE RELATED TO YORICK?
The hour of our death

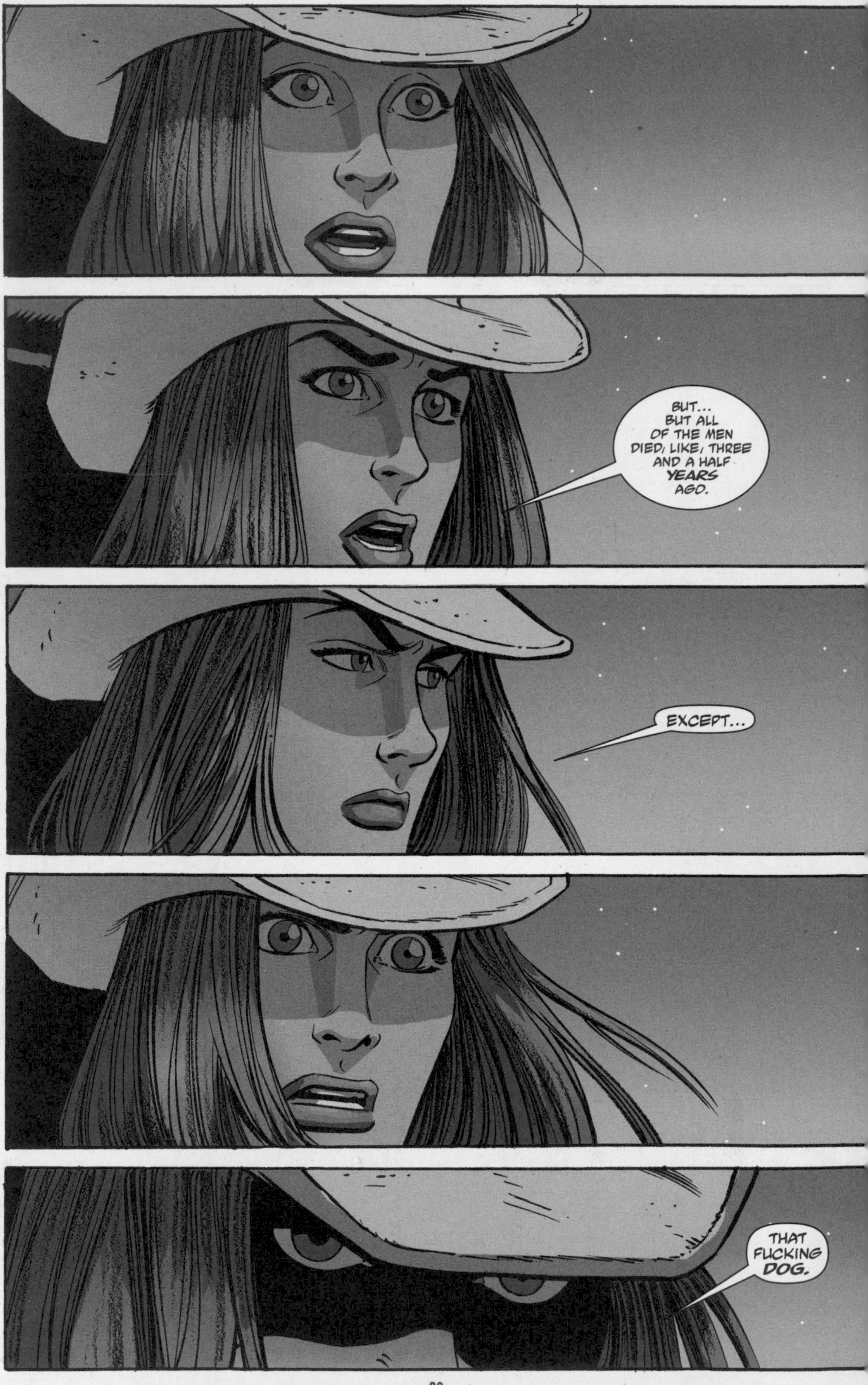
BUT...
BUT ALL OF THE MEN DIED, LIKE, THREE AND A HALF YEARS AGO.
EXCEPT...
THAT FUCKING DOG.

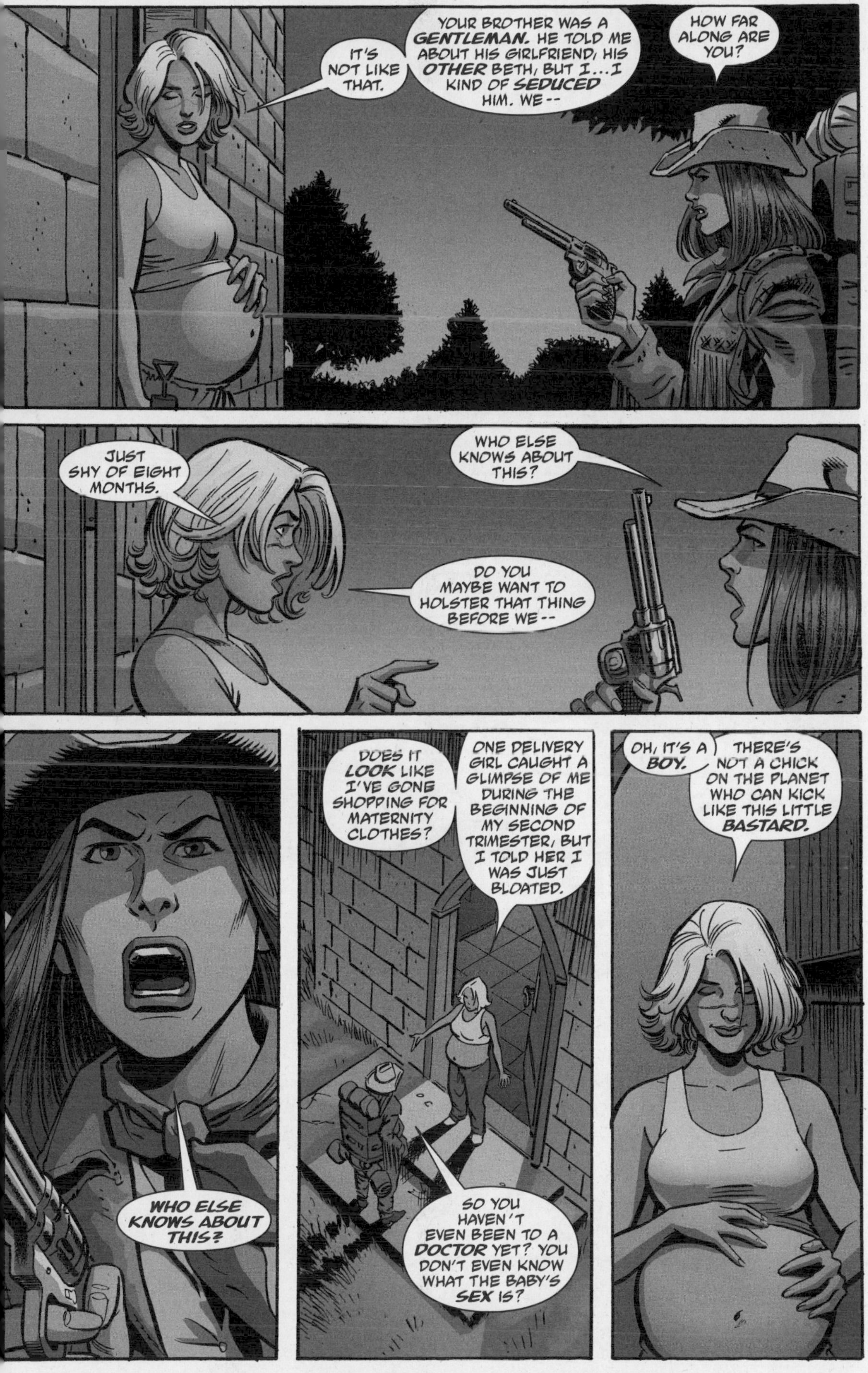
IT'S NOT LIKE THAT.
YOUR BROTHER WAS A GENTLEMAN. HE TOLD ME ABOUT HIS GIRLFRIEND, HIS OTHER BETH, BUT I... I KIND OF SEDUCED HIM. WE --
HOW FAR ALONG ARE YOU?
JUST SHY OF EIGHT MONTHS.
WHO ELSE KNOWS ABOUT THIS?
DO YOU MAYBE WANT TO HOLSTER THAT THING BEFORE WE --
WHO ELSE KNOWS ABOUT THIS?
DOES IT LOOK LIKE I'VE GONE SHOPPING FOR MATERNITY CLOTHES?
ONE DELIVERY GIRL CAUGHT A GLIMPSE OF ME DURING THE BEGINNING OF MY SECOND TRIMESTER, BUT I TOLD HER I WAS JUST BLOATED.
SO YOU HAVEN'T EVEN BEEN TO A DOCTOR YET? YOU DON'T EVEN KNOW WHAT THE BABY'S SEX IS?
OH, IT'S A BOY.
THERE'S NOT A CHICK ON THE PLANET WHO CAN KICK LIKE THIS LITTLE BASTARD.

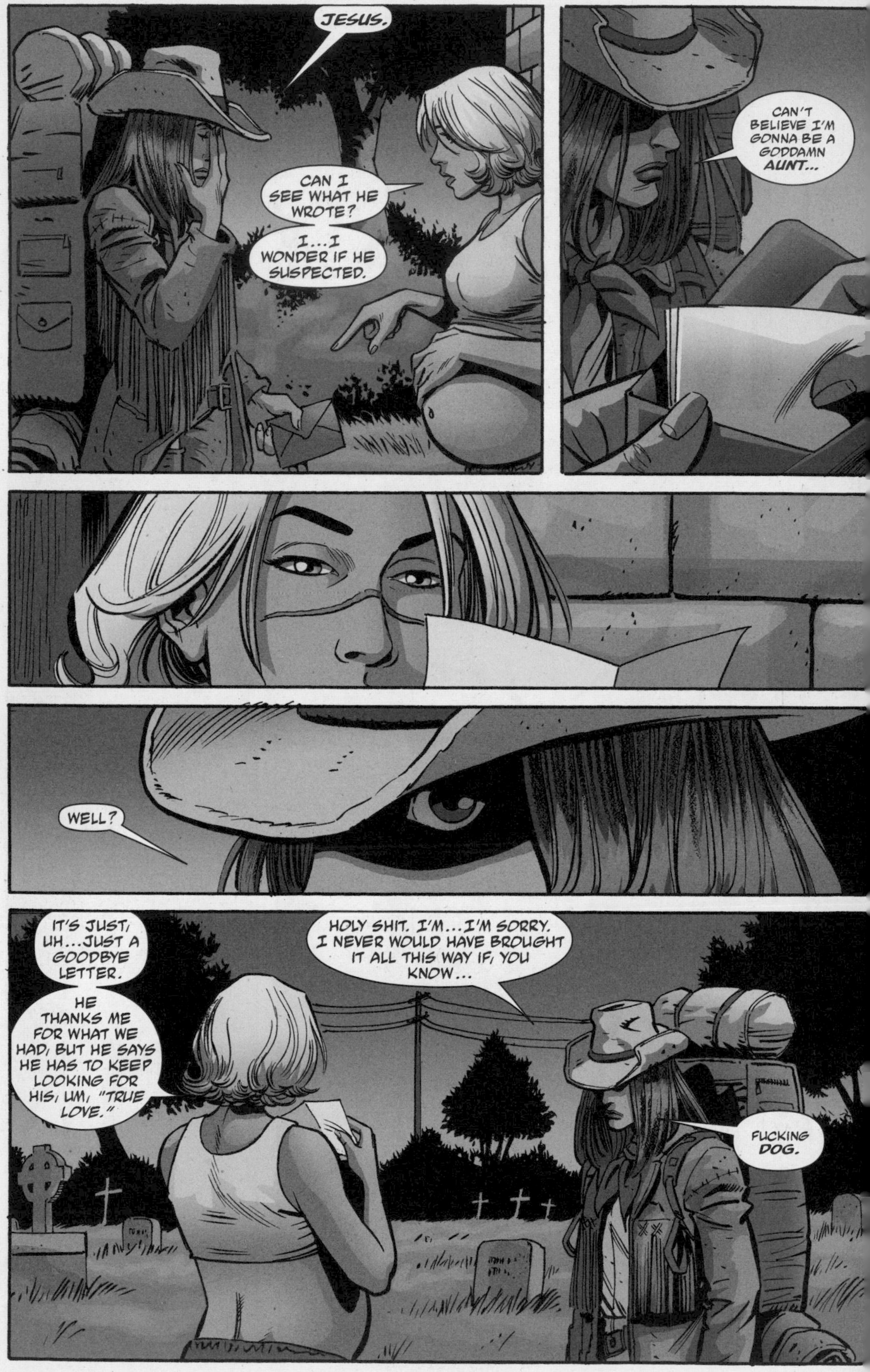
JESUS.
CAN I SEE WHAT HE WROTE?
I...I WONDER IF HE SUSPECTED.
CAN'T BELIEVE I'M GONNA BE A GODDAMN AUNT...
WELL?
IT'S JUST, UH...JUST A GOODBYE LETTER.
HE THANKS ME FOR WHAT WE HAD, BUT HE SAYS HE HAS TO KEEP LOOKING FOR HIS, UM, "TRUE LOVE."
HOLY SHIT. I'M...I'M SORRY. I NEVER WOULD HAVE BROUGHT IT ALL THIS WAY IF, YOU KNOW...
FUCKING DOG.

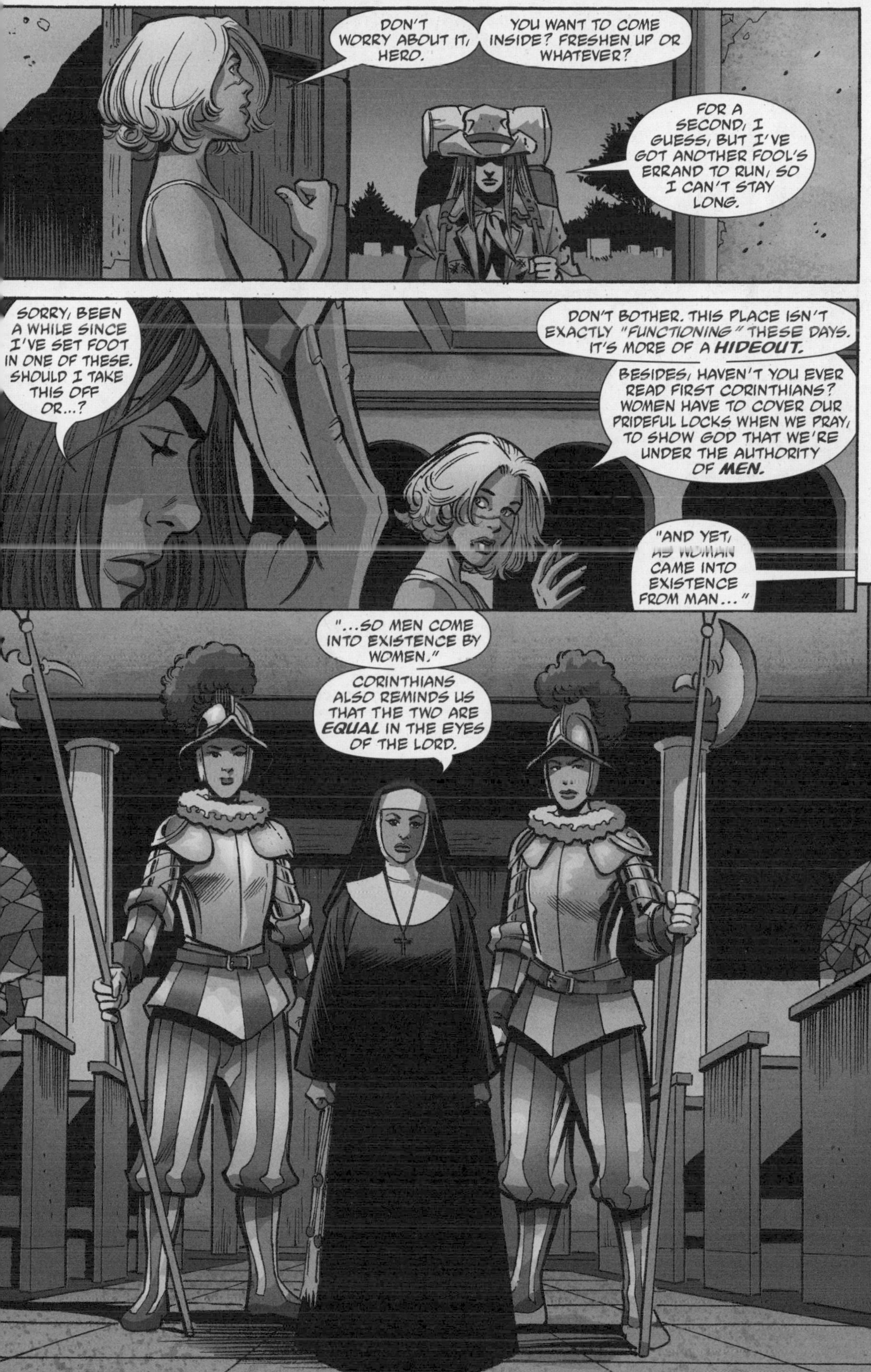
DON'T WORRY ABOUT IT, HERO.
YOU WANT TO COME INSIDE? FRESHEN UP OR WHATEVER?
FOR A SECOND, I GUESS, BUT I'VE GOT ANOTHER FOOL'S ERRAND TO RUN, SO I CAN'T STAY LONG.
SORRY, BEEN A WHILE SINCE I'VE SET FOOT IN ONE OF THESE. SHOULD I TAKE THIS OFF OR...?
DON'T BOTHER. THIS PLACE ISN'T EXACTLY "FUNCTIONING" THESE DAYS. IT'S MORE OF A **HIDEOUT.**
BESIDES, HAVEN'T YOU EVER READ FIRST CORINTHIANS? WOMEN HAVE TO COVER OUR PRIDEFUL LOCKS WHEN WE PRAY, TO SHOW GOD THAT WE'RE UNDER THE AUTHORITY OF **MEN.**
"AND YET, AS WOMAN CAME INTO EXISTENCE FROM MAN..."
"...SO MEN COME INTO EXISTENCE BY WOMEN."
CORINTHIANS ALSO REMINDS US THAT THE TWO ARE **EQUAL** IN THE EYES OF THE LORD.

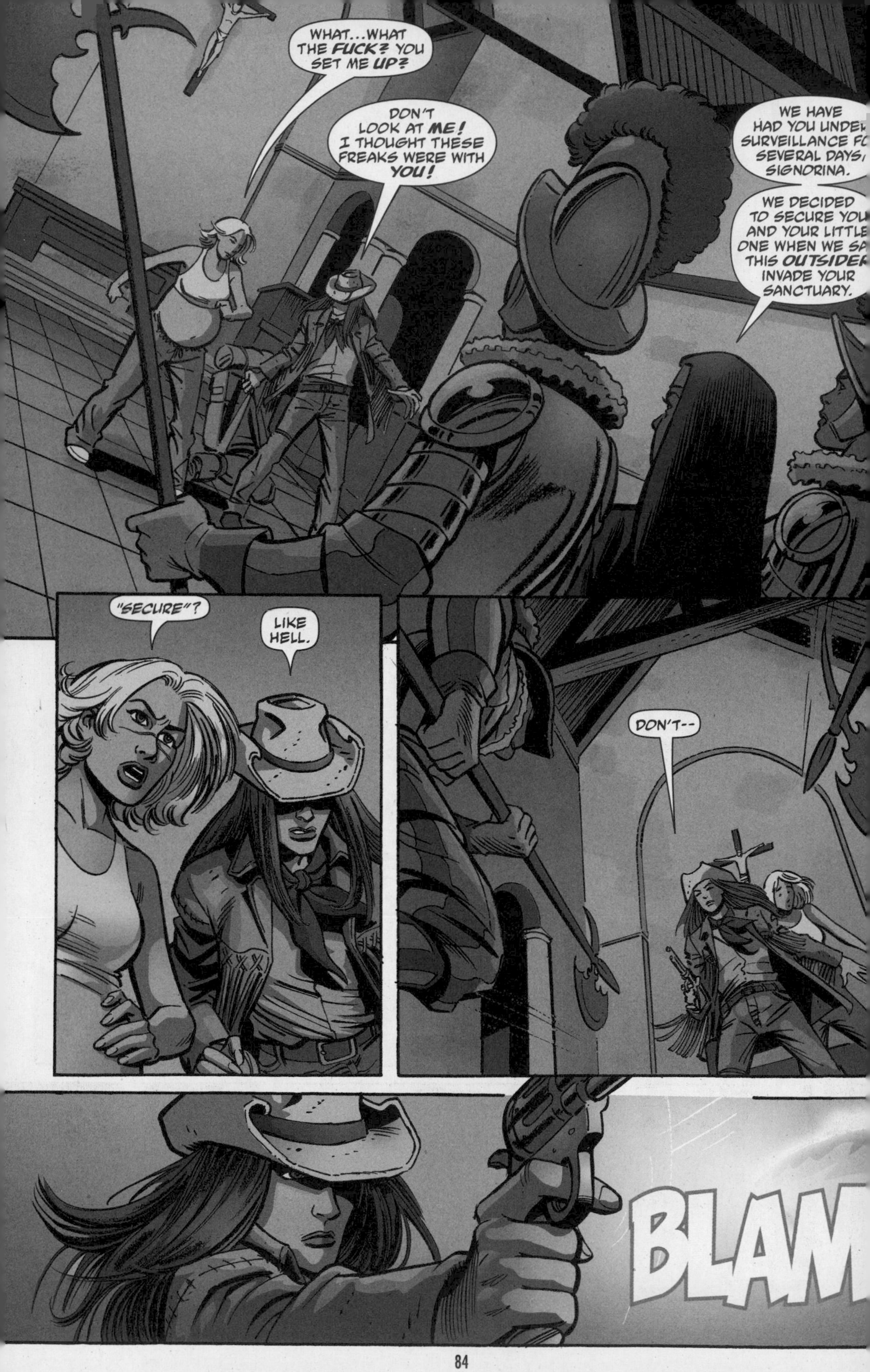

WHAT...WHAT THE FUCK? YOU SET ME UP?
DON'T LOOK AT ME! I THOUGHT THESE FREAKS WERE WITH YOU!
WE HAVE HAD YOU UNDER SURVEILLANCE FO SEVERAL DAYS, SIGNORINA.
WE DECIDED TO SECURE YOU AND YOUR LITTLE ONE WHEN WE SA THIS OUTSIDER INVADE YOUR SANCTUARY.
"SECURE"?
LIKE HELL.
DON'T--
BLAM

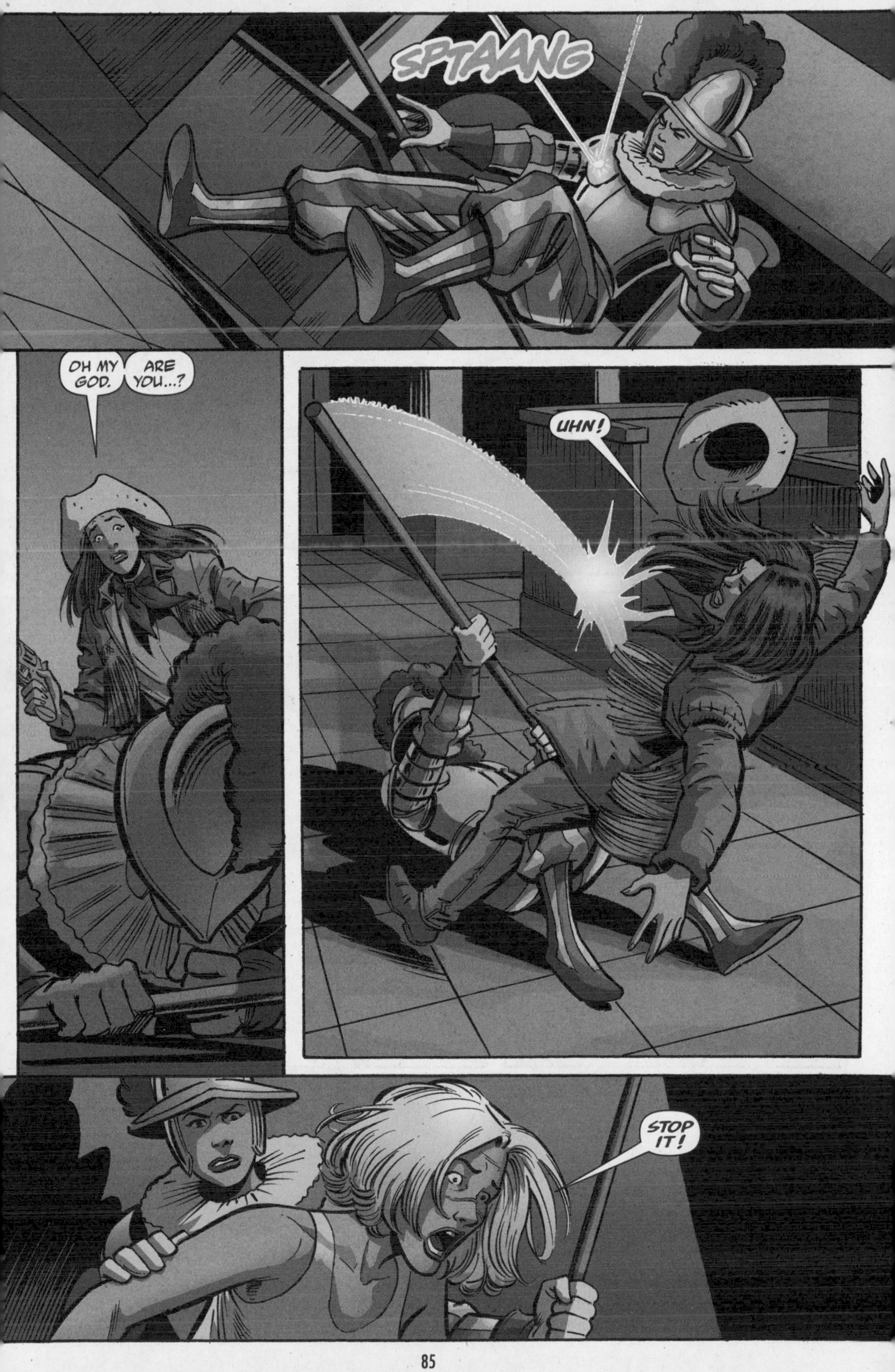
SPTAANG
OH MY GOD.
ARE YOU...?
UHN!
STOP IT!

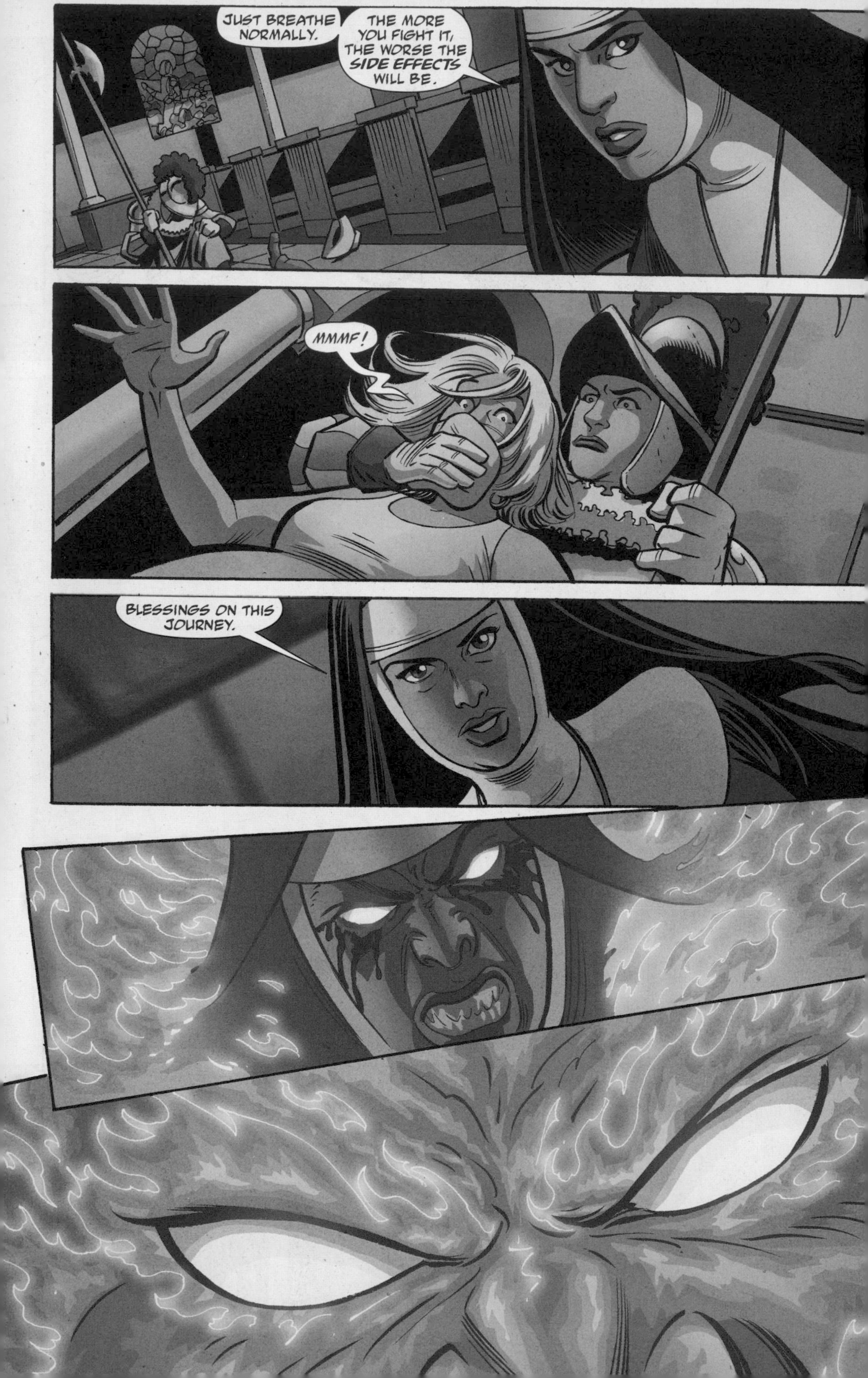
JUST BREATHE NORMALLY.
THE MORE YOU FIGHT IT, THE WORSE THE SIDE EFFECTS WILL BE.
MMMF!
BLESSINGS ON THIS JOURNEY.

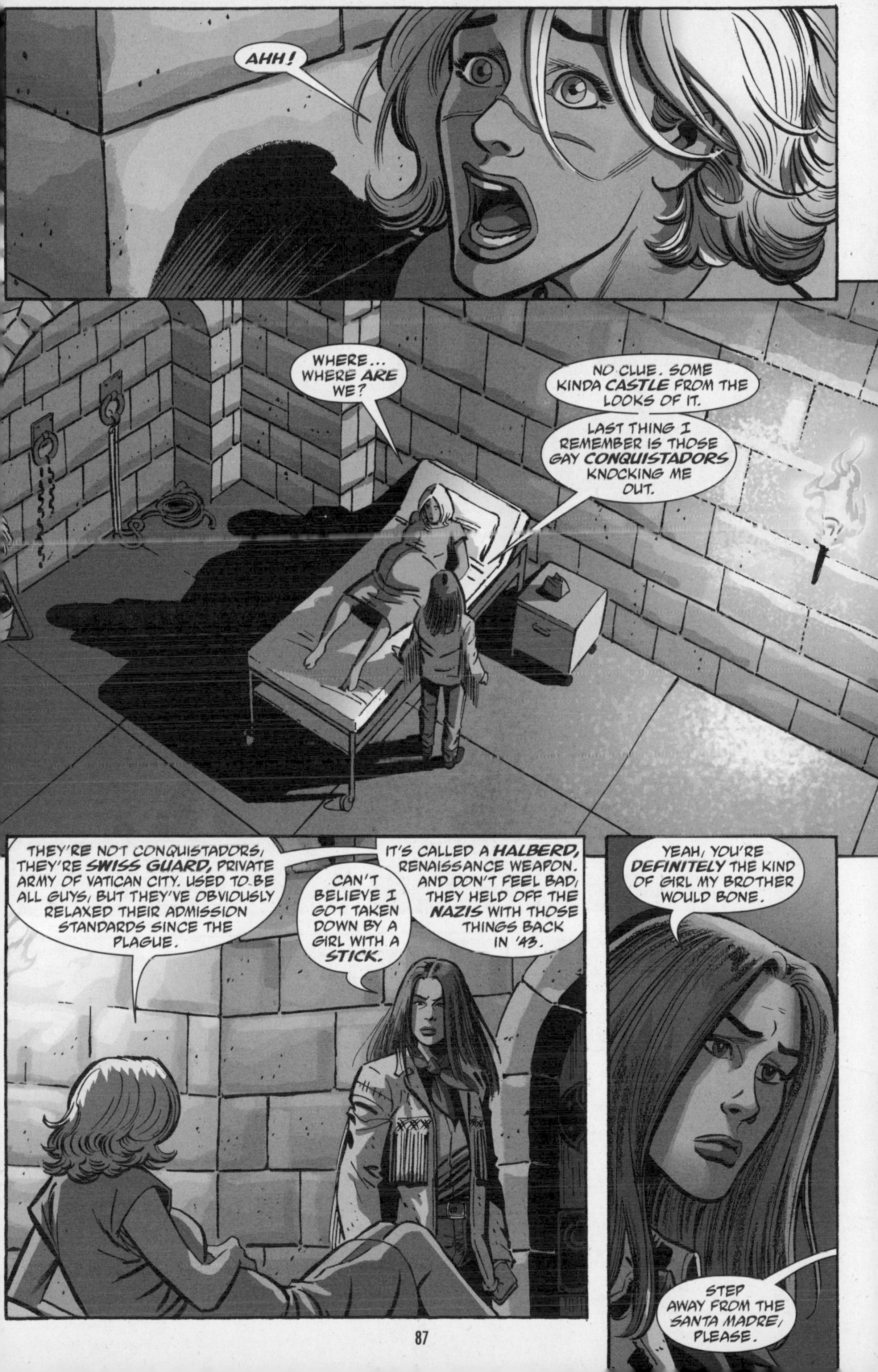
AHH!
WHERE... WHERE ARE WE?
NO CLUE. SOME KINDA CASTLE FROM THE LOOKS OF IT.
LAST THING I REMEMBER IS THOSE GAY CONQUISTADORS KNOCKING ME OUT.
THEY'RE NOT CONQUISTADORS, THEY'RE SWISS GUARD, PRIVATE ARMY OF VATICAN CITY. USED TO BE ALL GUYS, BUT THEY'VE OBVIOUSLY RELAXED THEIR ADMISSION STANDARDS SINCE THE PLAGUE.
CAN'T BELIEVE I GOT TAKEN DOWN BY A GIRL WITH A STICK.
IT'S CALLED A HALBERD, RENAISSANCE WEAPON. AND DON'T FEEL BAD, THEY HELD OFF THE NAZIS WITH THOSE THINGS BACK IN '43.
YEAH, YOU'RE DEFINITELY THE KIND OF GIRL MY BROTHER WOULD BONE.
STEP AWAY FROM THE SANTA MADRE, PLEASE.

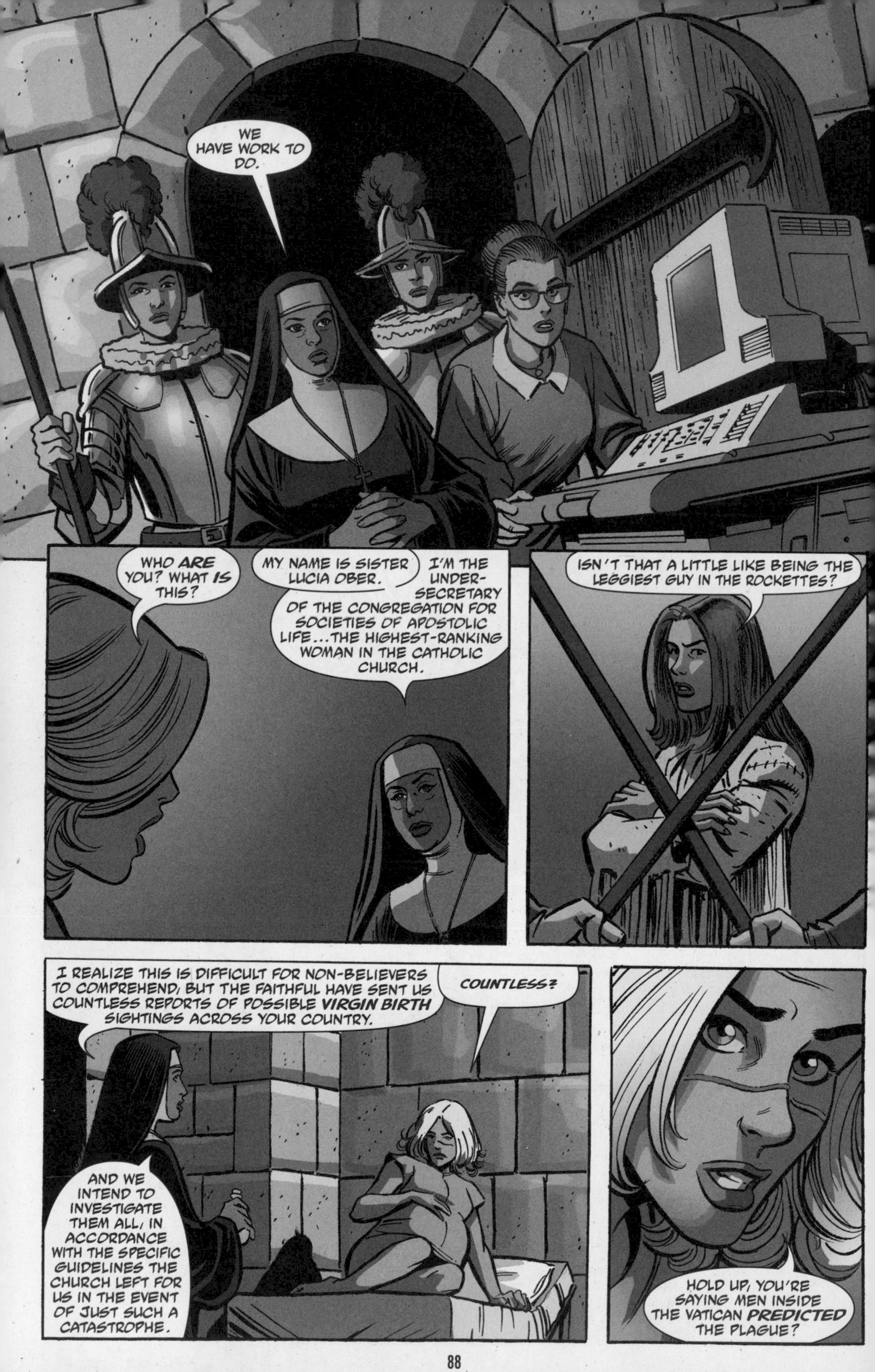
WE HAVE WORK TO DO.
WHO ARE YOU? WHAT IS THIS?
MY NAME IS SISTER LUCIA OBER.
I'M THE UNDER-SECRETARY OF THE CONGREGATION FOR SOCIETIES OF APOSTOLIC LIFE... THE HIGHEST-RANKING WOMAN IN THE CATHOLIC CHURCH.
ISN'T THAT A LITTLE LIKE BEING THE LEGGIEST GUY IN THE ROCKETTES?
I REALIZE THIS IS DIFFICULT FOR NON-BELIEVERS TO COMPREHEND, BUT THE FAITHFUL HAVE SENT US COUNTLESS REPORTS OF POSSIBLE VIRGIN BIRTH SIGHTINGS ACROSS YOUR COUNTRY.
COUNTLESS?
AND WE INTEND TO INVESTIGATE THEM ALL, IN ACCORDANCE WITH THE SPECIFIC GUIDELINES THE CHURCH LEFT FOR US IN THE EVENT OF JUST SUCH A CATASTROPHE.
HOLD UP, YOU'RE SAYING MEN INSIDE THE VATICAN PREDICTED THE PLAGUE?

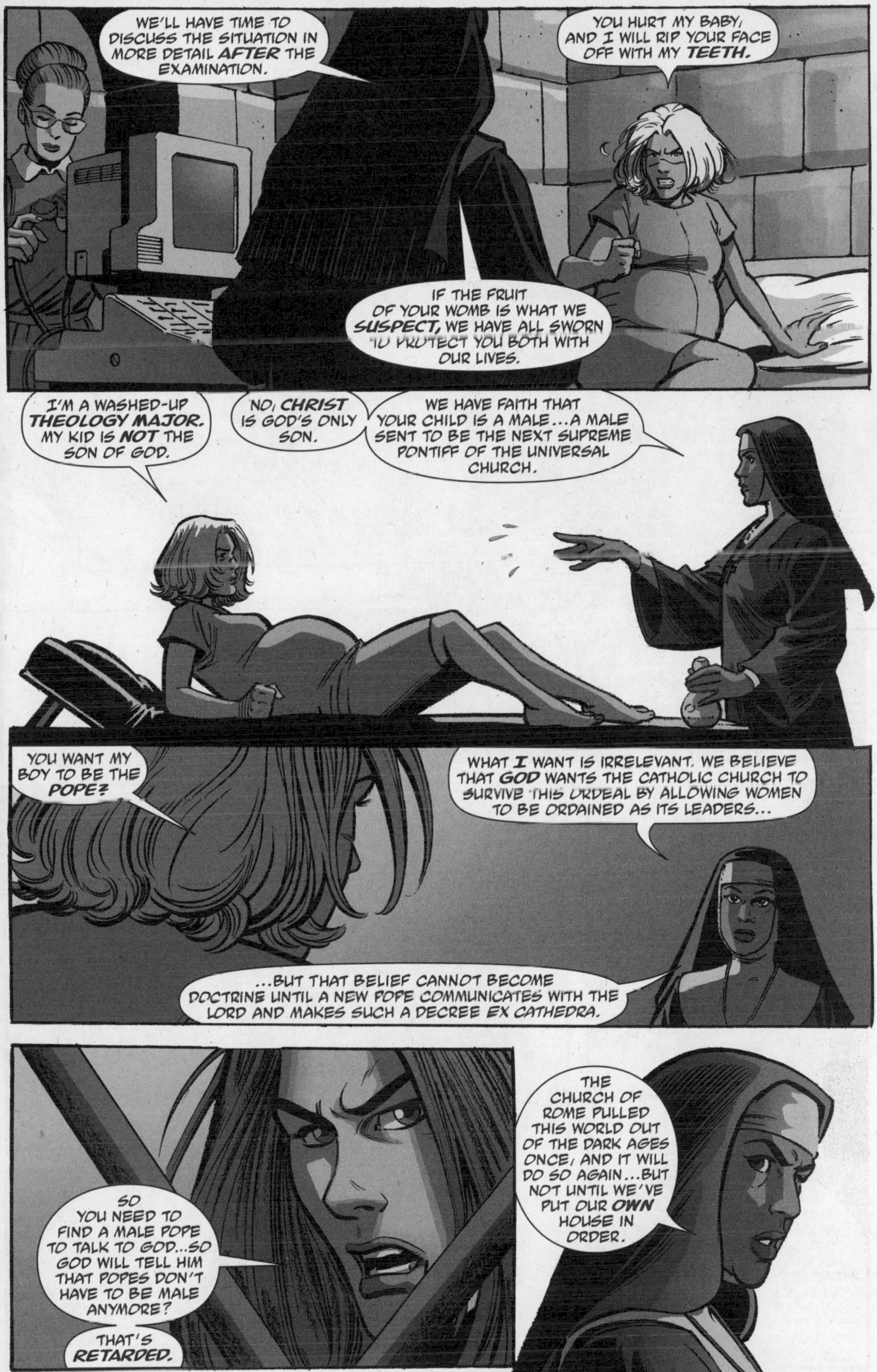
WE'LL HAVE TIME TO DISCUSS THE SITUATION IN MORE DETAIL AFTER THE EXAMINATION.
YOU HURT MY BABY, AND I WILL RIP YOUR FACE OFF WITH MY TEETH.
IF THE FRUIT OF YOUR WOMB IS WHAT WE SUSPECT, WE HAVE ALL SWORN TO PROTECT YOU BOTH WITH OUR LIVES.
I'M A WASHED-UP THEOLOGY MAJOR. MY KID IS NOT THE SON OF GOD.
NO, CHRIST IS GOD'S ONLY SON.
WE HAVE FAITH THAT YOUR CHILD IS A MALE...A MALE SENT TO BE THE NEXT SUPREME PONTIFF OF THE UNIVERSAL CHURCH.
YOU WANT MY BOY TO BE THE POPE?
WHAT I WANT IS IRRELEVANT. WE BELIEVE THAT GOD WANTS THE CATHOLIC CHURCH TO SURVIVE THIS ORDEAL BY ALLOWING WOMEN TO BE ORDAINED AS ITS LEADERS...
...BUT THAT BELIEF CANNOT BECOME DOCTRINE UNTIL A NEW POPE COMMUNICATES WITH THE LORD AND MAKES SUCH A DECREE EX CATHEDRA.
SO YOU NEED TO FIND A MALE POPE TO TALK TO GOD...SO GOD WILL TELL HIM THAT POPES DON'T HAVE TO BE MALE ANYMORE?
THAT'S RETARDED.
THE CHURCH OF ROME PULLED THIS WORLD OUT OF THE DARK AGES ONCE, AND IT WILL DO SO AGAIN...BUT NOT UNTIL WE'VE PUT OUR OWN HOUSE IN ORDER.

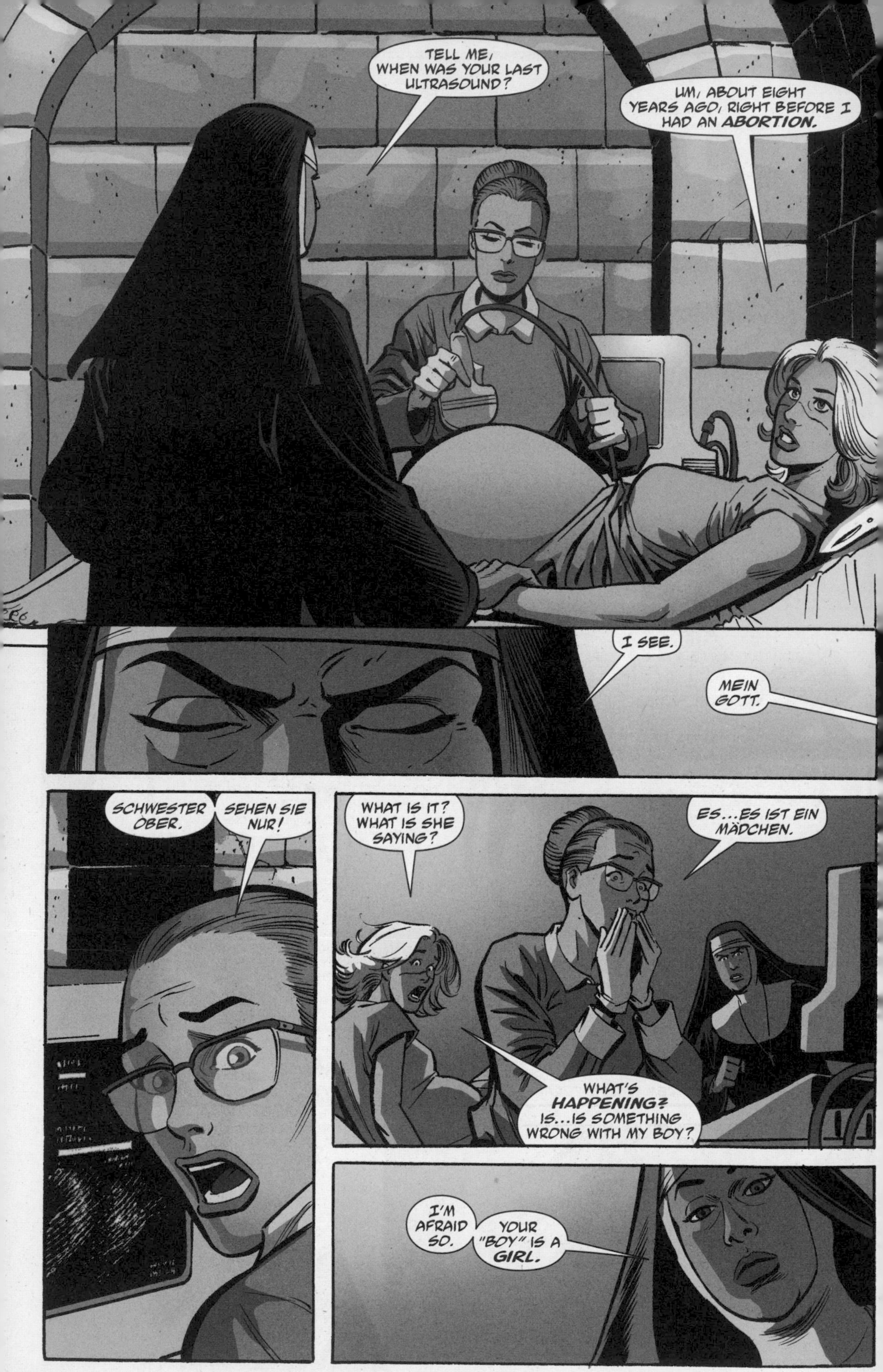
TELL ME, WHEN WAS YOUR LAST ULTRASOUND?
UM, ABOUT EIGHT YEARS AGO, RIGHT BEFORE I HAD AN **ABORTION.**
I SEE.
MEIN GOTT.
SCHWESTER OBER.
SEHEN SIE NUR!
WHAT IS IT? WHAT IS SHE SAYING?
ES...ES IST EIN MÄDCHEN.
WHAT'S **HAPPENING?** IS...IS SOMETHING WRONG WITH MY BOY?
I'M AFRAID SO.
YOUR "BOY" IS A **GIRL.**

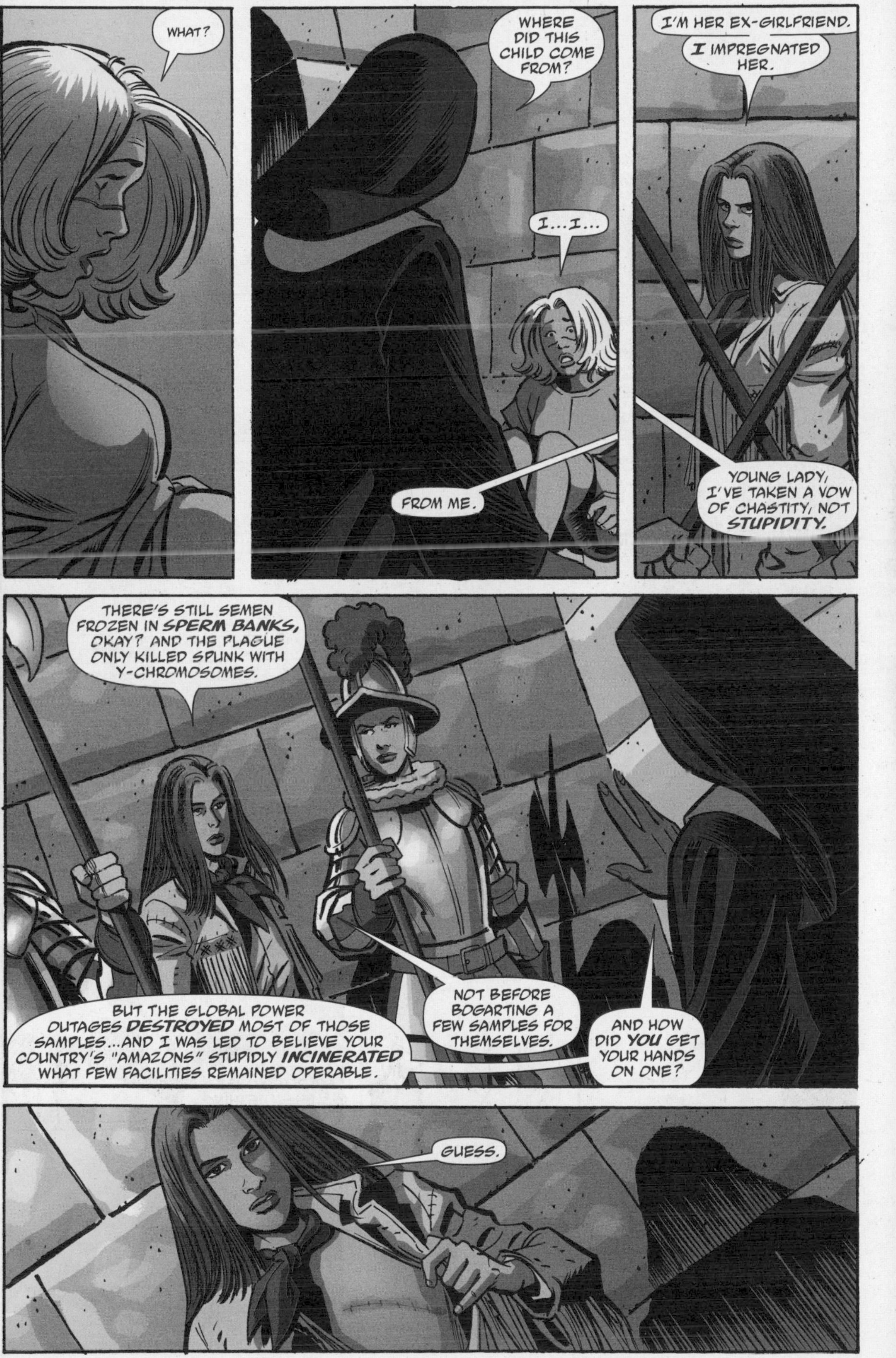
WHAT?
WHERE DID THIS CHILD COME FROM?
I...I...
FROM ME.
I'M HER EX-GIRLFRIEND.
I IMPREGNATED HER.
YOUNG LADY, I'VE TAKEN A VOW OF CHASTITY, NOT STUPIDITY.
THERE'S STILL SEMEN FROZEN IN SPERM BANKS, OKAY? AND THE PLAGUE ONLY KILLED SPUNK WITH Y-CHROMOSOMES.
BUT THE GLOBAL POWER OUTAGES DESTROYED MOST OF THOSE SAMPLES...AND I WAS LED TO BELIEVE YOUR COUNTRY'S "AMAZONS" STUPIDLY INCINERATED WHAT FEW FACILITIES REMAINED OPERABLE.
NOT BEFORE BOGARTING A FEW SAMPLES FOR THEMSELVES.
AND HOW DID YOU GET YOUR HANDS ON ONE?
GUESS.

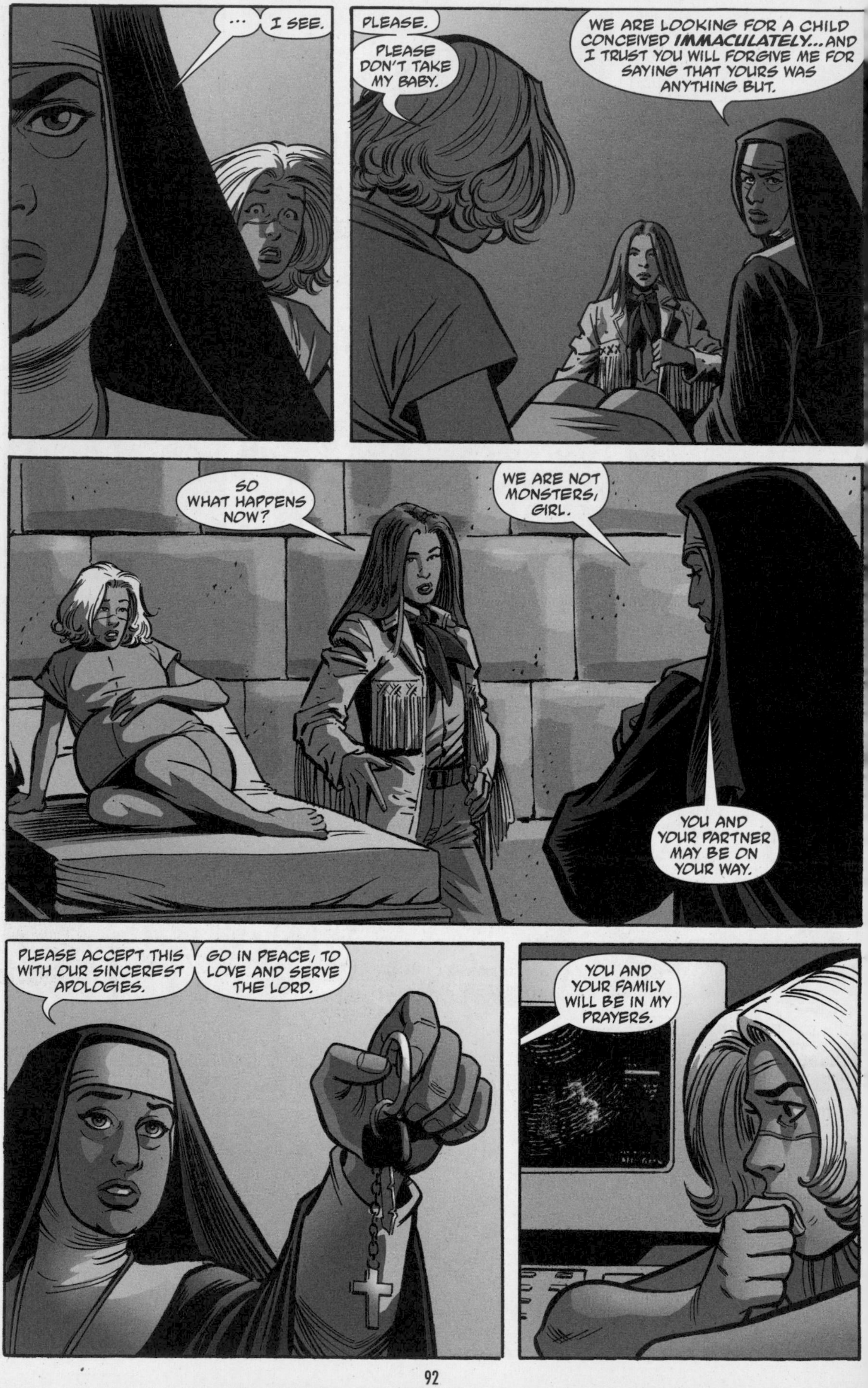
...
I SEE.
PLEASE.
PLEASE DON'T TAKE MY BABY.
WE ARE LOOKING FOR A CHILD CONCEIVED **IMMACULATELY...** AND I TRUST YOU WILL FORGIVE ME FOR SAYING THAT YOURS WAS ANYTHING BUT.
SO WHAT HAPPENS NOW?
WE ARE NOT MONSTERS, GIRL.
YOU AND YOUR PARTNER MAY BE ON YOUR WAY.
PLEASE ACCEPT THIS WITH OUR SINCEREST APOLOGIES.
GO IN PEACE, TO LOVE AND SERVE THE LORD.
YOU AND YOUR FAMILY WILL BE IN MY PRAYERS.

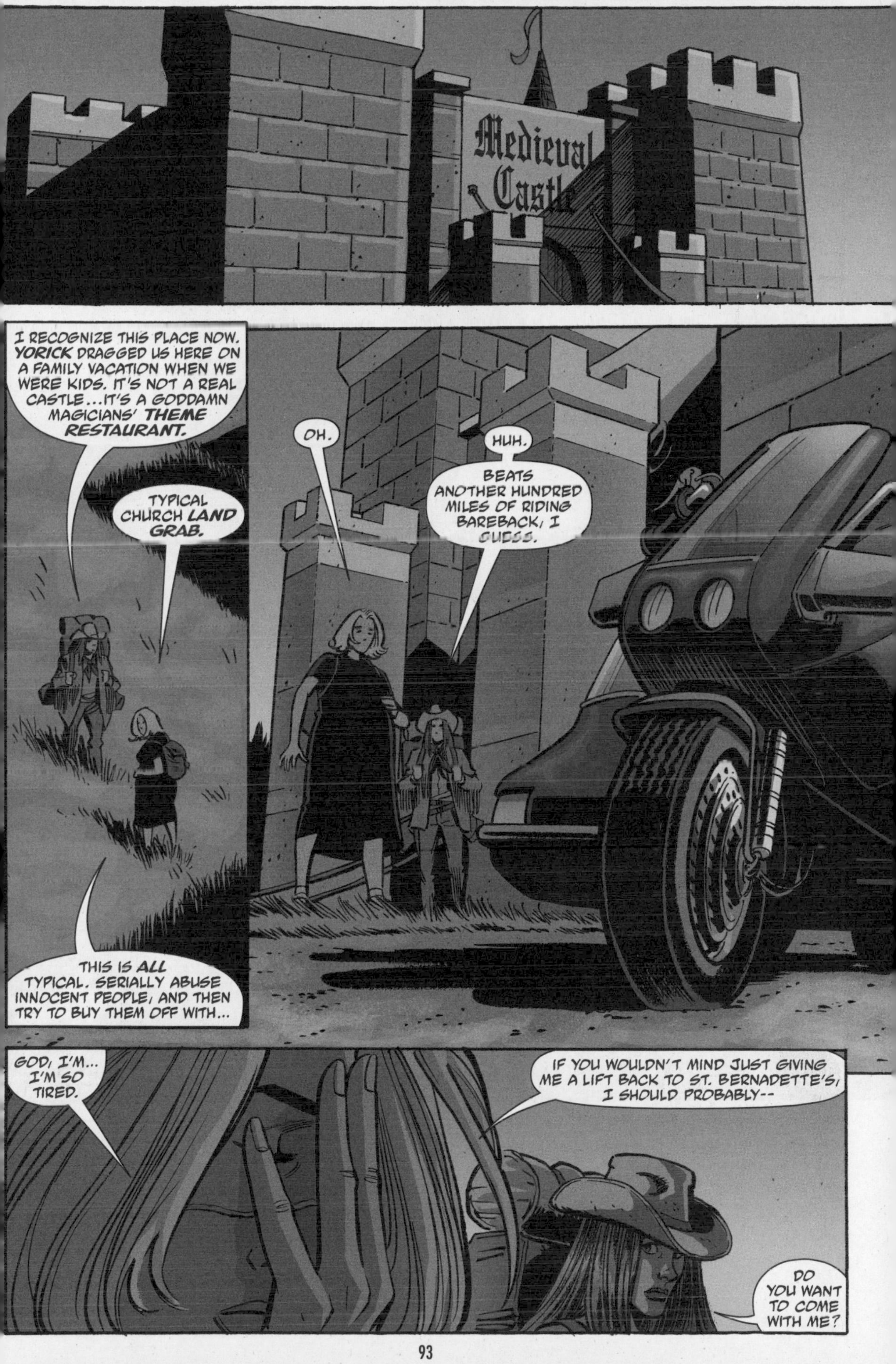
Medieval Castle
I RECOGNIZE THIS PLACE NOW. YORICK DRAGGED US HERE ON A FAMILY VACATION WHEN WE WERE KIDS. IT'S NOT A REAL CASTLE... IT'S A GODDAMN MAGICIANS' THEME RESTAURANT.
OH.
HUH.
BEATS ANOTHER HUNDRED MILES OF RIDING BAREBACK, I GUESS.
TYPICAL CHURCH LAND GRAB.
THIS IS ALL TYPICAL. SERIALLY ABUSE INNOCENT PEOPLE, AND THEN TRY TO BUY THEM OFF WITH...
GOD, I'M... I'M SO TIRED.
IF YOU WOULDN'T MIND JUST GIVING ME A LIFT BACK TO ST. BERNADETTE'S, I SHOULD PROBABLY--
DO YOU WANT TO COME WITH ME?

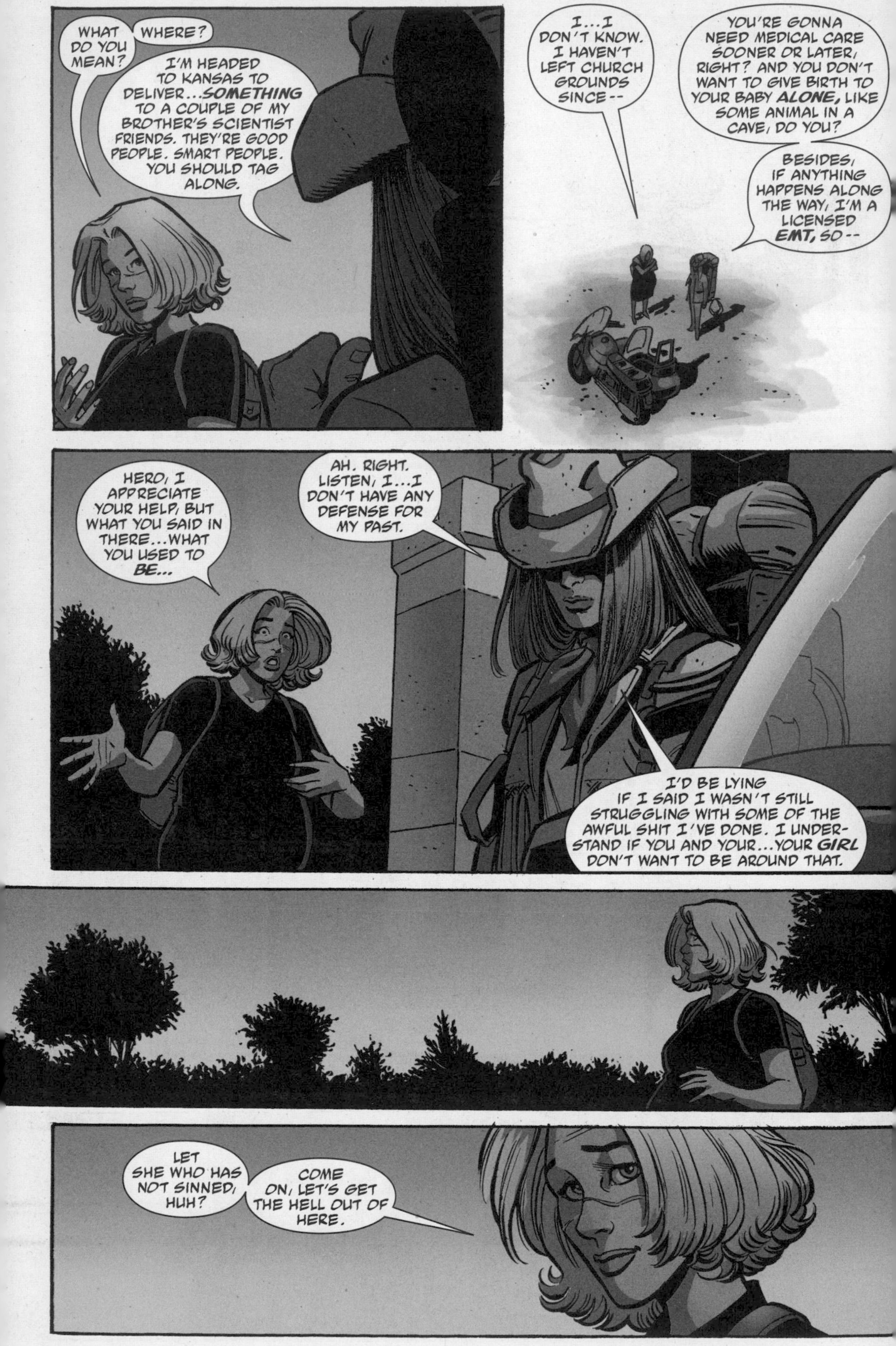
WHAT DO YOU MEAN?
WHERE?
I'M HEADED TO KANSAS TO DELIVER...SOMETHING TO A COUPLE OF MY BROTHER'S SCIENTIST FRIENDS. THEY'RE GOOD PEOPLE. SMART PEOPLE. YOU SHOULD TAG ALONG.
I...I DON'T KNOW. I HAVEN'T LEFT CHURCH GROUNDS SINCE --
YOU'RE GONNA NEED MEDICAL CARE SOONER OR LATER, RIGHT? AND YOU DON'T WANT TO GIVE BIRTH TO YOUR BABY ALONE, LIKE SOME ANIMAL IN A CAVE, DO YOU?
BESIDES, IF ANYTHING HAPPENS ALONG THE WAY, I'M A LICENSED EMT, SO --
HERO, I APPRECIATE YOUR HELP, BUT WHAT YOU SAID IN THERE...WHAT YOU USED TO BE...
AH. RIGHT. LISTEN, I...I DON'T HAVE ANY DEFENSE FOR MY PAST.
I'D BE LYING IF I SAID I WASN'T STILL STRUGGLING WITH SOME OF THE AWFUL SHIT I'VE DONE. I UNDERSTAND IF YOU AND YOUR...YOUR GIRL DON'T WANT TO BE AROUND THAT.
LET SHE WHO HAS NOT SINNED, HUH?
COME ON, LET'S GET THE HELL OUT OF HERE.

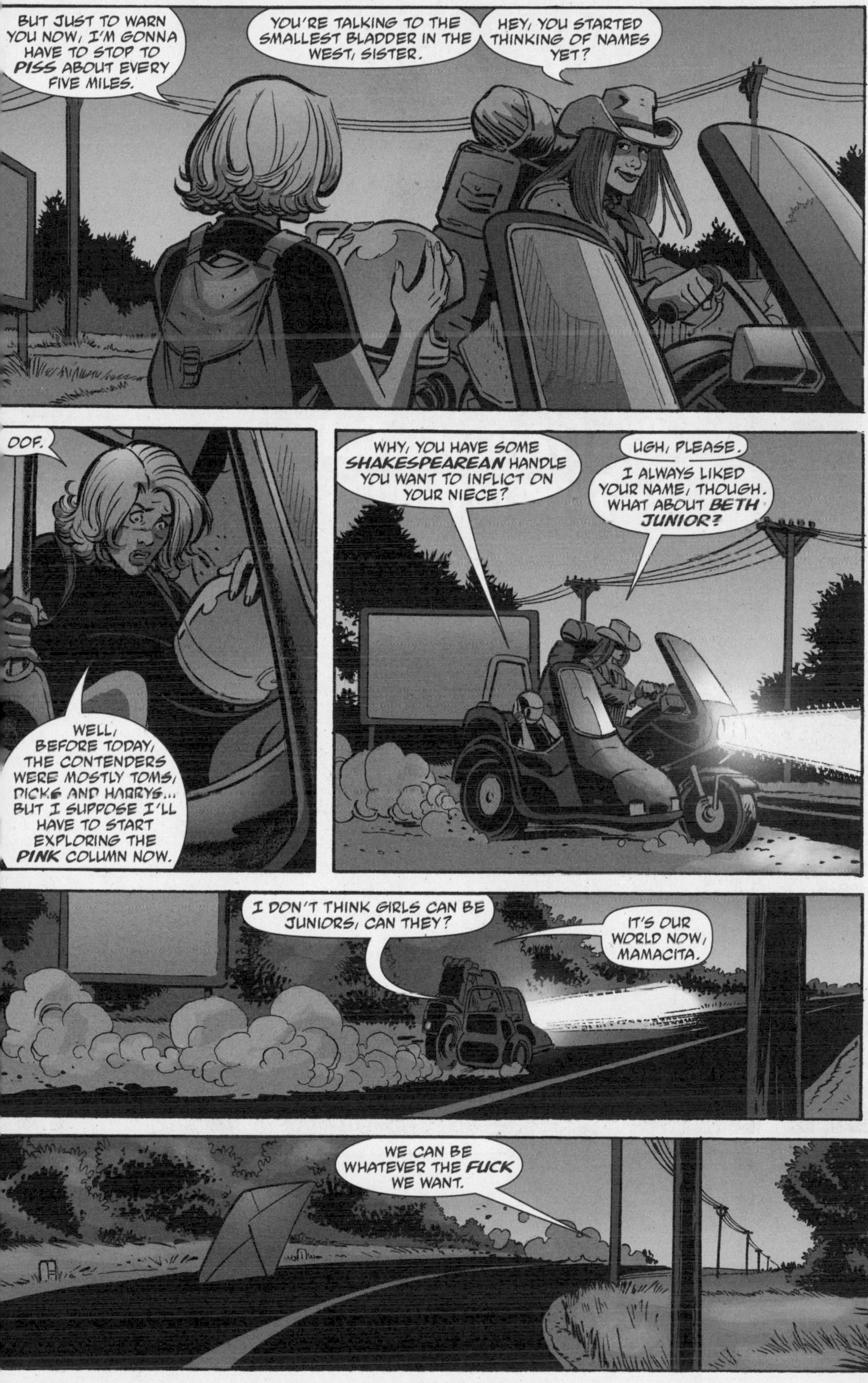
BUT JUST TO WARN YOU NOW, I'M GONNA HAVE TO STOP TO PISS ABOUT EVERY FIVE MILES.
YOU'RE TALKING TO THE SMALLEST BLADDER IN THE WEST, SISTER.
HEY, YOU STARTED THINKING OF NAMES YET?
OOF.
WELL, BEFORE TODAY, THE CONTENDERS WERE MOSTLY TOMS, DICKS AND HARRYS... BUT I SUPPOSE I'LL HAVE TO START EXPLORING THE PINK COLUMN NOW.
WHY, YOU HAVE SOME SHAKESPEAREAN HANDLE YOU WANT TO INFLICT ON YOUR NIECE?
UGH, PLEASE.
I ALWAYS LIKED YOUR NAME, THOUGH. WHAT ABOUT BETH JUNIOR?
I DON'T THINK GIRLS CAN BE JUNIORS, CAN THEY?
IT'S OUR WORLD NOW, MAMACITA.
WE CAN BE WHATEVER THE FUCK WE WANT.

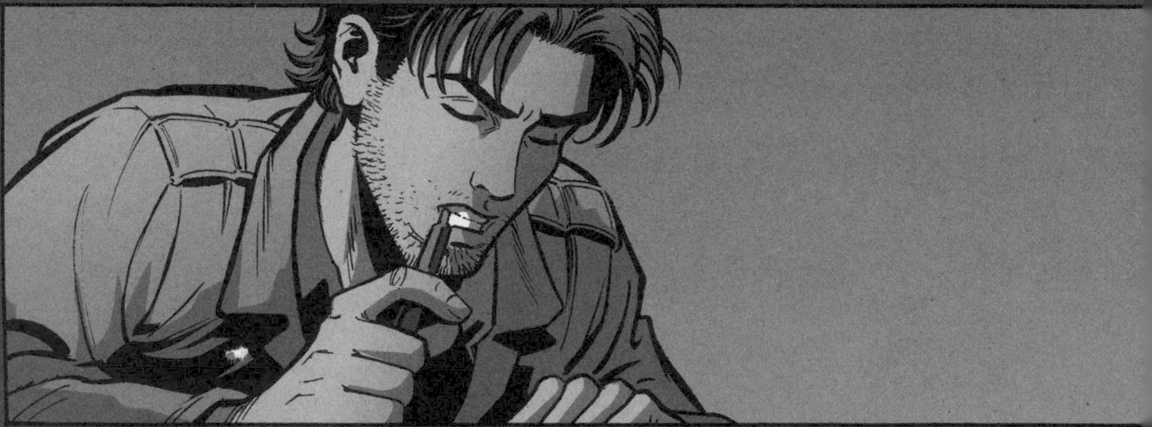

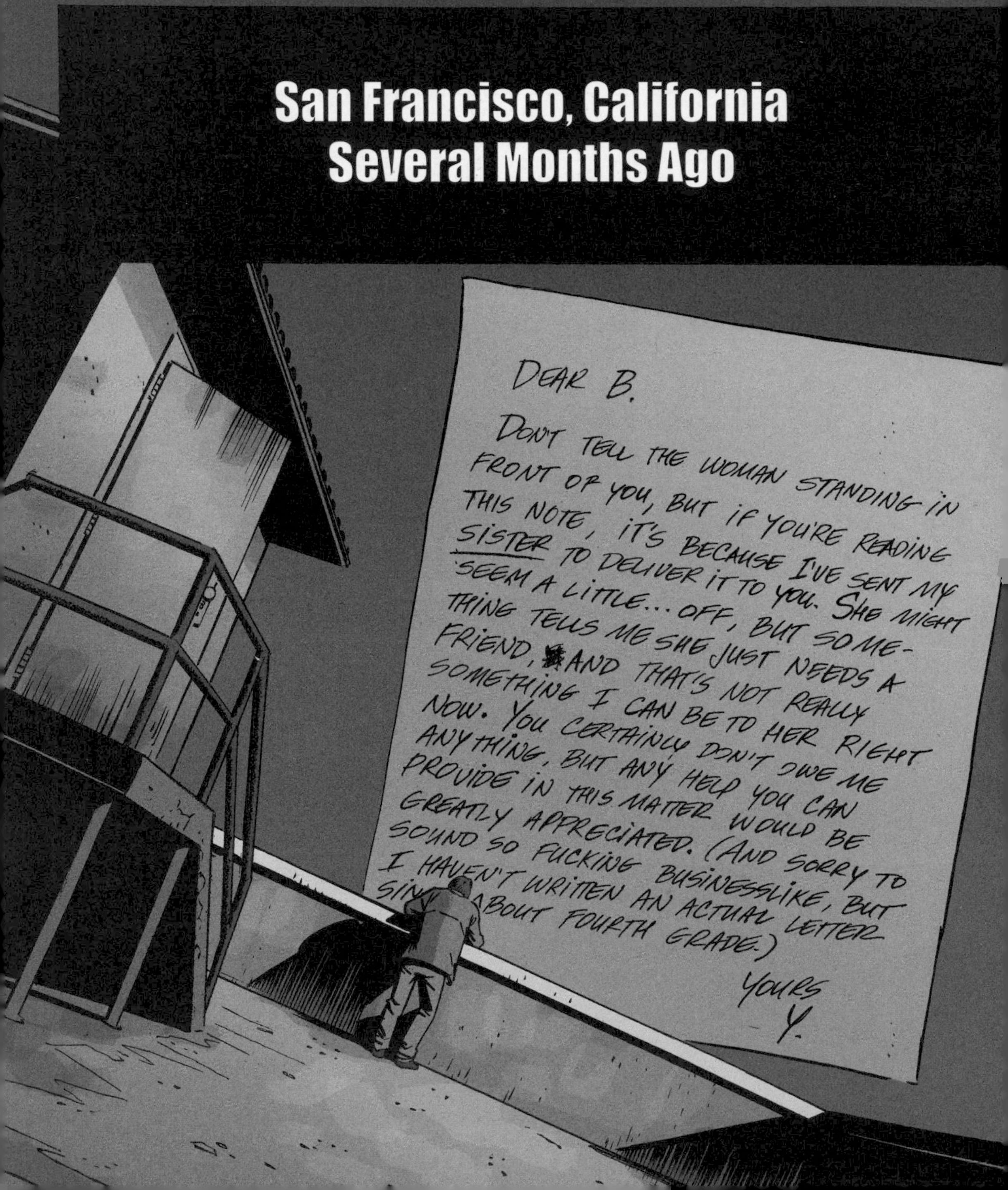
San Francisco, California
Several Months Ago
DEAR B.
DON'T TELL THE WOMAN STANDING IN
FRONT OF YOU, BUT IF YOU'RE READING
THIS NOTE, IT'S BECAUSE I'VE SENT MY
SISTER TO DELIVER IT TO YOU. SHE MIGHT
SEEM A LITTLE... OFF, BUT SOME-
THING TELLS ME SHE JUST NEEDS A
FRIEND, AND THAT'S NOT REALLY
SOMETHING I CAN BE TO HER RIGHT
NOW. YOU CERTAINLY DON'T OWE ME
ANYTHING, BUT ANY HELP YOU CAN
PROVIDE IN THIS MATTER WOULD BE
GREATLY APPRECIATED. (AND SORRY TO
SOUND SO FUCKING BUSINESSLIKE, BUT
I HAVEN'T WRITTEN AN ACTUAL LETTER
SIN ABOUT FOURTH GRADE.)
YOURS
-Y.

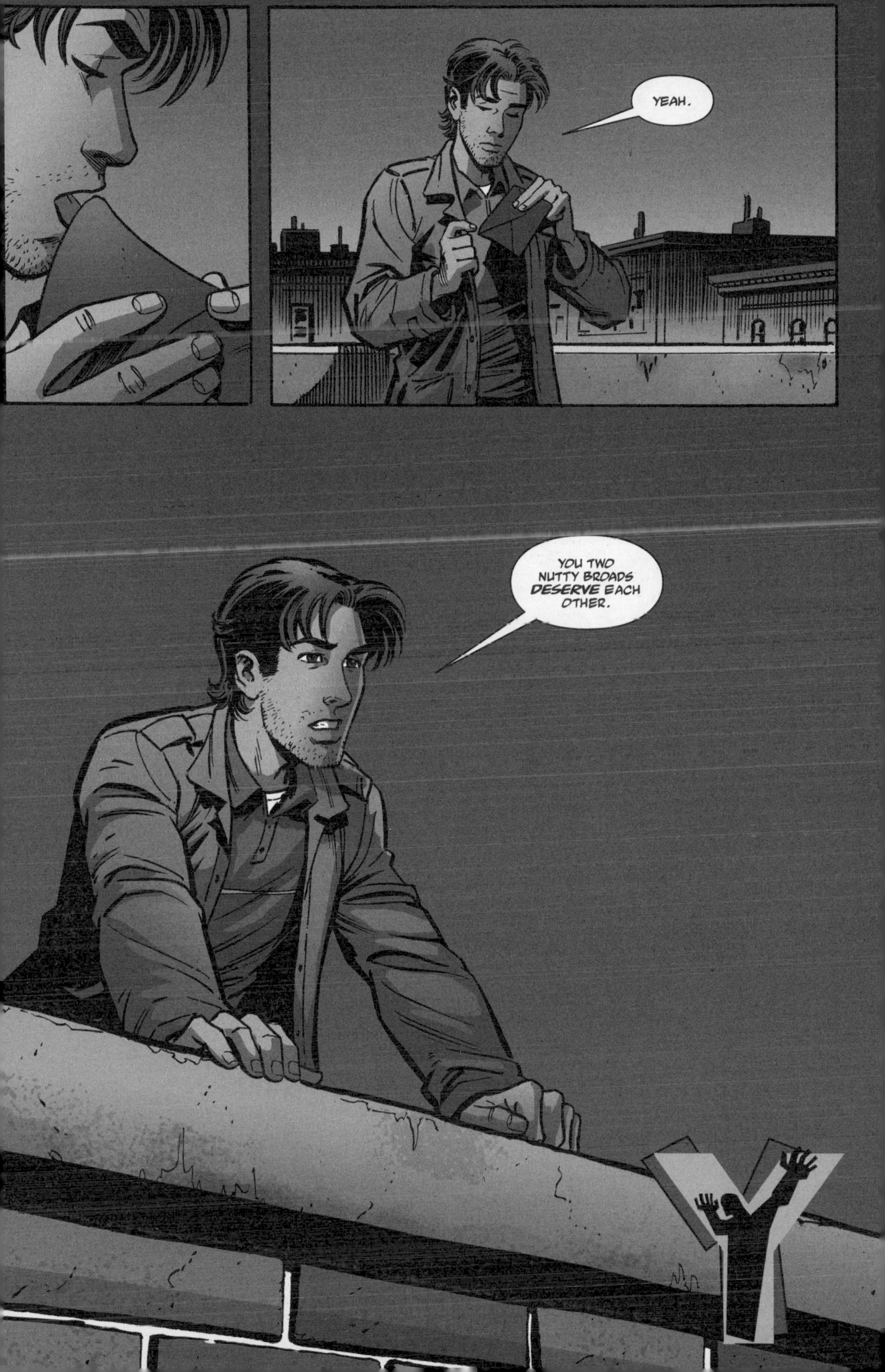
YEAH.
YOU TWO NUTTY BROADS **DESERVE** EACH OTHER.

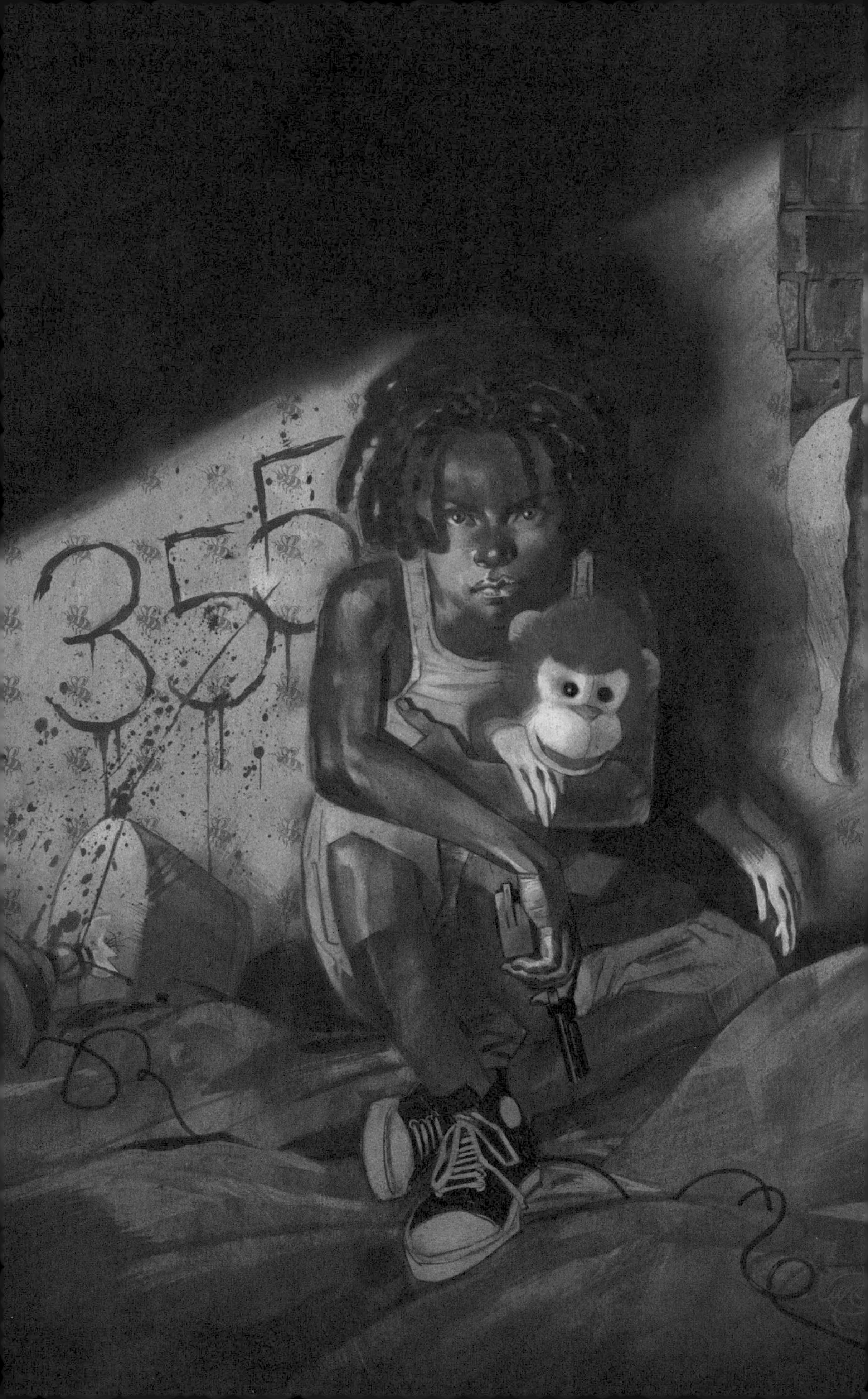
355

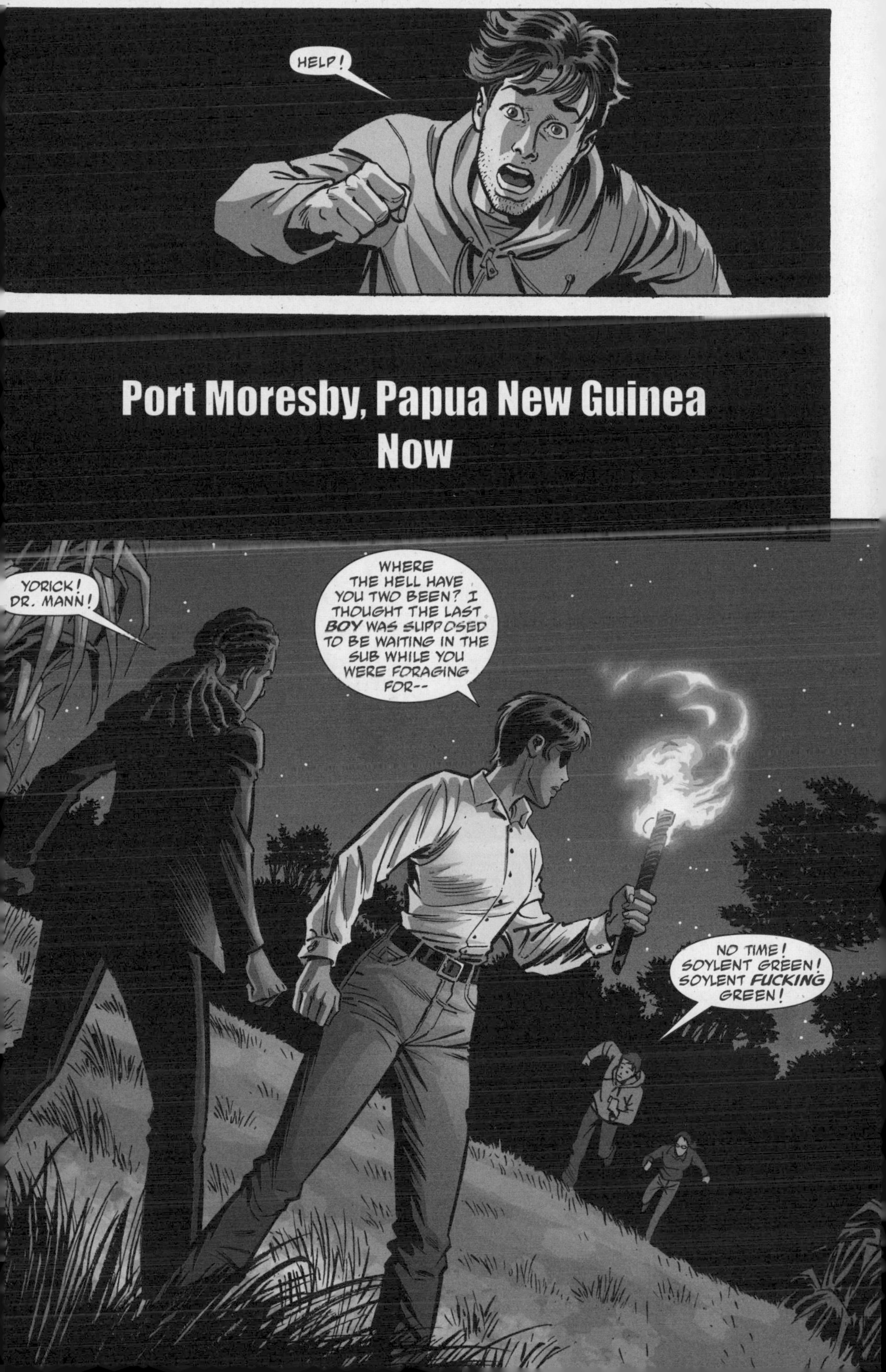
HELP!
Port Moresby, Papua New Guinea
Now
YORICK! DR. MANN!
WHERE THE HELL HAVE YOU TWO BEEN? I THOUGHT THE LAST BOY WAS SUPPOSED TO BE WAITING IN THE SUB WHILE YOU WERE FORAGING FOR--
NO TIME! SOYLENT GREEN! SOYLENT FUCKING GREEN!

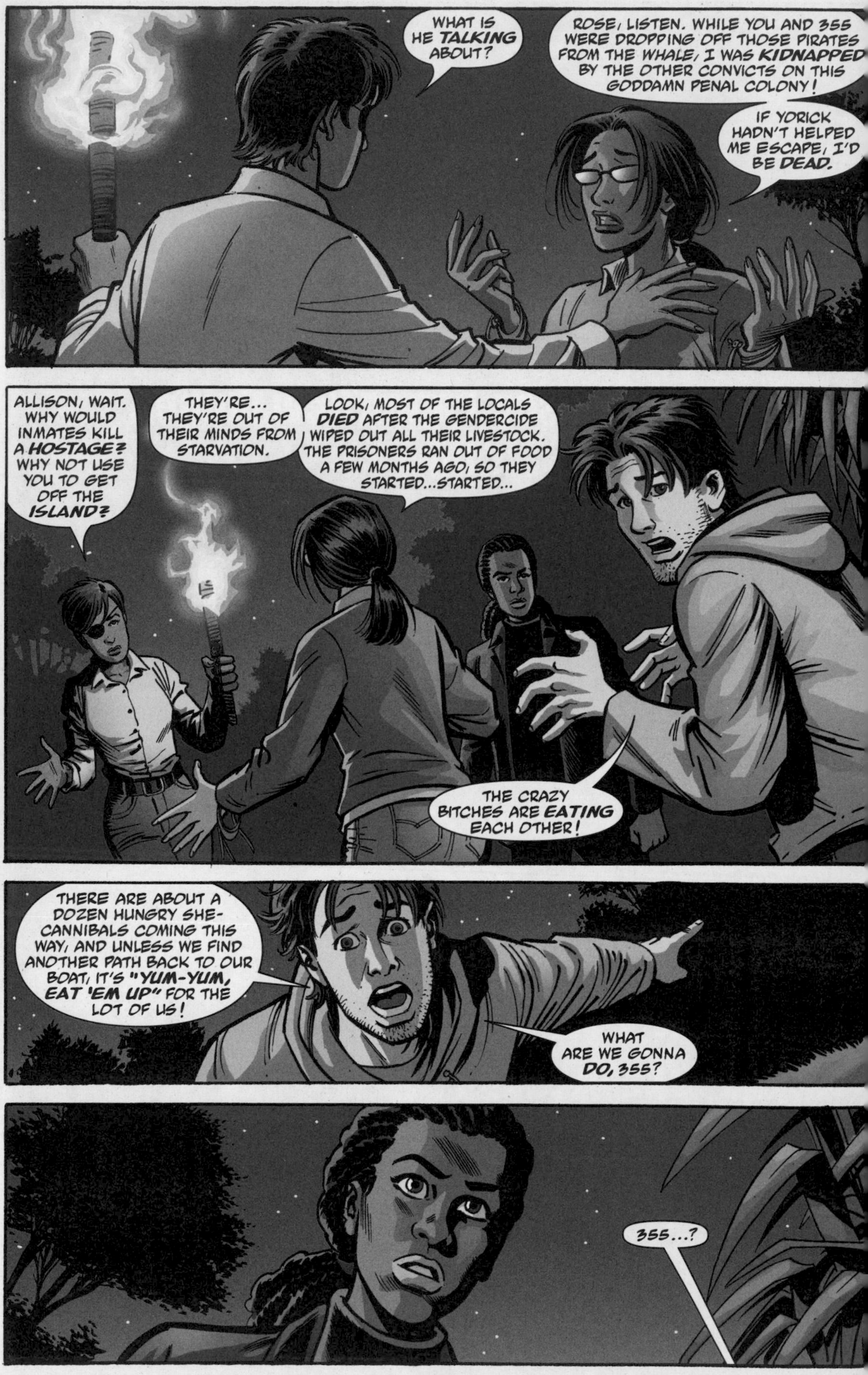
WHAT IS HE TALKING ABOUT?
ROSE, LISTEN. WHILE YOU AND 355 WERE DROPPING OFF THOSE PIRATES FROM THE WHALE, I WAS KIDNAPPED BY THE OTHER CONVICTS ON THIS GODDAMN PENAL COLONY!
IF YORICK HADN'T HELPED ME ESCAPE, I'D BE DEAD.
ALLISON, WAIT. WHY WOULD INMATES KILL A HOSTAGE? WHY NOT USE YOU TO GET OFF THE ISLAND?
THEY'RE... THEY'RE OUT OF THEIR MINDS FROM STARVATION.
LOOK, MOST OF THE LOCALS DIED AFTER THE GENDERCIDE WIPED OUT ALL THEIR LIVESTOCK. THE PRISONERS RAN OUT OF FOOD A FEW MONTHS AGO, SO THEY STARTED...STARTED...
THE CRAZY BITCHES ARE EATING EACH OTHER!
THERE ARE ABOUT A DOZEN HUNGRY SHE-CANNIBALS COMING THIS WAY, AND UNLESS WE FIND ANOTHER PATH BACK TO OUR BOAT, IT'S "YUM-YUM, EAT 'EM UP" FOR THE LOT OF US!
WHAT ARE WE GONNA DO, 355?
355...?

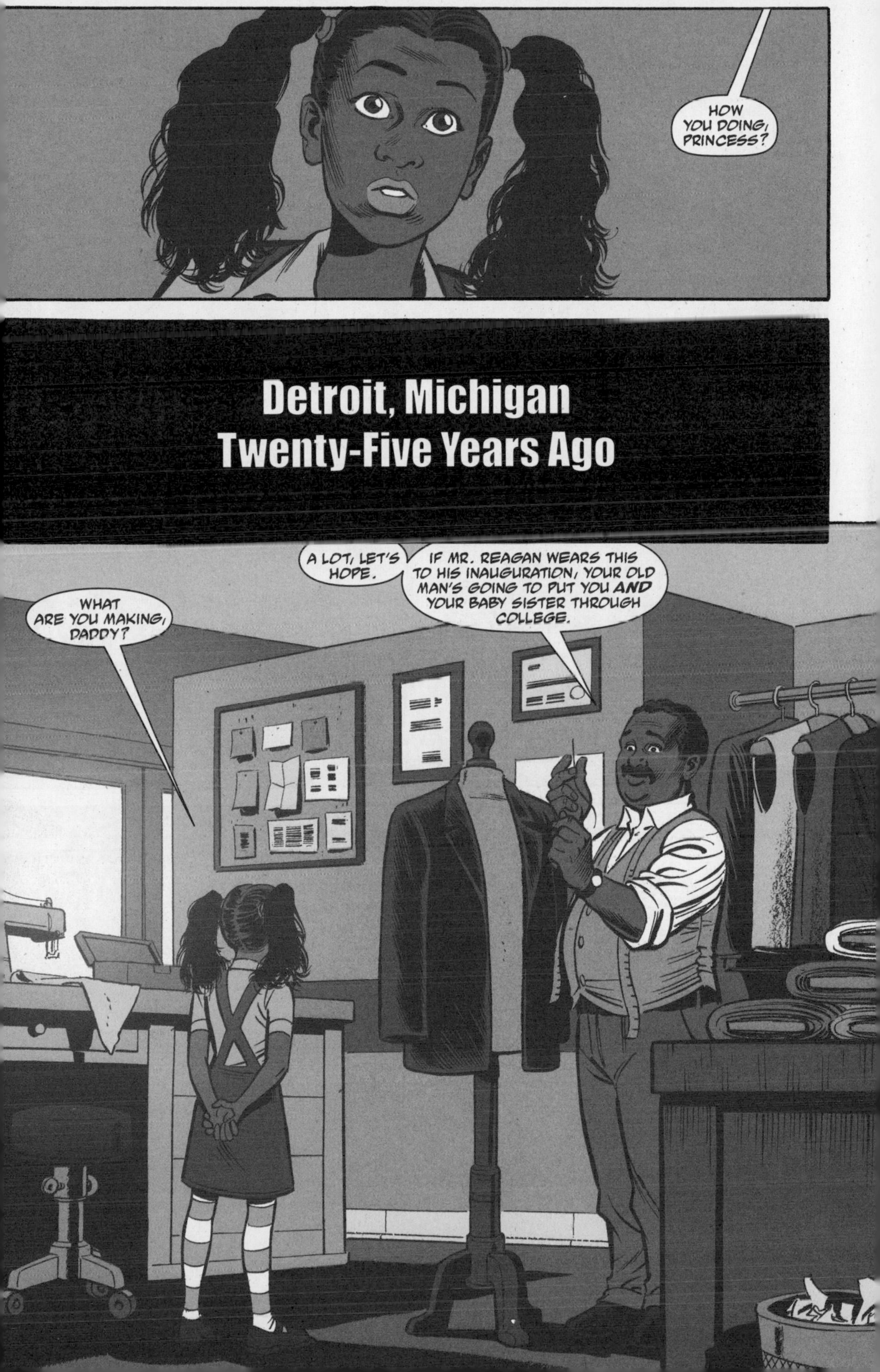
HOW YOU DOING, PRINCESS?
Detroit, Michigan
Twenty-Five Years Ago
WHAT ARE YOU MAKING, DADDY?
A LOT, LET'S HOPE.
IF MR. REAGAN WEARS THIS TO HIS INAUGURATION, YOUR OLD MAN'S GOING TO PUT YOU **AND** YOUR BABY SISTER THROUGH COLLEGE.

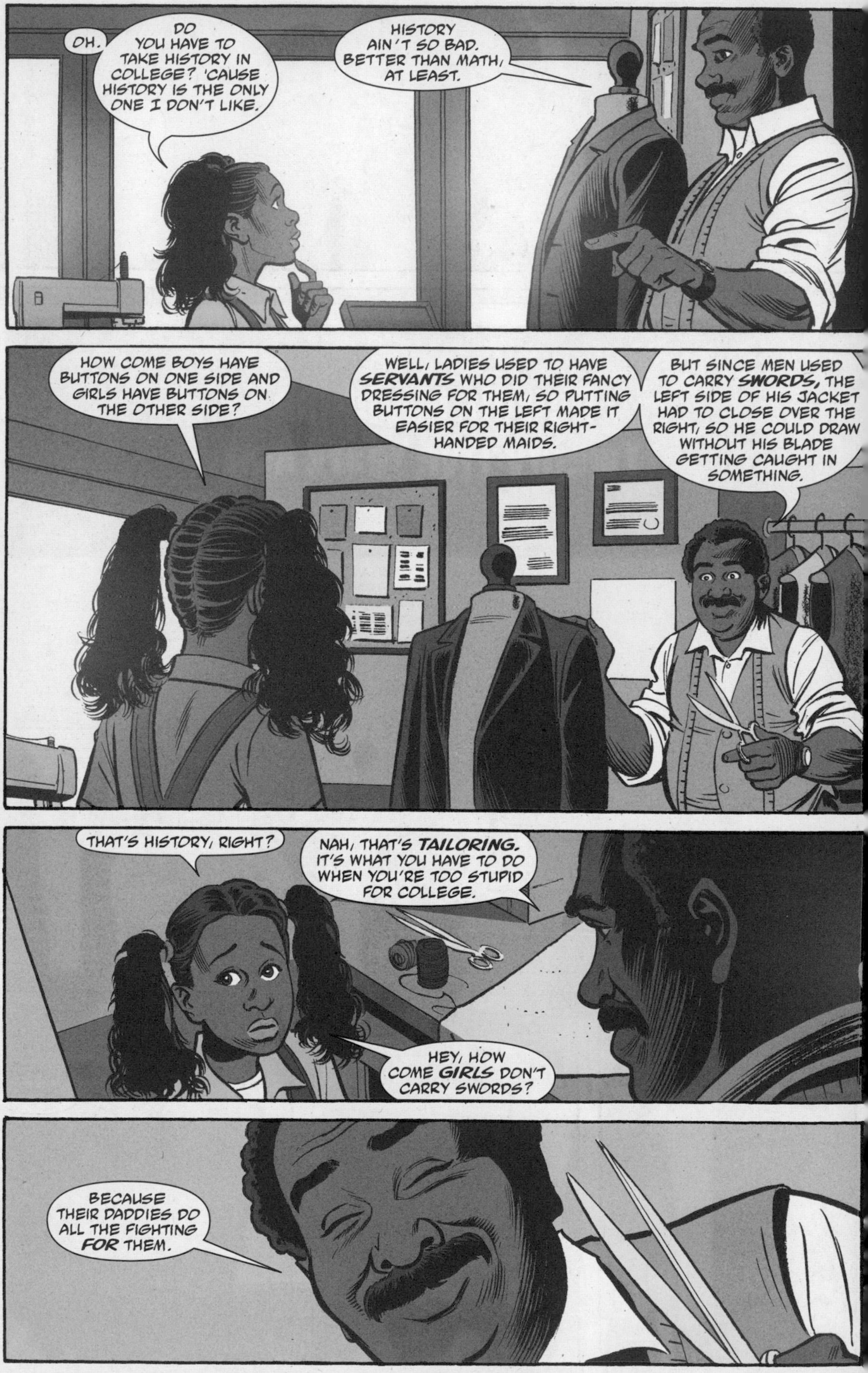
OH.
DO YOU HAVE TO TAKE HISTORY IN COLLEGE? 'CAUSE HISTORY IS THE ONLY ONE I DON'T LIKE.
HISTORY AIN'T SO BAD. BETTER THAN MATH, AT LEAST.
HOW COME BOYS HAVE BUTTONS ON ONE SIDE AND GIRLS HAVE BUTTONS ON THE OTHER SIDE?
WELL, LADIES USED TO HAVE **SERVANTS** WHO DID THEIR FANCY DRESSING FOR THEM, SO PUTTING BUTTONS ON THE LEFT MADE IT EASIER FOR THEIR RIGHT-HANDED MAIDS.
BUT SINCE MEN USED TO CARRY **SWORDS,** THE LEFT SIDE OF HIS JACKET HAD TO CLOSE OVER THE RIGHT, SO HE COULD DRAW WITHOUT HIS BLADE GETTING CAUGHT IN SOMETHING.
THAT'S HISTORY, RIGHT?
NAH, THAT'S **TAILORING.** IT'S WHAT YOU HAVE TO DO WHEN YOU'RE TOO STUPID FOR COLLEGE.
HEY, HOW COME **GIRLS** DON'T CARRY SWORDS?
BECAUSE THEIR DADDIES DO ALL THE FIGHTING **FOR** THEM.

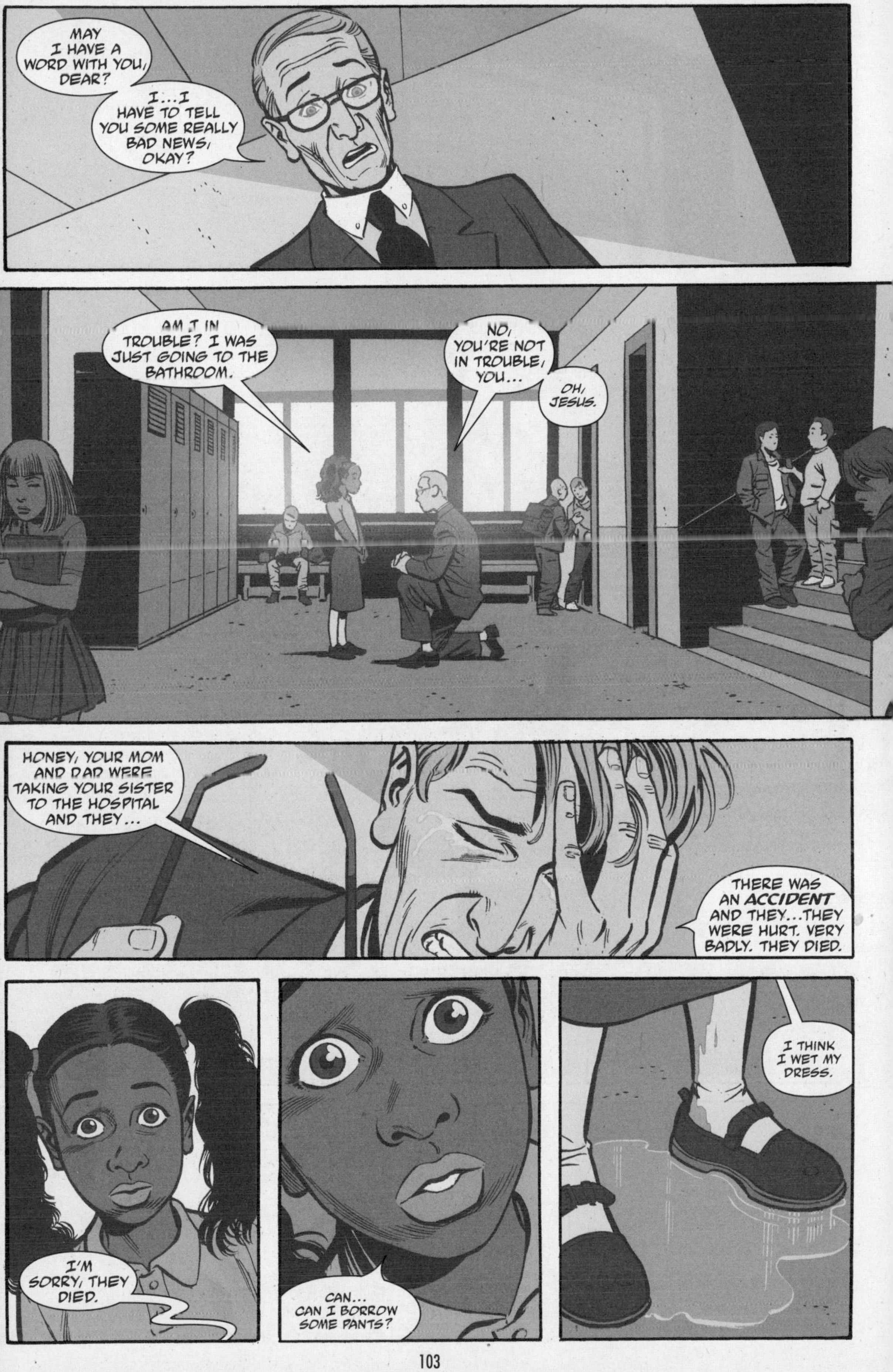
MAY I HAVE A WORD WITH YOU, DEAR?
I...I HAVE TO TELL YOU SOME REALLY BAD NEWS, OKAY?
AM I IN TROUBLE? I WAS JUST GOING TO THE BATHROOM.
NO, YOU'RE NOT IN TROUBLE, YOU...
OH, JESUS.
HONEY, YOUR MOM AND DAD WERE TAKING YOUR SISTER TO THE HOSPITAL AND THEY...
THERE WAS AN ACCIDENT AND THEY...THEY WERE HURT. VERY BADLY. THEY DIED.
I'M SORRY, THEY DIED.
CAN... CAN I BORROW SOME PANTS?
I THINK I WET MY DRESS.

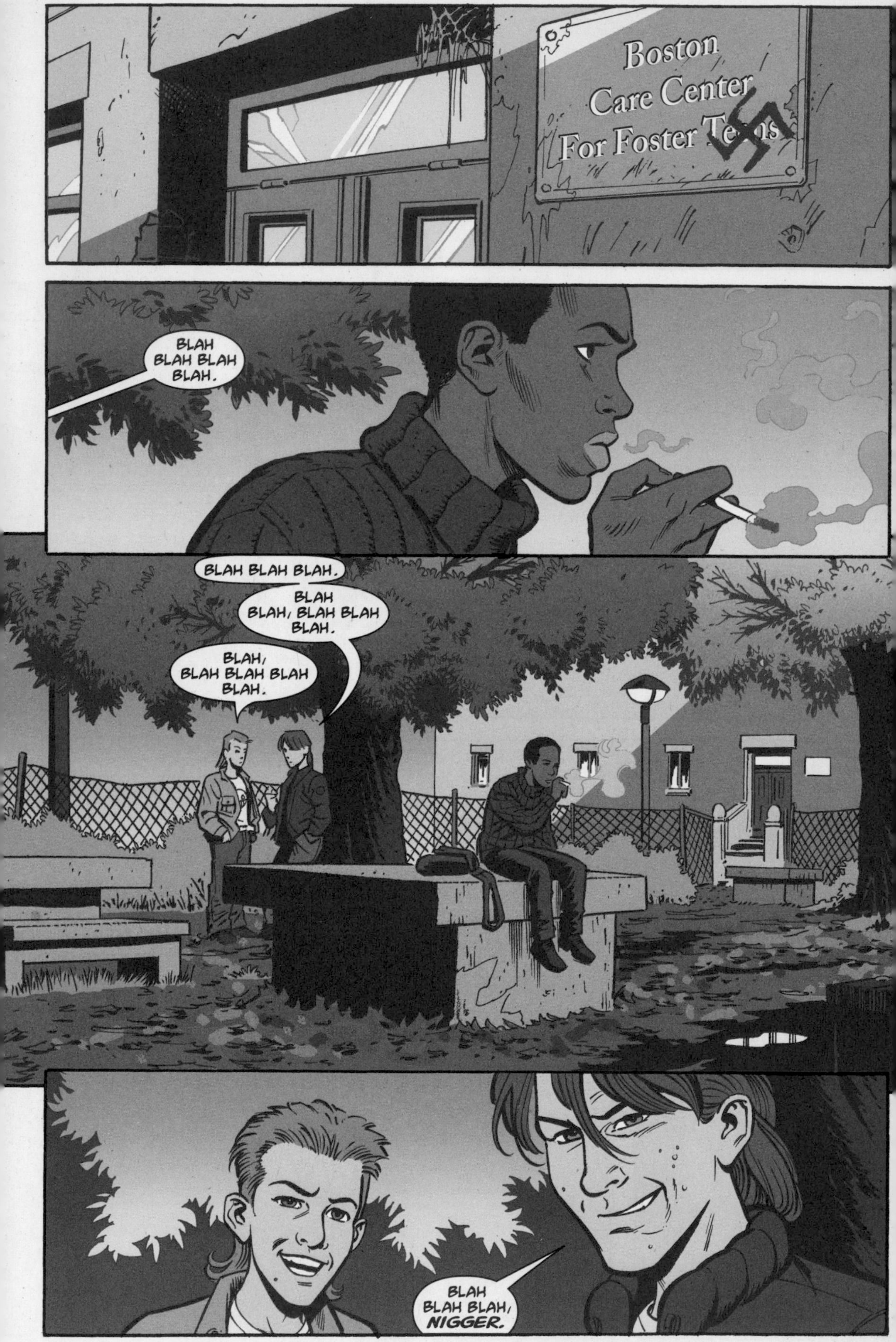
Boston
Care Center
For Foster Teens
BLAH BLAH BLAH BLAH.
BLAH BLAH BLAH.
BLAH BLAH, BLAH BLAH BLAH.
BLAH, BLAH BLAH BLAH BLAH.
BLAH BLAH BLAH, NIGGER.

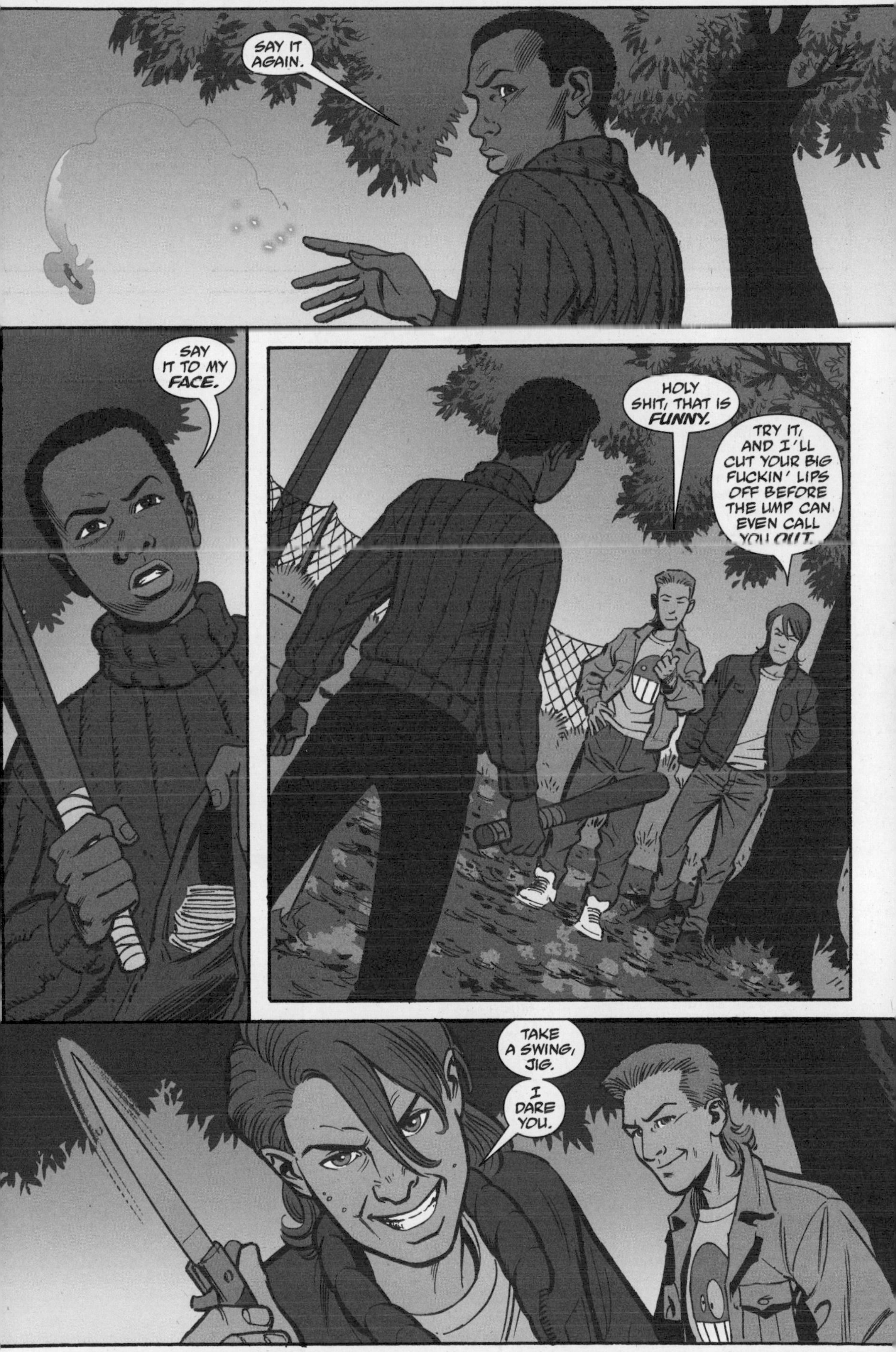
SAY IT AGAIN.
SAY IT TO MY FACE.
HOLY SHIT, THAT IS FUNNY.
TRY IT, AND I'LL CUT YOUR BIG FUCKIN' LIPS OFF BEFORE THE UMP CAN EVEN CALL YOU OUT.
TAKE A SWING, JIG.
I DARE YOU.

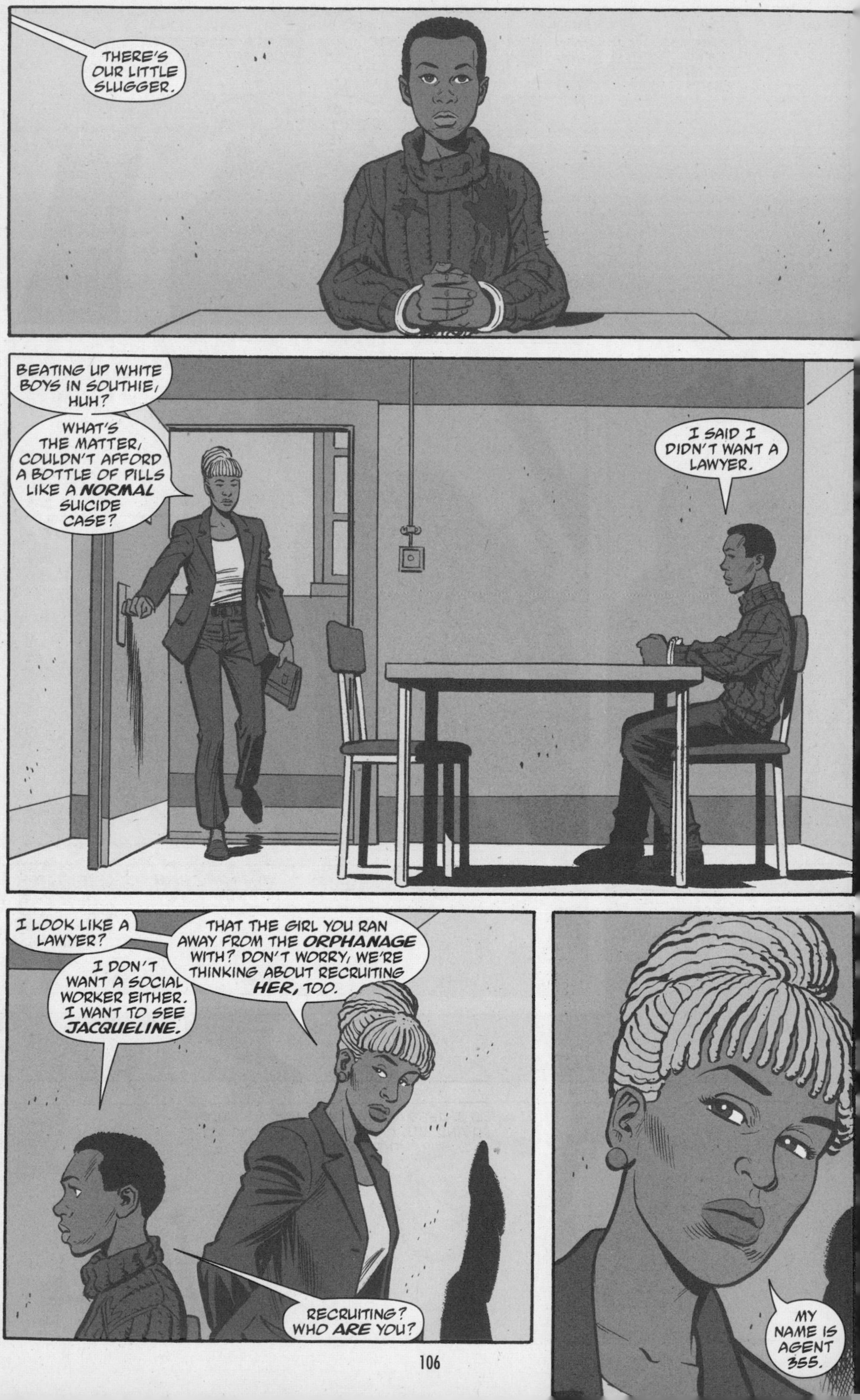
THERE'S OUR LITTLE SLUGGER.
BEATING UP WHITE BOYS IN SOUTHIE, HUH?
WHAT'S THE MATTER, COULDN'T AFFORD A BOTTLE OF PILLS LIKE A NORMAL SUICIDE CASE?
I SAID I DIDN'T WANT A LAWYER.
I LOOK LIKE A LAWYER?
I DON'T WANT A SOCIAL WORKER EITHER. I WANT TO SEE JACQUELINE.
THAT THE GIRL YOU RAN AWAY FROM THE ORPHANAGE WITH? DON'T WORRY, WE'RE THINKING ABOUT RECRUITING HER, TOO.
RECRUITING? WHO ARE YOU?
MY NAME IS AGENT 355.

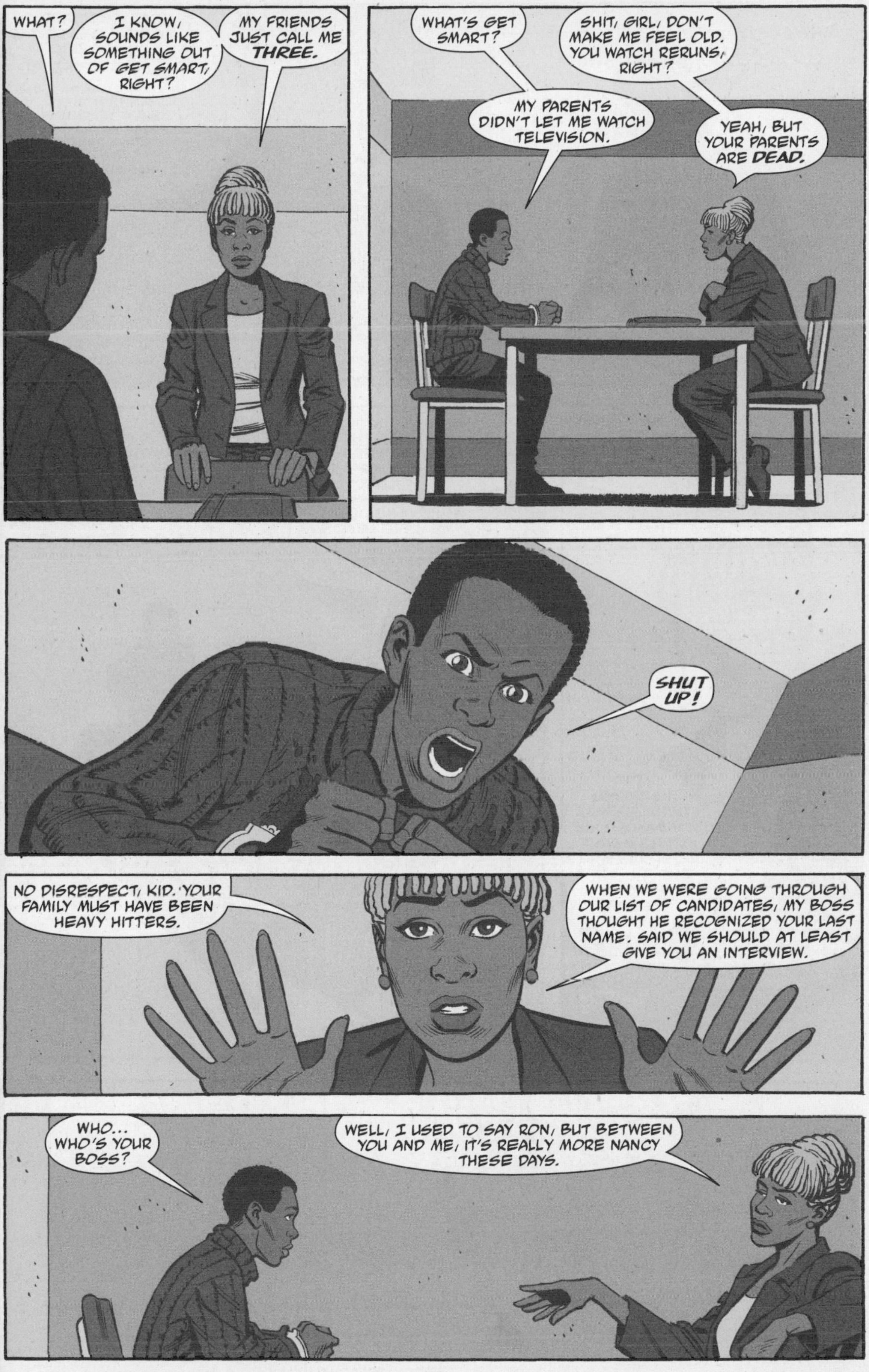
WHAT?
I KNOW, SOUNDS LIKE SOMETHING OUT OF GET SMART, RIGHT?
MY FRIENDS JUST CALL ME THREE.
WHAT'S GET SMART?
SHIT, GIRL, DON'T MAKE ME FEEL OLD. YOU WATCH RERUNS, RIGHT?
MY PARENTS DIDN'T LET ME WATCH TELEVISION.
YEAH, BUT YOUR PARENTS ARE DEAD.
SHUT UP!
NO DISRESPECT, KID. YOUR FAMILY MUST HAVE BEEN HEAVY HITTERS.
WHEN WE WERE GOING THROUGH OUR LIST OF CANDIDATES, MY BOSS THOUGHT HE RECOGNIZED YOUR LAST NAME. SAID WE SHOULD AT LEAST GIVE YOU AN INTERVIEW.
WHO... WHO'S YOUR BOSS?
WELL, I USED TO SAY RON, BUT BETWEEN YOU AND ME, IT'S REALLY MORE NANCY THESE DAYS.

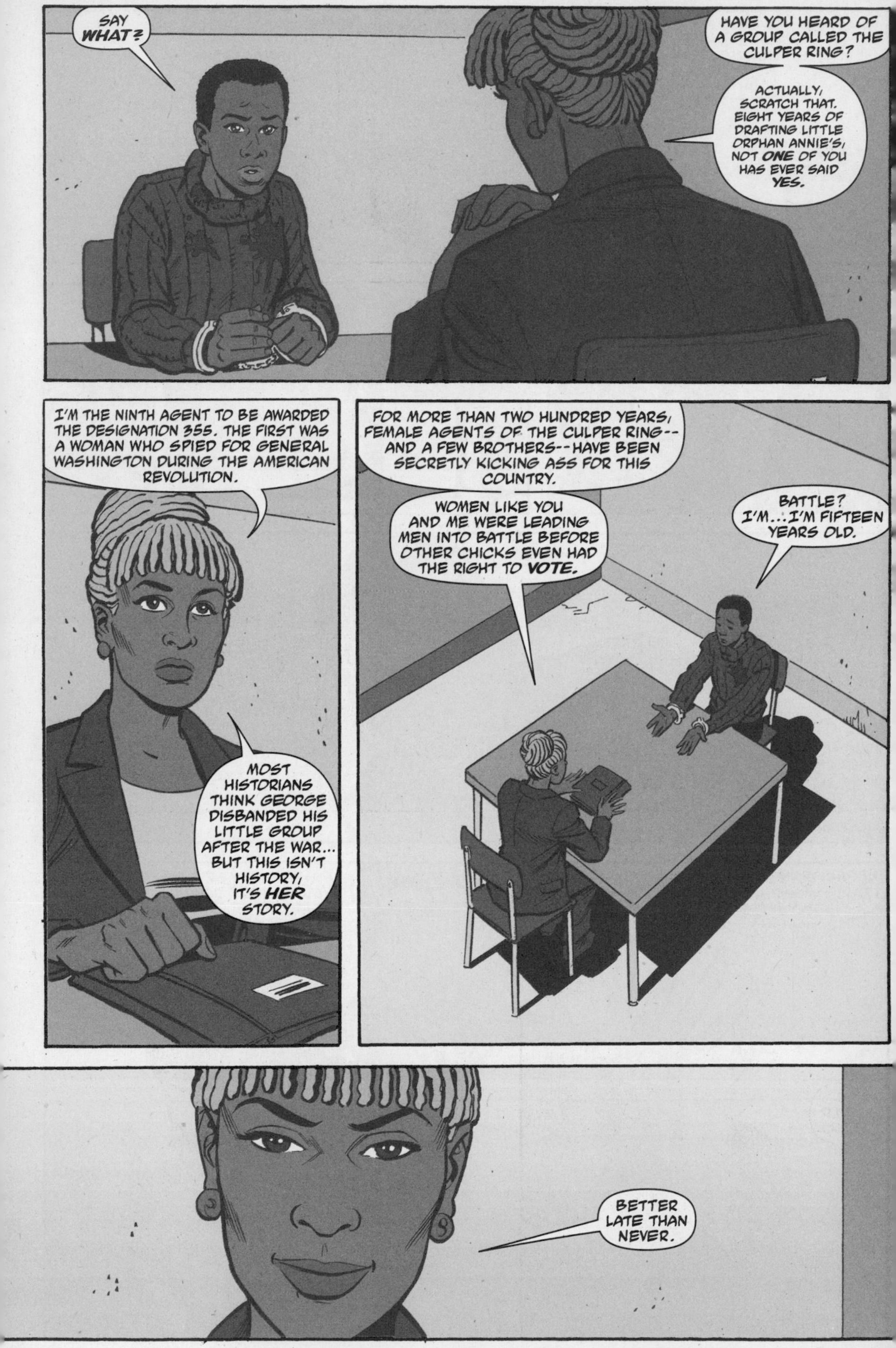
SAY WHAT?
HAVE YOU HEARD OF A GROUP CALLED THE CULPER RING?
ACTUALLY, SCRATCH THAT. EIGHT YEARS OF DRAFTING LITTLE ORPHAN ANNIE'S, NOT ONE OF YOU HAS EVER SAID YES.
I'M THE NINTH AGENT TO BE AWARDED THE DESIGNATION 355. THE FIRST WAS A WOMAN WHO SPIED FOR GENERAL WASHINGTON DURING THE AMERICAN REVOLUTION.
MOST HISTORIANS THINK GEORGE DISBANDED HIS LITTLE GROUP AFTER THE WAR... BUT THIS ISN'T HISTORY, IT'S HER STORY.
FOR MORE THAN TWO HUNDRED YEARS, FEMALE AGENTS OF THE CULPER RING-- AND A FEW BROTHERS--HAVE BEEN SECRETLY KICKING ASS FOR THIS COUNTRY.
WOMEN LIKE YOU AND ME WERE LEADING MEN INTO BATTLE BEFORE OTHER CHICKS EVEN HAD THE RIGHT TO VOTE.
BATTLE? I'M...I'M FIFTEEN YEARS OLD.
BETTER LATE THAN NEVER.

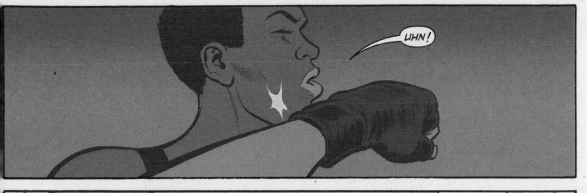

UHN!

NOT SO TOUGH WITHOUT THE **BAT**, ARE YOU?

SCREW YOU, THREE.

NINE TIMES OUT OF TEN, A MAN IS GONNA BE STRONGER THAN YOU. BIOLOGY'S A BITCH, BUT THERE YOU GO.

FORGET WHAT YOU SAW ON *CHARLIE'S ANGELS,* EVEN AN **AVERAGE** GUY IS USUALLY GONNA BE ABLE TO OVER-POWER YOU.

I TOLD YOU...

...I DON'T **WATCH** TV.

UNF!

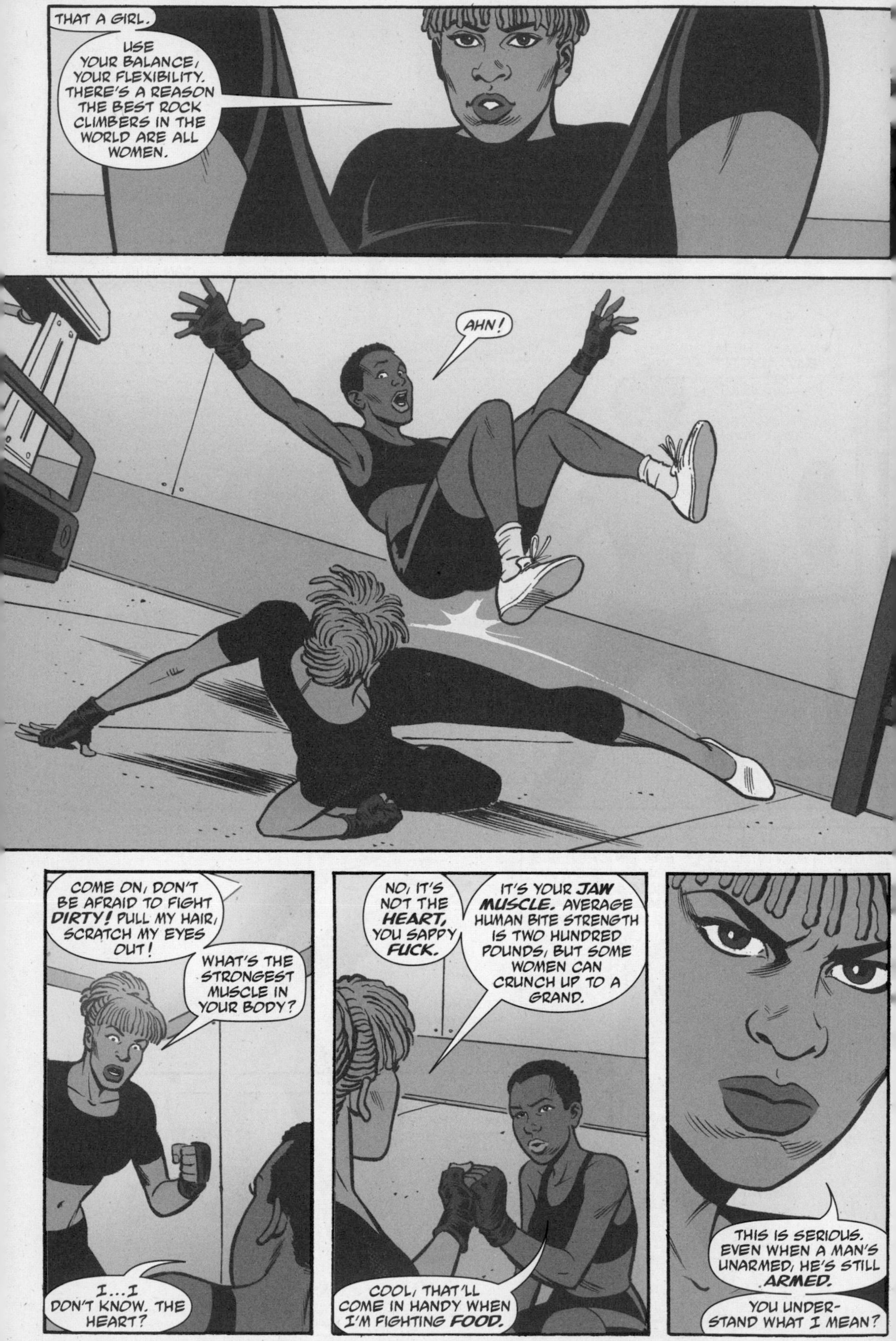
THAT A GIRL.
USE YOUR BALANCE, YOUR FLEXIBILITY. THERE'S A REASON THE BEST ROCK CLIMBERS IN THE WORLD ARE ALL WOMEN.
AHN!
COME ON, DON'T BE AFRAID TO FIGHT DIRTY! PULL MY HAIR, SCRATCH MY EYES OUT!
WHAT'S THE STRONGEST MUSCLE IN YOUR BODY?
I...I DON'T KNOW. THE HEART?
NO, IT'S NOT THE HEART, YOU SAPPY FUCK.
IT'S YOUR JAW MUSCLE. AVERAGE HUMAN BITE STRENGTH IS TWO HUNDRED POUNDS, BUT SOME WOMEN CAN CRUNCH UP TO A GRAND.
COOL, THAT'LL COME IN HANDY WHEN I'M FIGHTING FOOD.
THIS IS SERIOUS. EVEN WHEN A MAN'S UNARMED, HE'S STILL ARMED.
YOU UNDER-STAND WHAT I MEAN?

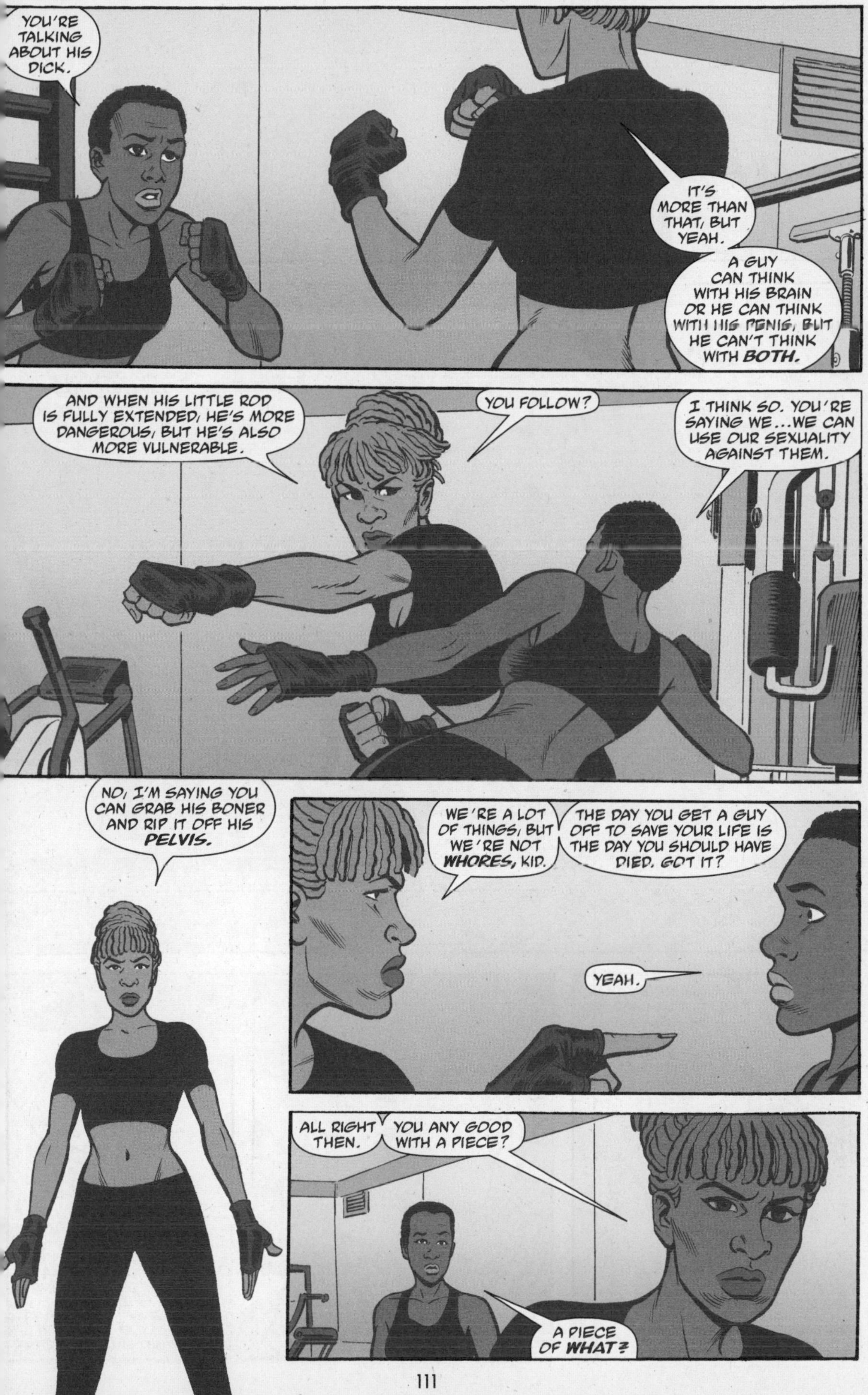
YOU'RE TALKING ABOUT HIS DICK.
IT'S MORE THAN THAT, BUT YEAH.
A GUY CAN THINK WITH HIS BRAIN OR HE CAN THINK WITH HIS PENIS, BUT HE CAN'T THINK WITH **BOTH.**
AND WHEN HIS LITTLE ROD IS FULLY EXTENDED, HE'S MORE DANGEROUS, BUT HE'S ALSO MORE VULNERABLE.
YOU FOLLOW?
I THINK SO. YOU'RE SAYING WE... WE CAN USE OUR SEXUALITY AGAINST THEM.
NO, I'M SAYING YOU CAN GRAB HIS BONER AND RIP IT OFF HIS **PELVIS.**
WE'RE A LOT OF THINGS, BUT WE'RE NOT **WHORES,** KID.
THE DAY YOU GET A GUY OFF TO SAVE YOUR LIFE IS THE DAY YOU SHOULD HAVE DIED. GOT IT?
YEAH.
ALL RIGHT THEN.
YOU ANY GOOD WITH A PIECE?
A PIECE OF **WHAT?**

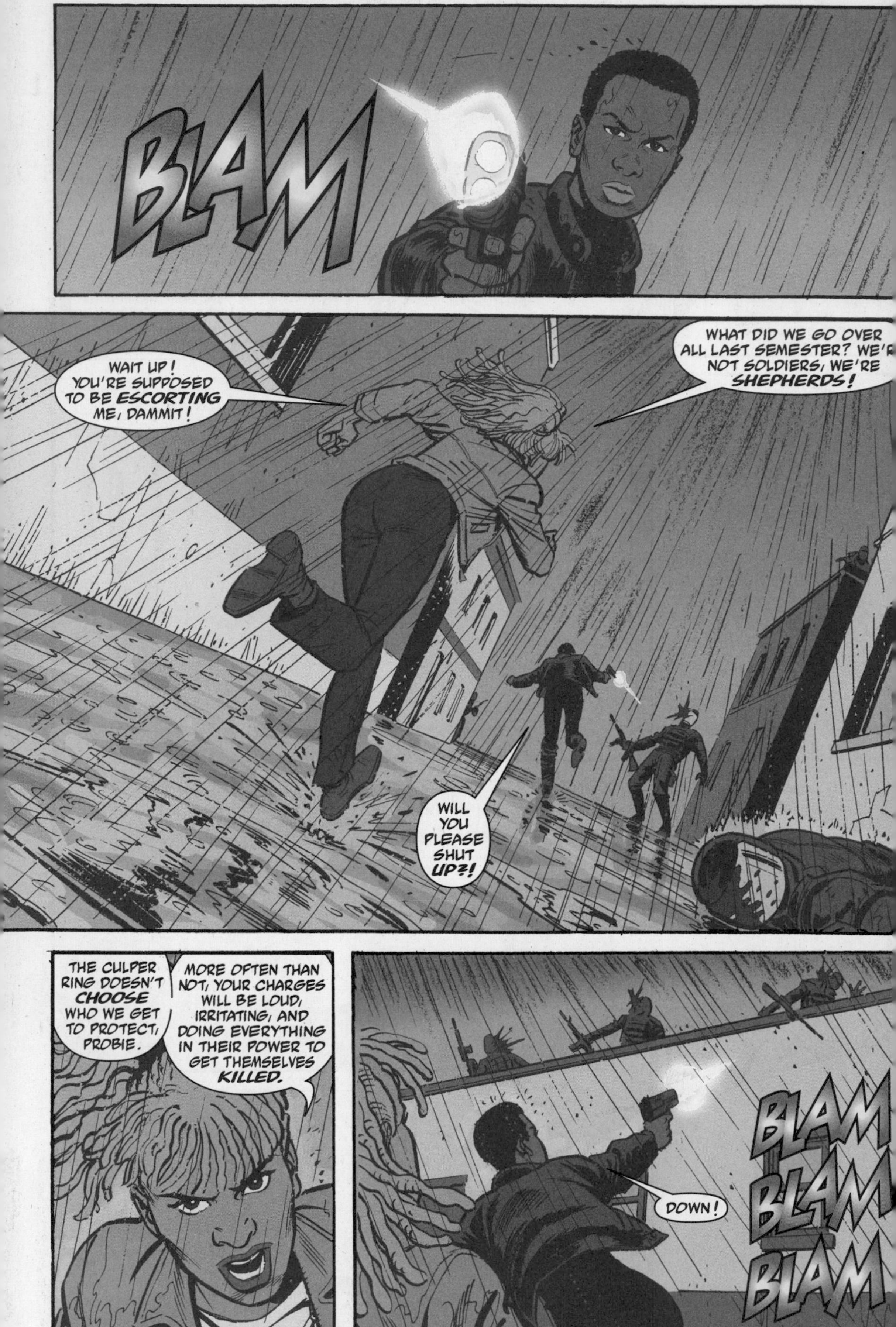

BLAM
WAIT UP! YOU'RE SUPPOSED TO BE ESCORTING ME, DAMMIT!
WHAT DID WE GO OVER ALL LAST SEMESTER? WE'R NOT SOLDIERS, WE'RE SHEPHERDS!
WILL YOU PLEASE SHUT UP?!
THE CULPER RING DOESN'T CHOOSE WHO WE GET TO PROTECT, PROBIE.
MORE OFTEN THAN NOT, YOUR CHARGES WILL BE LOUD, IRRITATING, AND DOING EVERYTHING IN THEIR POWER TO GET THEMSELVES KILLED.
DOWN!
BLAM
BLAM
BLAM

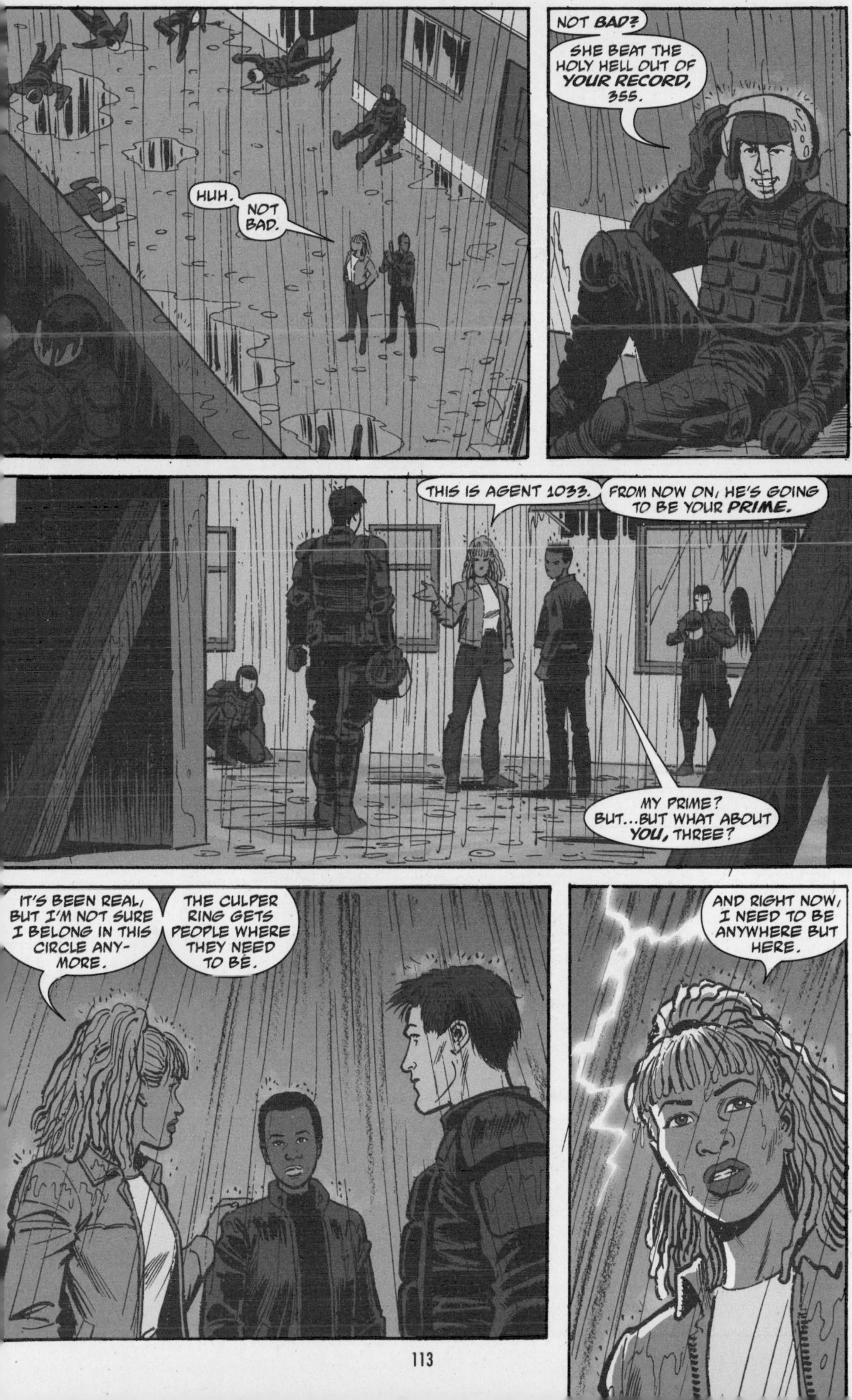
HUH. NOT BAD.
NOT BAD?
SHE BEAT THE HOLY HELL OUT OF YOUR RECORD, 355.
THIS IS AGENT 1033.
FROM NOW ON, HE'S GOING TO BE YOUR PRIME.
MY PRIME? BUT...BUT WHAT ABOUT YOU, THREE?
IT'S BEEN REAL, BUT I'M NOT SURE I BELONG IN THIS CIRCLE ANY-MORE.
THE CULPER RING GETS PEOPLE WHERE THEY NEED TO BE.
AND RIGHT NOW, I NEED TO BE ANYWHERE BUT HERE.

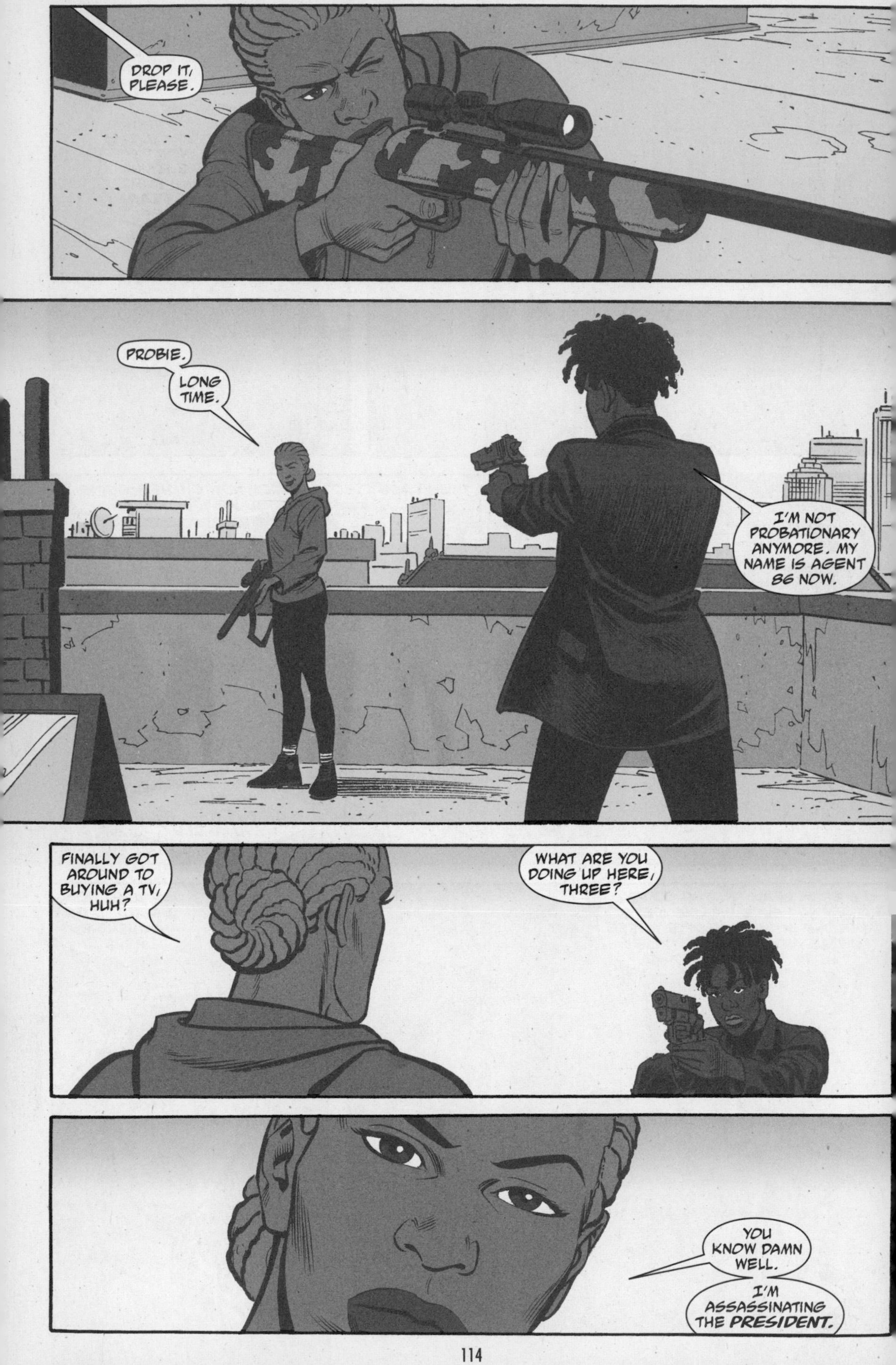

DROP IT, PLEASE.
PROBIE.
LONG TIME.
I'M NOT PROBATIONARY ANYMORE. MY NAME IS AGENT 86 NOW.
FINALLY GOT AROUND TO BUYING A TV, HUH?
WHAT ARE YOU DOING UP HERE, THREE?
YOU KNOW DAMN WELL.
I'M ASSASSINATING THE *PRESIDENT.*

SO IT'S TRUE?
YOU'VE DEFECTED TO THE SETAUKET RING?
BULLSHIT. IT'S THIS COUNTRY THAT'S DEFECTED FROM ME.
HOW CAN YOU TAKE ORDERS FROM THAT BASTARD?
AFTER WHAT HE DID TO THAT...THAT GIRL? IN THE FUCKING OVAL OFFICE?
THAT'S A REASON TO KILL A MAN?
SURE, BUT IT'S NOT MY ONLY REASON. THIS GOES DEEPER THAN YOU COULD IMAGINE, KID. I'VE SEEN THE DOSSIERS.
IT'S NOT JUST THE COMMANDER IN CHIEF. THERE ARE MEN IN THIS WORLD WHO WON'T STOP UNTIL THEY'VE FOUND A WAY TO BRING EVERY WOMAN ON THE PLANET TO HER KNEES.
AGENT 711 WARNED ME YOU'D CHANGED. SHE SAYS YOU'RE SICK, DELUSIONAL.
I DON'T WANT TO FIGHT YOU, SWEETIE PIE.
WHY DON'T YOU HOLSTER YOUR WEAPON SO WE CAN TALK ABOUT THIS LIKE THE CIVILIZED WOMEN WE ARE?

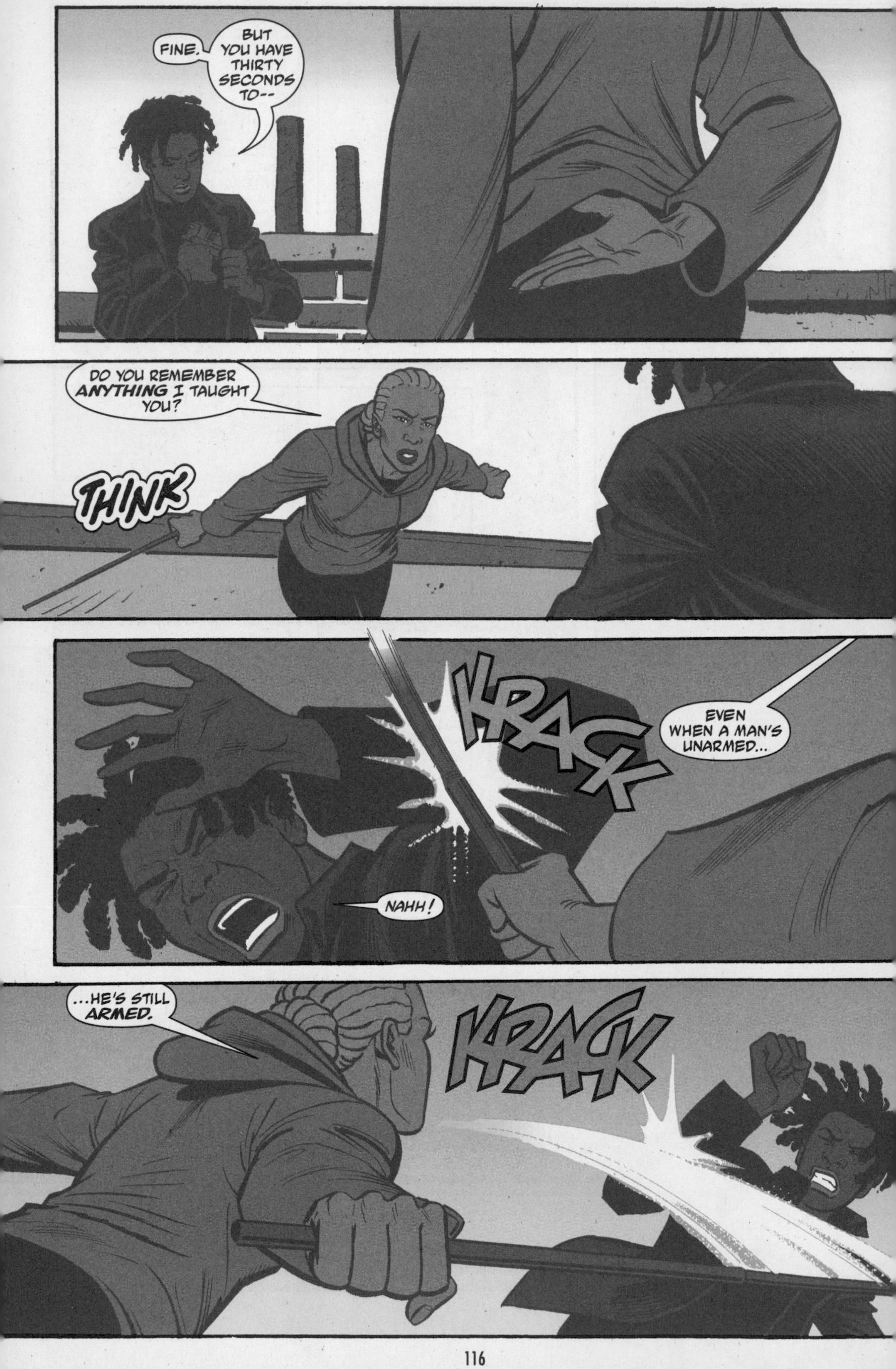
FINE.
BUT YOU HAVE THIRTY SECONDS TO--
DO YOU REMEMBER ANYTHING I TAUGHT YOU?
THINK
KRACK
EVEN WHEN A MAN'S UNARMED...
NAHH!
...HE'S STILL ARMED.
KRACK

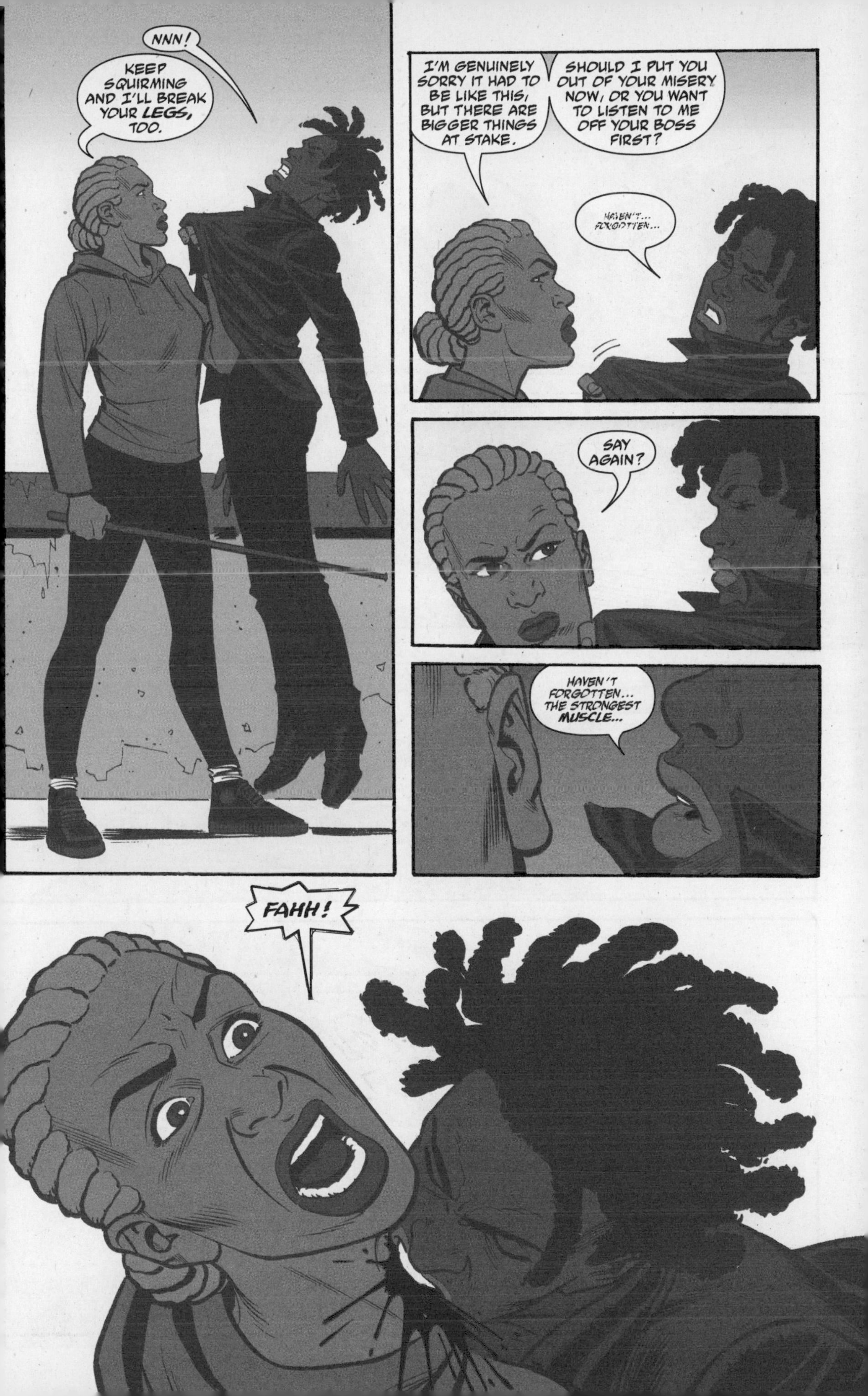
NNN!
KEEP SQUIRMING AND I'LL BREAK YOUR LEGS, TOO.
I'M GENUINELY SORRY IT HAD TO BE LIKE THIS, BUT THERE ARE BIGGER THINGS AT STAKE.
SHOULD I PUT YOU OUT OF YOUR MISERY NOW, OR YOU WANT TO LISTEN TO ME OFF YOUR BOSS FIRST?
HAVEN'T... FORGOTTEN...
SAY AGAIN?
HAVEN'T FORGOTTEN... THE STRONGEST MUSCLE...
FAHH!

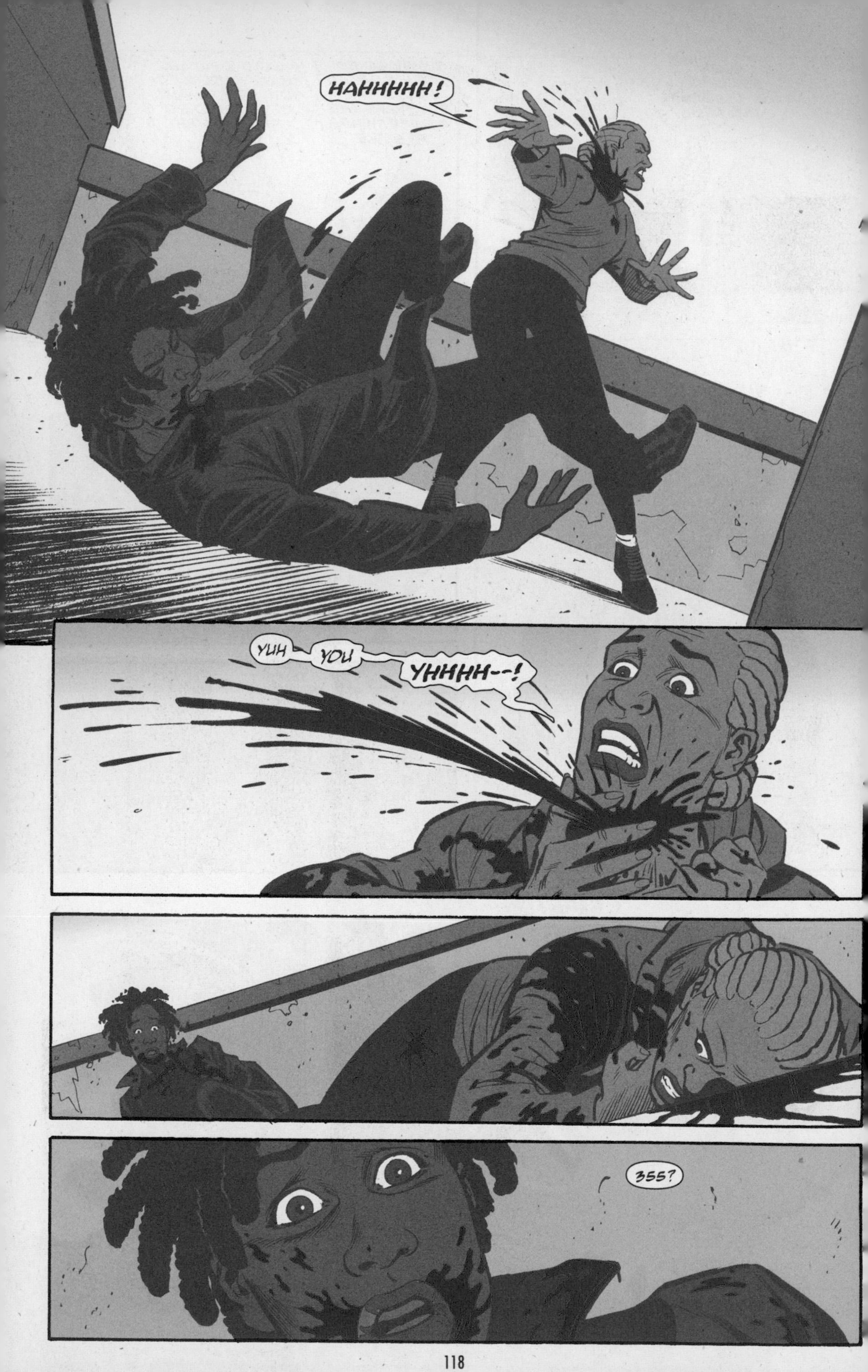
HAHHHHH!
YUH
YOU
YHHHH--!
355?

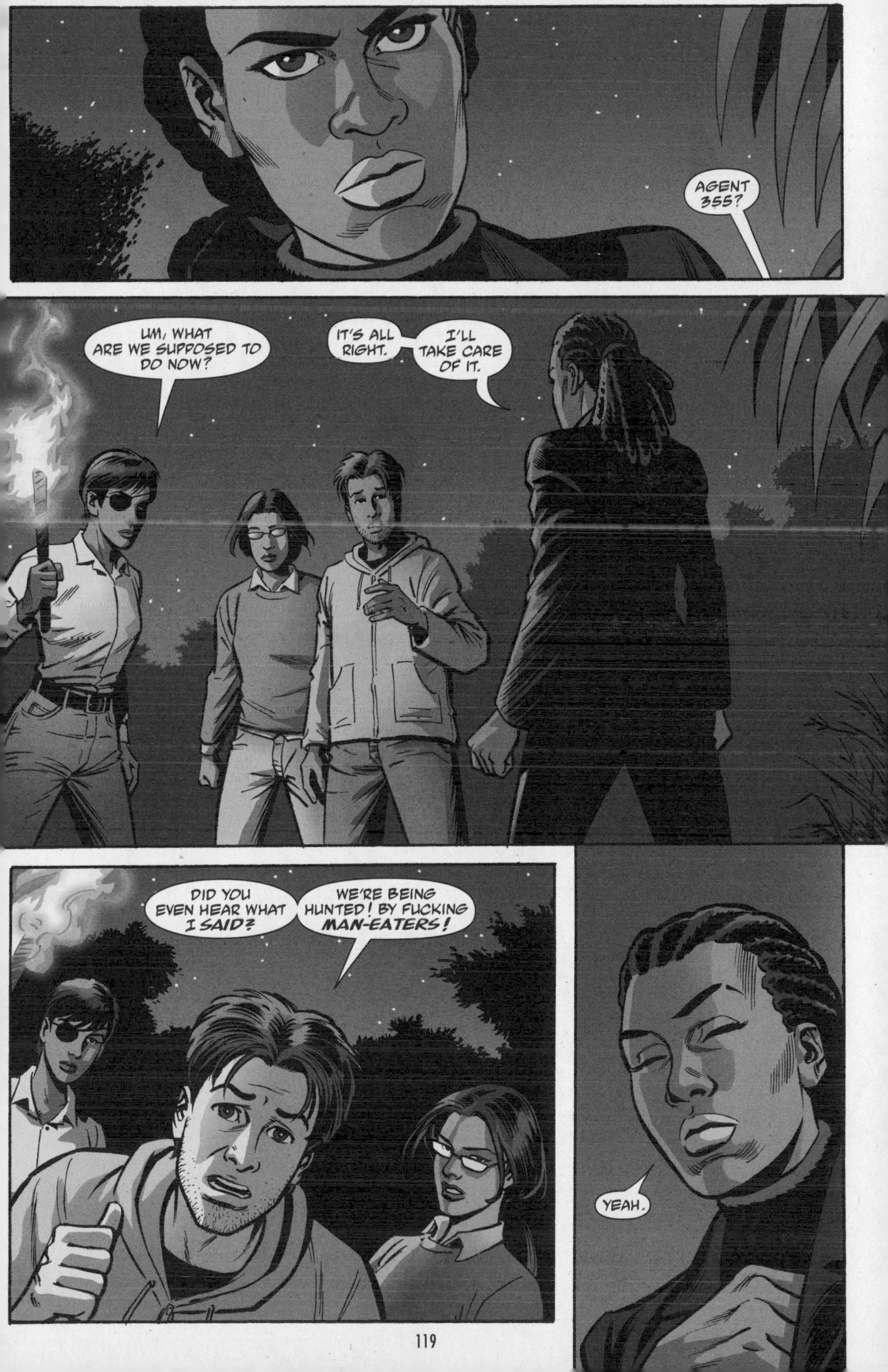
AGENT 355?
UM, WHAT ARE WE SUPPOSED TO DO NOW?
IT'S ALL RIGHT.
I'LL TAKE CARE OF IT.
DID YOU EVEN HEAR WHAT I SAID?
WE'RE BEING HUNTED! BY FUCKING MAN-EATERS!
YEAH.

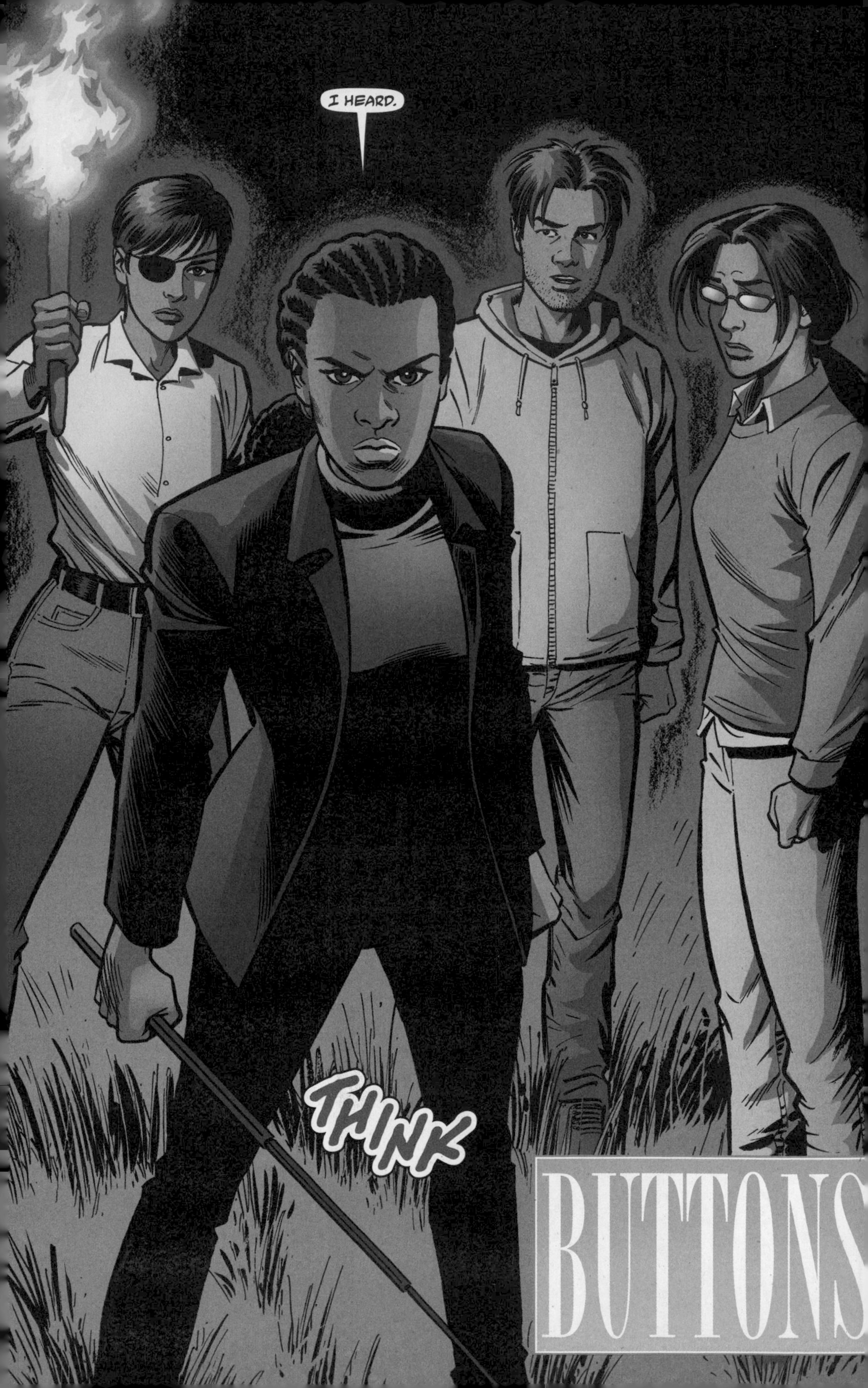
I HEARD.
THINK
BUTTONS

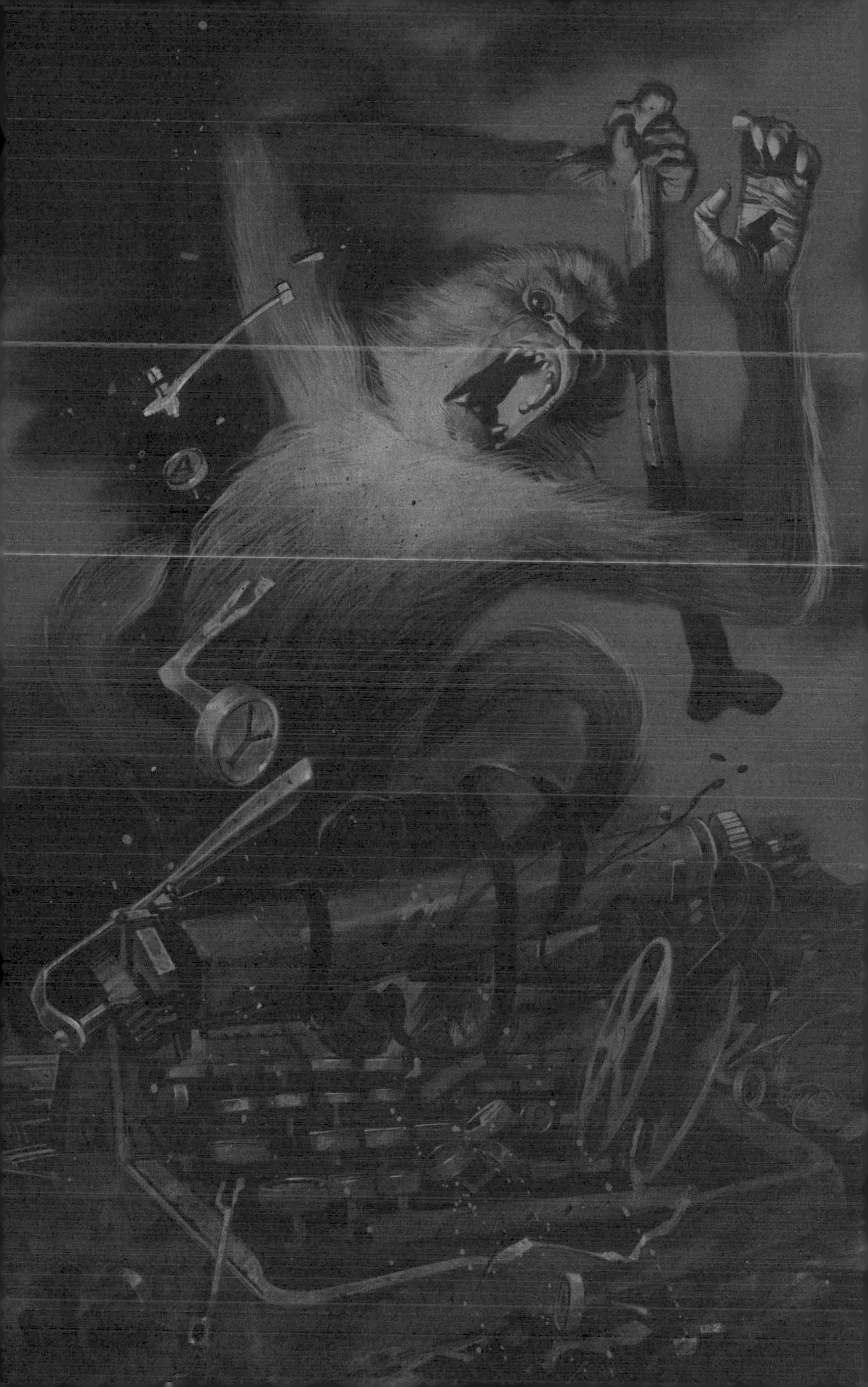

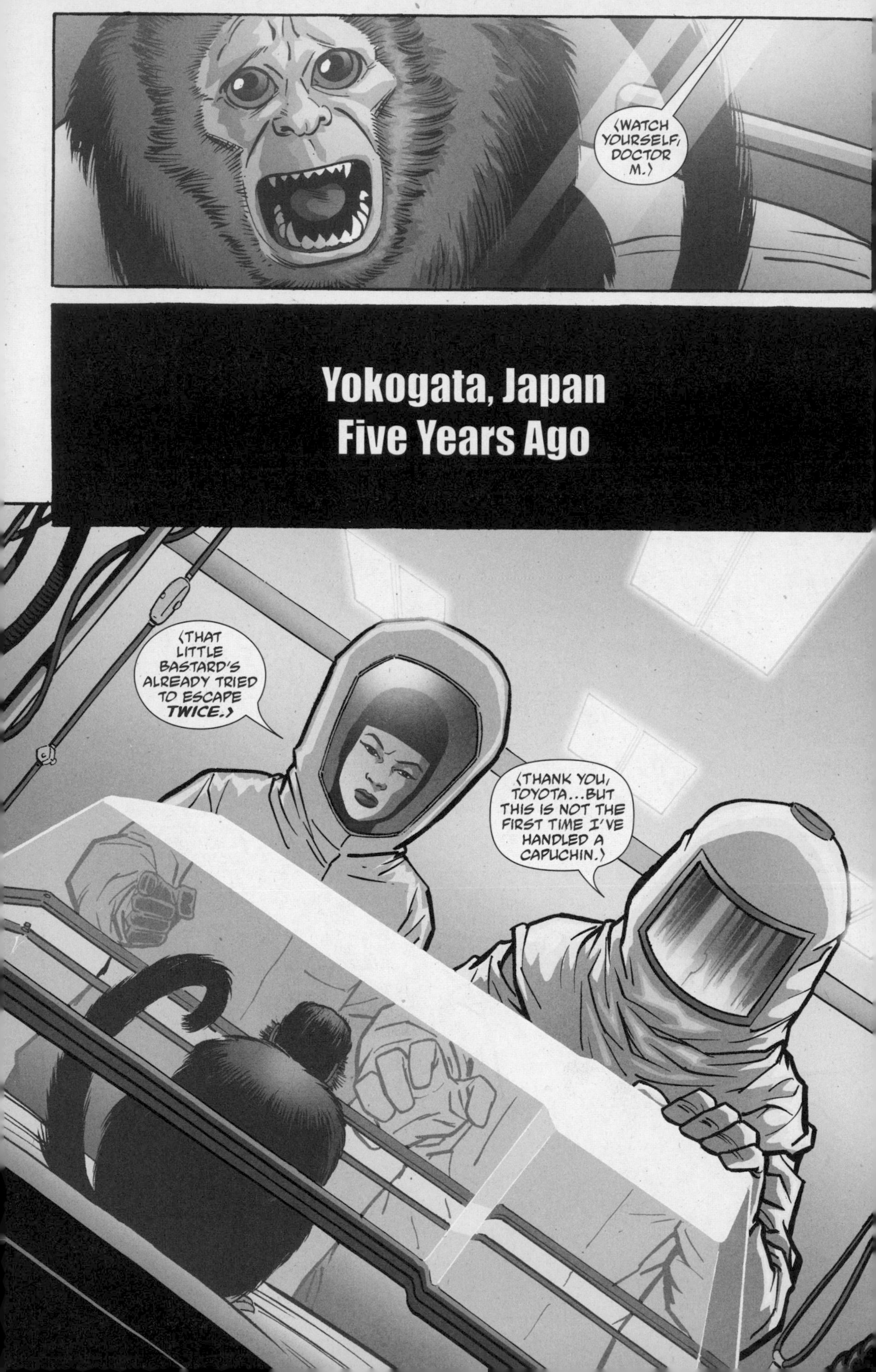
⟨WATCH YOURSELF, DOCTOR M.⟩
Yokogata, Japan
Five Years Ago
⟨THAT LITTLE BASTARD'S ALREADY TRIED TO ESCAPE *TWICE*.⟩
⟨THANK YOU, TOYOTA...BUT THIS IS NOT THE FIRST TIME I'VE HANDLED A CAPUCHIN.⟩

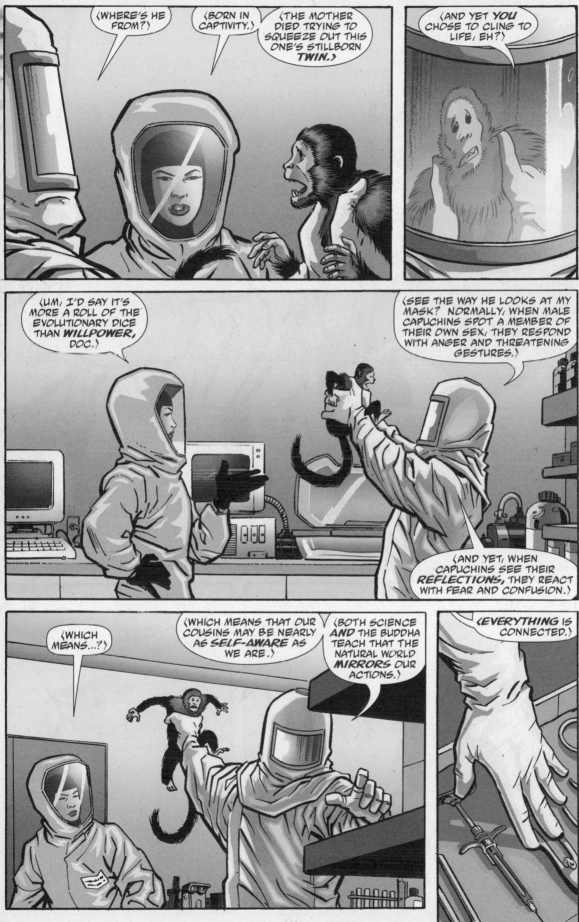

‹WHERE'S HE FROM?›

‹BORN IN CAPTIVITY.›

‹THE MOTHER DIED TRYING TO SQUEEZE OUT THIS ONE'S STILLBORN *TWIN.*›

‹AND YET *YOU* CHOSE TO CLING TO LIFE, EH?›

‹UM, I'D SAY IT'S MORE A ROLL OF THE EVOLUTIONARY DICE THAN *WILLPOWER,* DOC.›

‹SEE THE WAY HE LOOKS AT MY MASK? NORMALLY, WHEN MALE CAPUCHINS SPOT A MEMBER OF THEIR OWN SEX, THEY RESPOND WITH ANGER AND THREATENING GESTURES.›

‹AND YET, WHEN CAPUCHINS SEE THEIR *REFLECTIONS,* THEY REACT WITH FEAR AND CONFUSION.›

‹WHICH MEANS...?›

‹WHICH MEANS THAT OUR COUSINS MAY BE NEARLY AS *SELF-AWARE* AS WE ARE.›

‹BOTH SCIENCE *AND* THE BUDDHA TEACH THAT THE NATURAL WORLD *MIRRORS* OUR ACTIONS.›

‹*EVERYTHING* IS CONNECTED.›

123

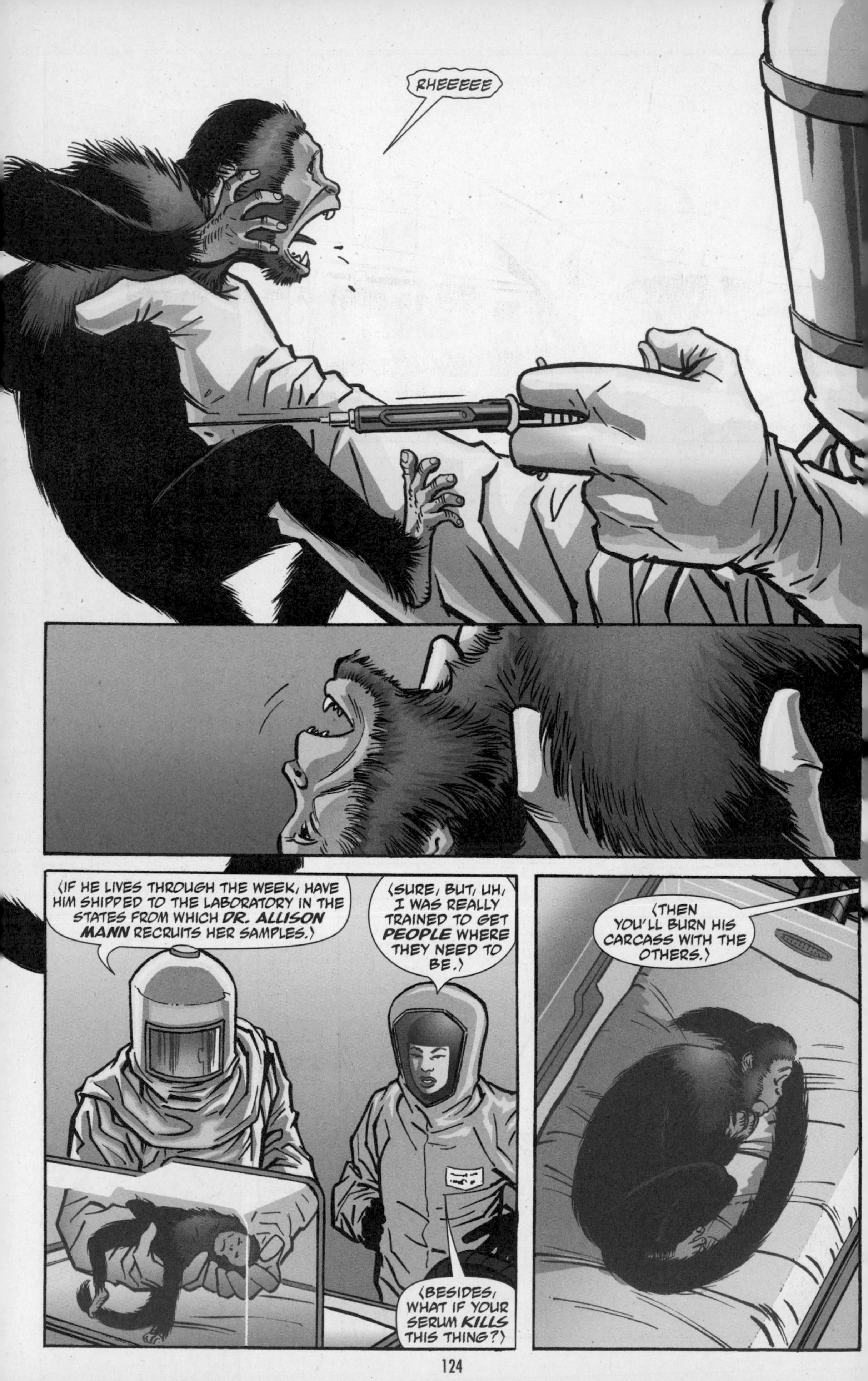
RHEEEEE
‹IF HE LIVES THROUGH THE WEEK, HAVE HIM SHIPPED TO THE LABORATORY IN THE STATES FROM WHICH DR. ALLISON MANN RECRUITS HER SAMPLES.›
‹SURE, BUT, UH, I WAS REALLY TRAINED TO GET PEOPLE WHERE THEY NEED TO BE.›
‹BESIDES, WHAT IF YOUR SERUM KILLS THIS THING?›
‹THEN YOU'LL BURN HIS CARCASS WITH THE OTHERS.›

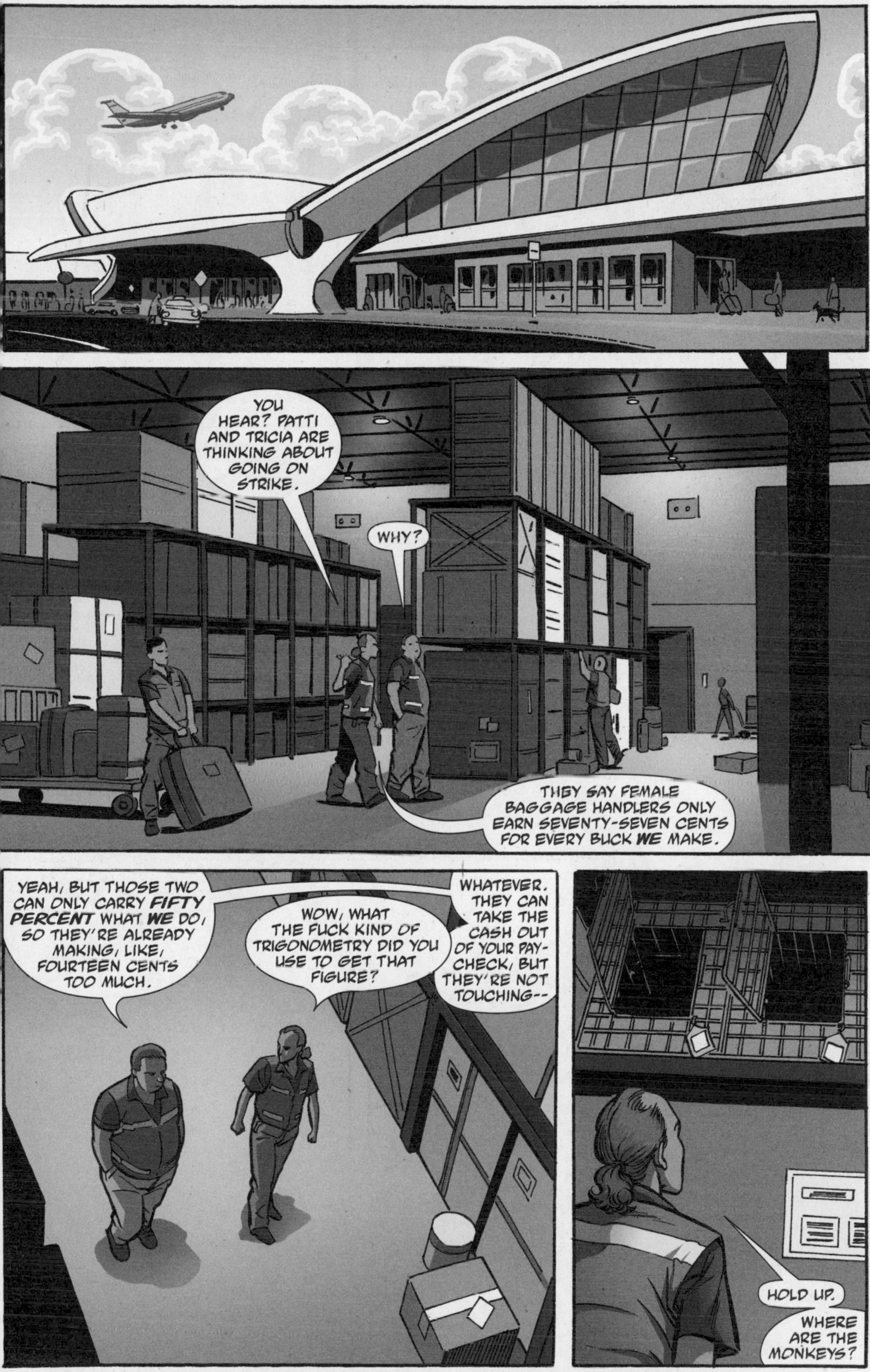

YOU HEAR? PATTI AND TRICIA ARE THINKING ABOUT GOING ON STRIKE.
WHY?
THEY SAY FEMALE BAGGAGE HANDLERS ONLY EARN SEVENTY-SEVEN CENTS FOR EVERY BUCK WE MAKE.
YEAH, BUT THOSE TWO CAN ONLY CARRY FIFTY PERCENT WHAT WE DO, SO THEY'RE ALREADY MAKING, LIKE, FOURTEEN CENTS TOO MUCH.
WOW, WHAT THE FUCK KIND OF TRIGONOMETRY DID YOU USE TO GET THAT FIGURE?
WHATEVER. THEY CAN TAKE THE CASH OUT OF YOUR PAY-CHECK, BUT THEY'RE NOT TOUCHING--
HOLD UP.
WHERE ARE THE MONKEYS?

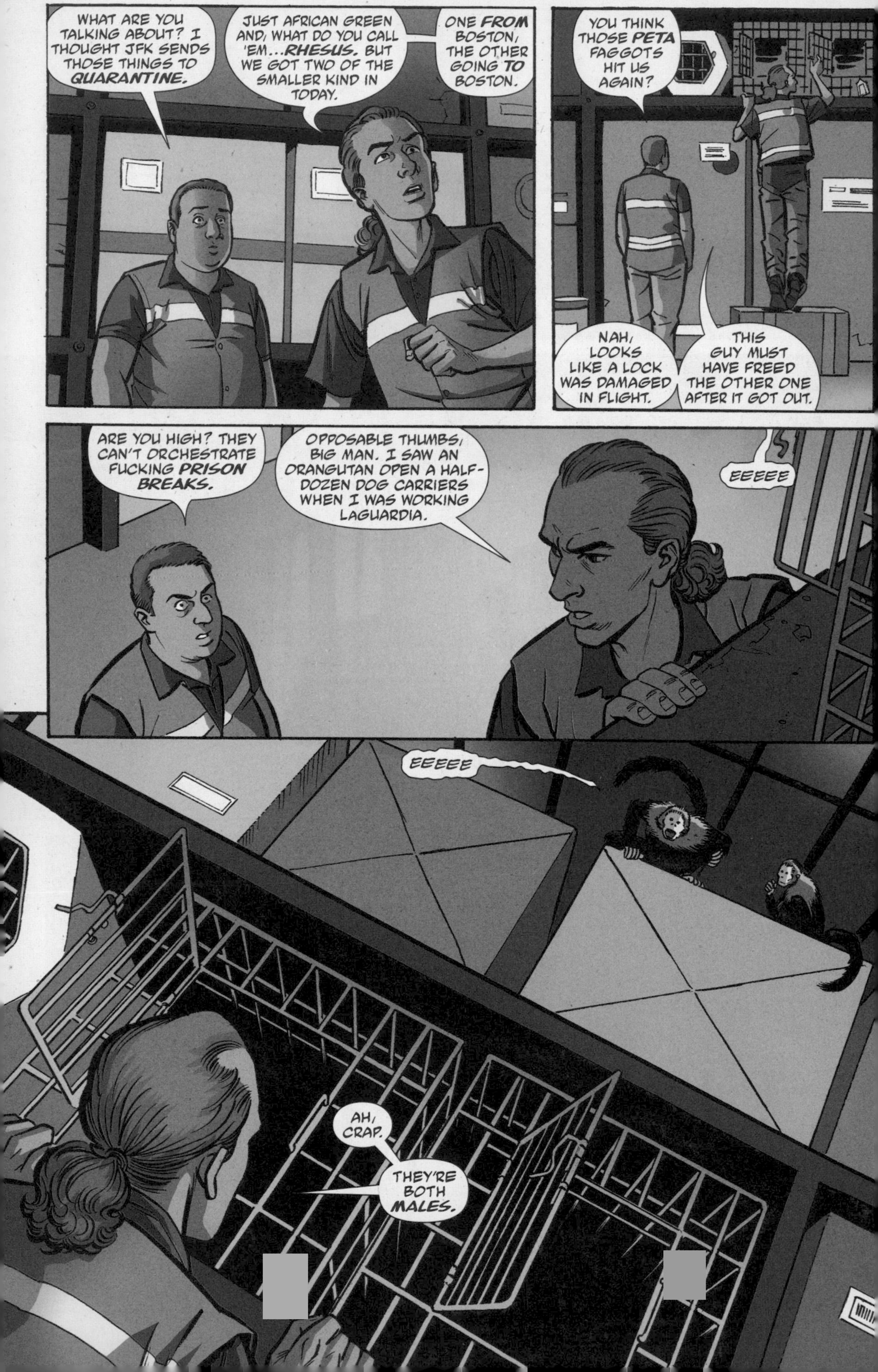

WHAT ARE YOU TALKING ABOUT? I THOUGHT JFK SENDS THOSE THINGS TO QUARANTINE.
JUST AFRICAN GREEN AND, WHAT DO YOU CALL 'EM...RHESUS. BUT WE GOT TWO OF THE SMALLER KIND IN TODAY.
ONE FROM BOSTON, THE OTHER GOING TO BOSTON.
YOU THINK THOSE PETA FAGGOTS HIT US AGAIN?
NAH, LOOKS LIKE A LOCK WAS DAMAGED IN FLIGHT.
THIS GUY MUST HAVE FREED THE OTHER ONE AFTER IT GOT OUT.
ARE YOU HIGH? THEY CAN'T ORCHESTRATE FUCKING PRISON BREAKS.
OPPOSABLE THUMBS, BIG MAN. I SAW AN ORANGUTAN OPEN A HALF-DOZEN DOG CARRIERS WHEN I WAS WORKING LAGUARDIA.
EEEEE
EEEEE
AH, CRAP.
THEY'RE BOTH MALES.

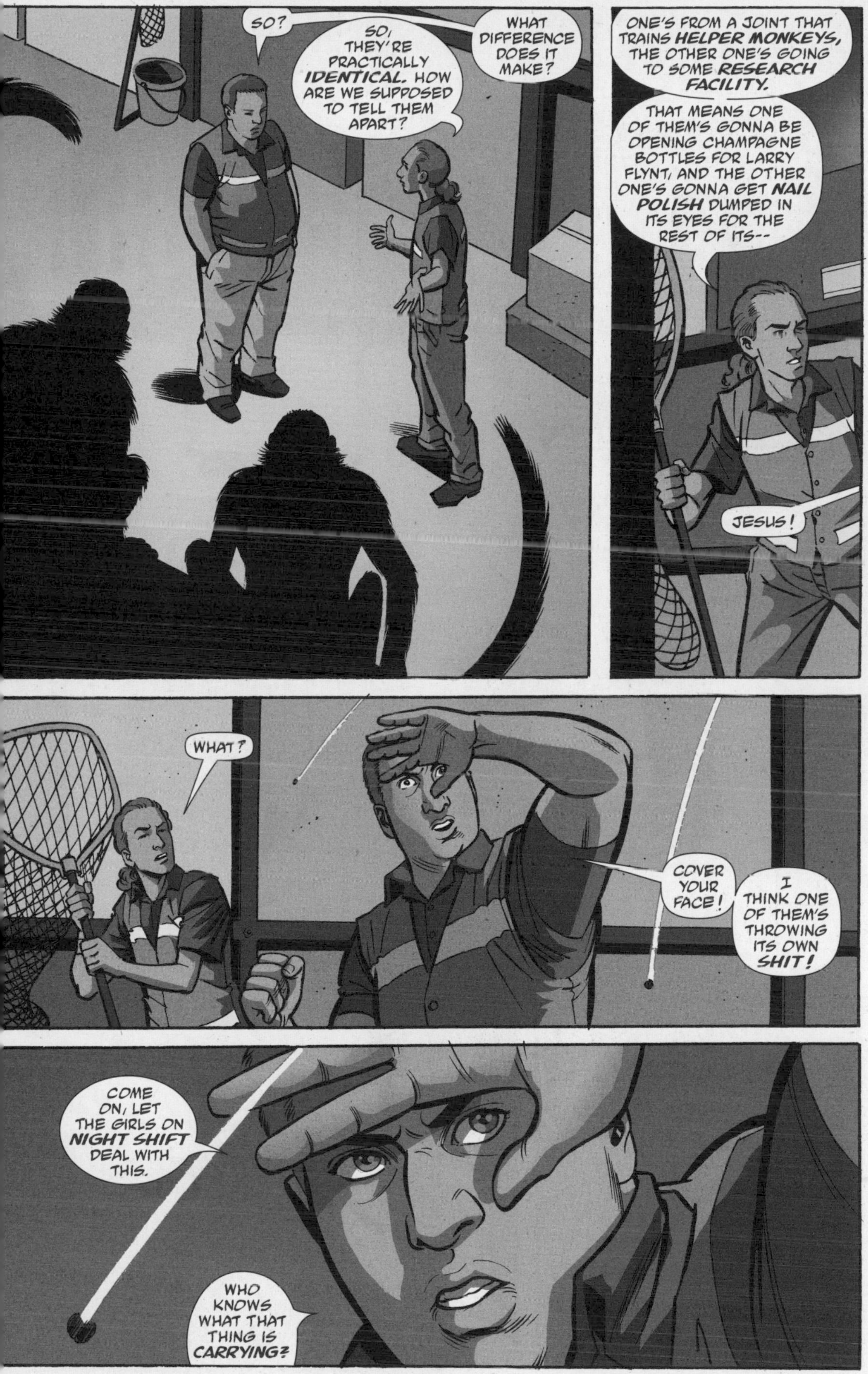
SO?
SO, THEY'RE PRACTICALLY IDENTICAL. HOW ARE WE SUPPOSED TO TELL THEM APART?
WHAT DIFFERENCE DOES IT MAKE?
ONE'S FROM A JOINT THAT TRAINS HELPER MONKEYS, THE OTHER ONE'S GOING TO SOME RESEARCH FACILITY.
THAT MEANS ONE OF THEM'S GONNA BE OPENING CHAMPAGNE BOTTLES FOR LARRY FLYNT, AND THE OTHER ONE'S GONNA GET NAIL POLISH DUMPED IN ITS EYES FOR THE REST OF ITS--
JESUS!
WHAT?
COVER YOUR FACE!
I THINK ONE OF THEM'S THROWING ITS OWN SHIT!
COME ON, LET THE GIRLS ON NIGHT SHIFT DEAL WITH THIS.
WHO KNOWS WHAT THAT THING IS CARRYING?

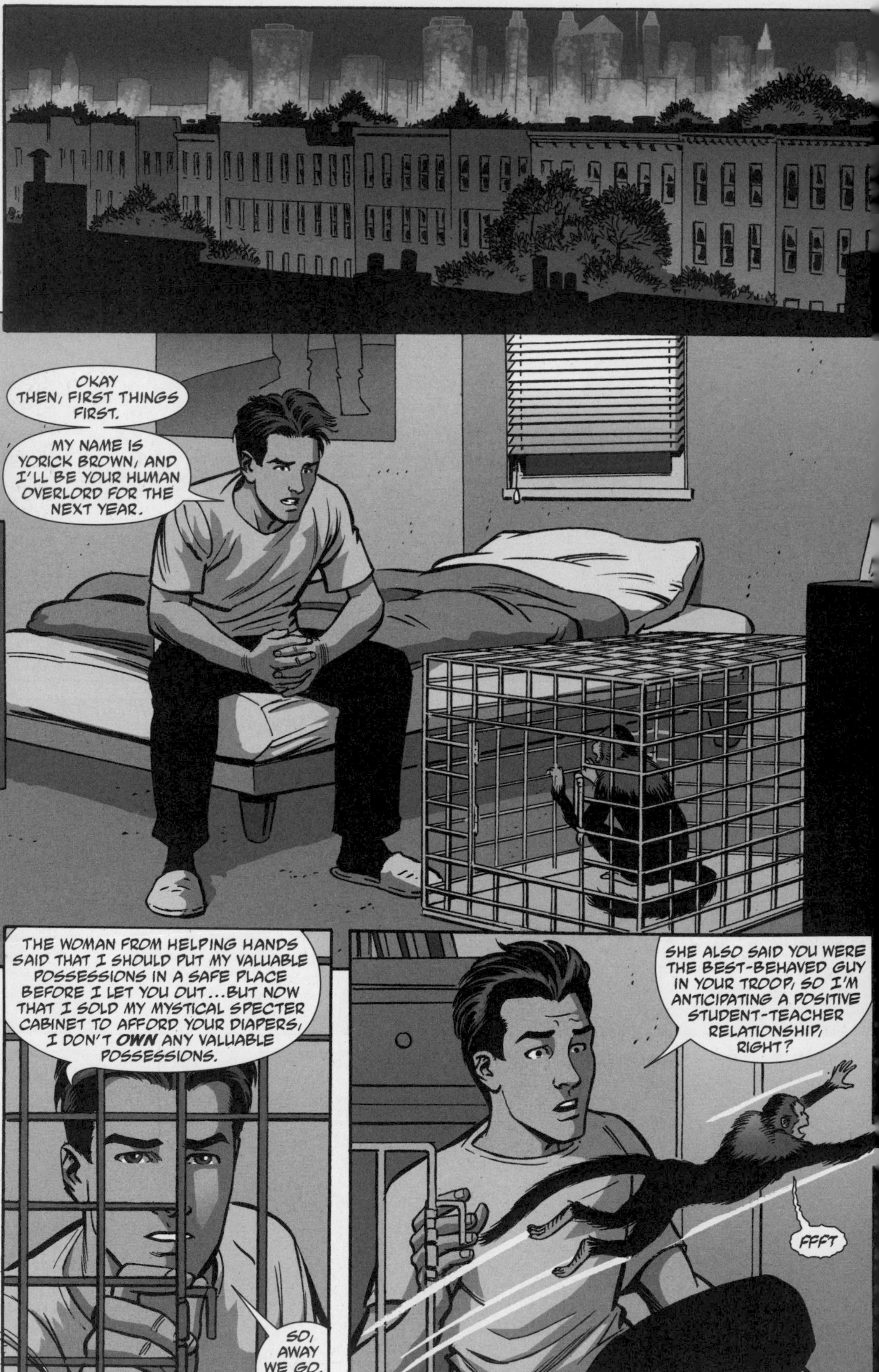
OKAY THEN, FIRST THINGS FIRST.
MY NAME IS YORICK BROWN, AND I'LL BE YOUR HUMAN OVERLORD FOR THE NEXT YEAR.
THE WOMAN FROM HELPING HANDS SAID THAT I SHOULD PUT MY VALUABLE POSSESSIONS IN A SAFE PLACE BEFORE I LET YOU OUT... BUT NOW THAT I SOLD MY MYSTICAL SPECTER CABINET TO AFFORD YOUR DIAPERS, I DON'T **OWN** ANY VALUABLE POSSESSIONS.
SO, AWAY WE GO.
SHE ALSO SAID YOU WERE THE BEST-BEHAVED GUY IN YOUR TROOP, SO I'M ANTICIPATING A POSITIVE STUDENT-TEACHER RELATIONSHIP, RIGHT?
FFFT

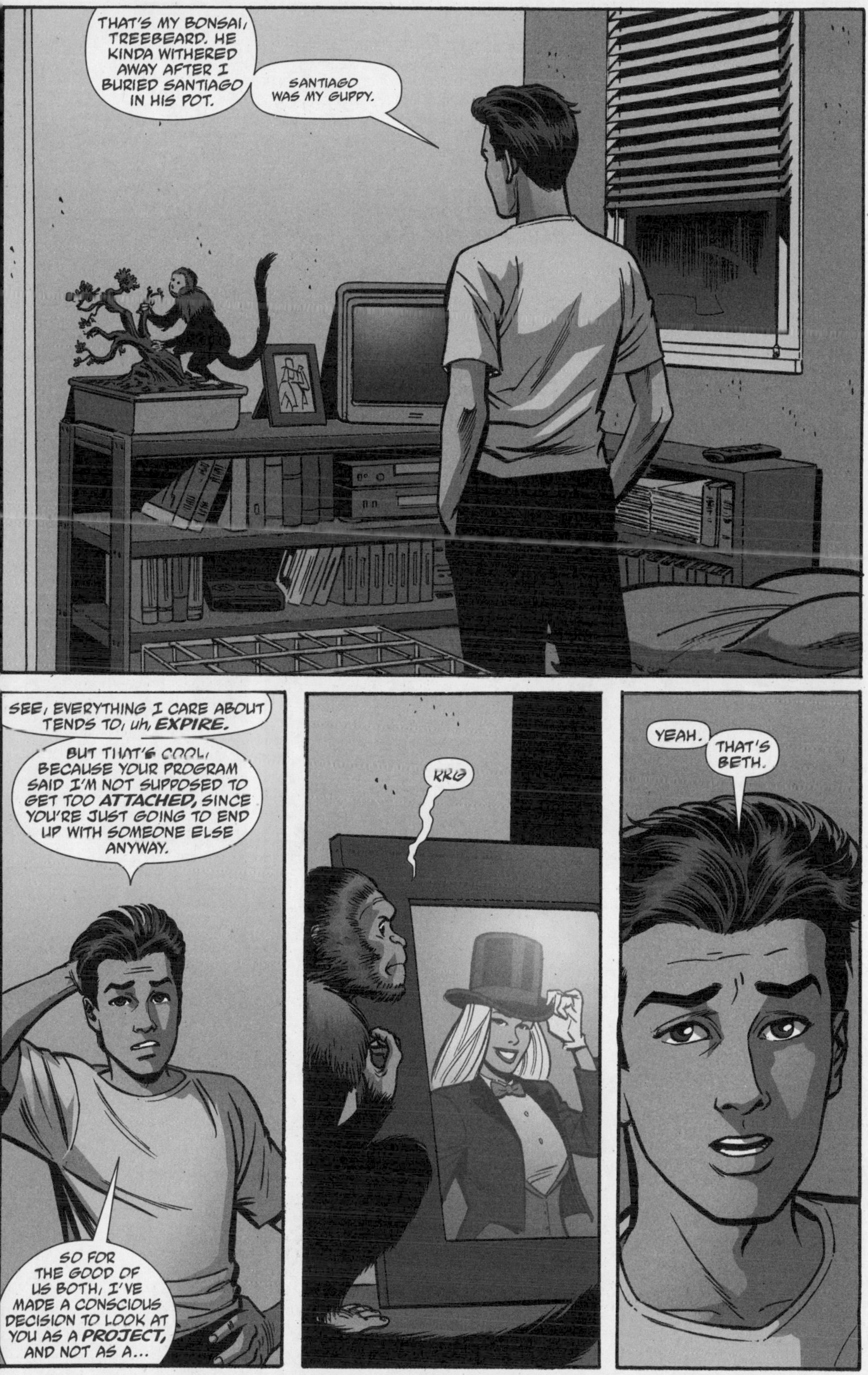
THAT'S MY BONSAI, TREEBEARD. HE KINDA WITHERED AWAY AFTER I BURIED SANTIAGO IN HIS POT.
SANTIAGO WAS MY GUPPY.
SEE, EVERYTHING I CARE ABOUT TENDS TO, uh, EXPIRE.
BUT THAT'S COOL, BECAUSE YOUR PROGRAM SAID I'M NOT SUPPOSED TO GET TOO ATTACHED, SINCE YOU'RE JUST GOING TO END UP WITH SOMEONE ELSE ANYWAY.
SO FOR THE GOOD OF US BOTH, I'VE MADE A CONSCIOUS DECISION TO LOOK AT YOU AS A PROJECT, AND NOT AS A...
KRG
YEAH.
THAT'S BETH.

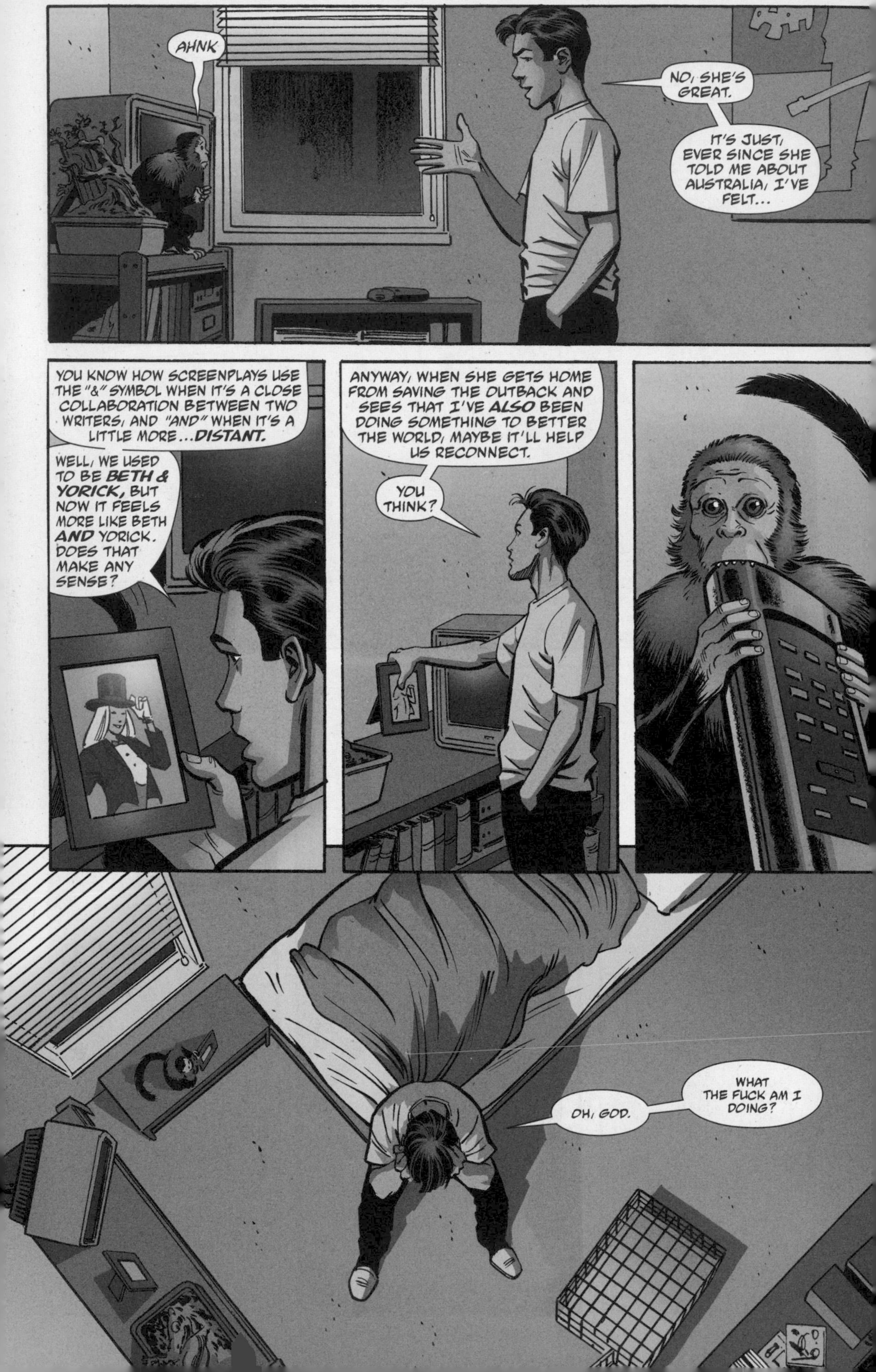
AHNK
NO, SHE'S GREAT.
IT'S JUST, EVER SINCE SHE TOLD ME ABOUT AUSTRALIA, I'VE FELT...
YOU KNOW HOW SCREENPLAYS USE THE "&" SYMBOL WHEN IT'S A CLOSE COLLABORATION BETWEEN TWO WRITERS, AND "AND" WHEN IT'S A LITTLE MORE...DISTANT.
WELL, WE USED TO BE BETH & YORICK, BUT NOW IT FEELS MORE LIKE BETH AND YORICK. DOES THAT MAKE ANY SENSE?
ANYWAY, WHEN SHE GETS HOME FROM SAVING THE OUTBACK AND SEES THAT I'VE ALSO BEEN DOING SOMETHING TO BETTER THE WORLD, MAYBE IT'LL HELP US RECONNECT.
YOU THINK?
OH, GOD.
WHAT THE FUCK AM I DOING?

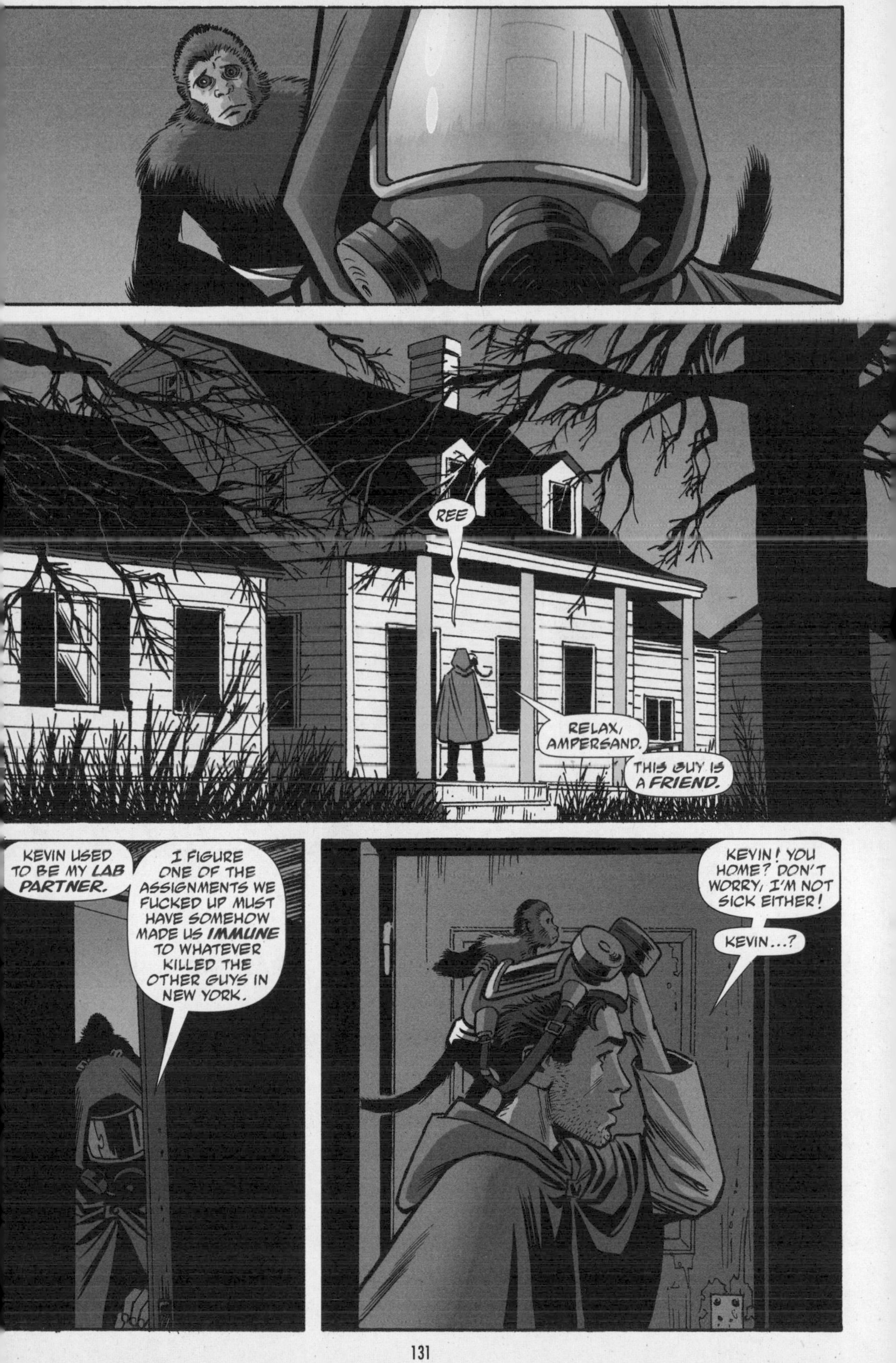
REE
RELAX, AMPERSAND.
THIS GUY IS A FRIEND.
KEVIN USED TO BE MY LAB PARTNER.
I FIGURE ONE OF THE ASSIGNMENTS WE FUCKED UP MUST HAVE SOMEHOW MADE US IMMUNE TO WHATEVER KILLED THE OTHER GUYS IN NEW YORK.
KEVIN! YOU HOME? DON'T WORRY, I'M NOT SICK EITHER!
KEVIN...?

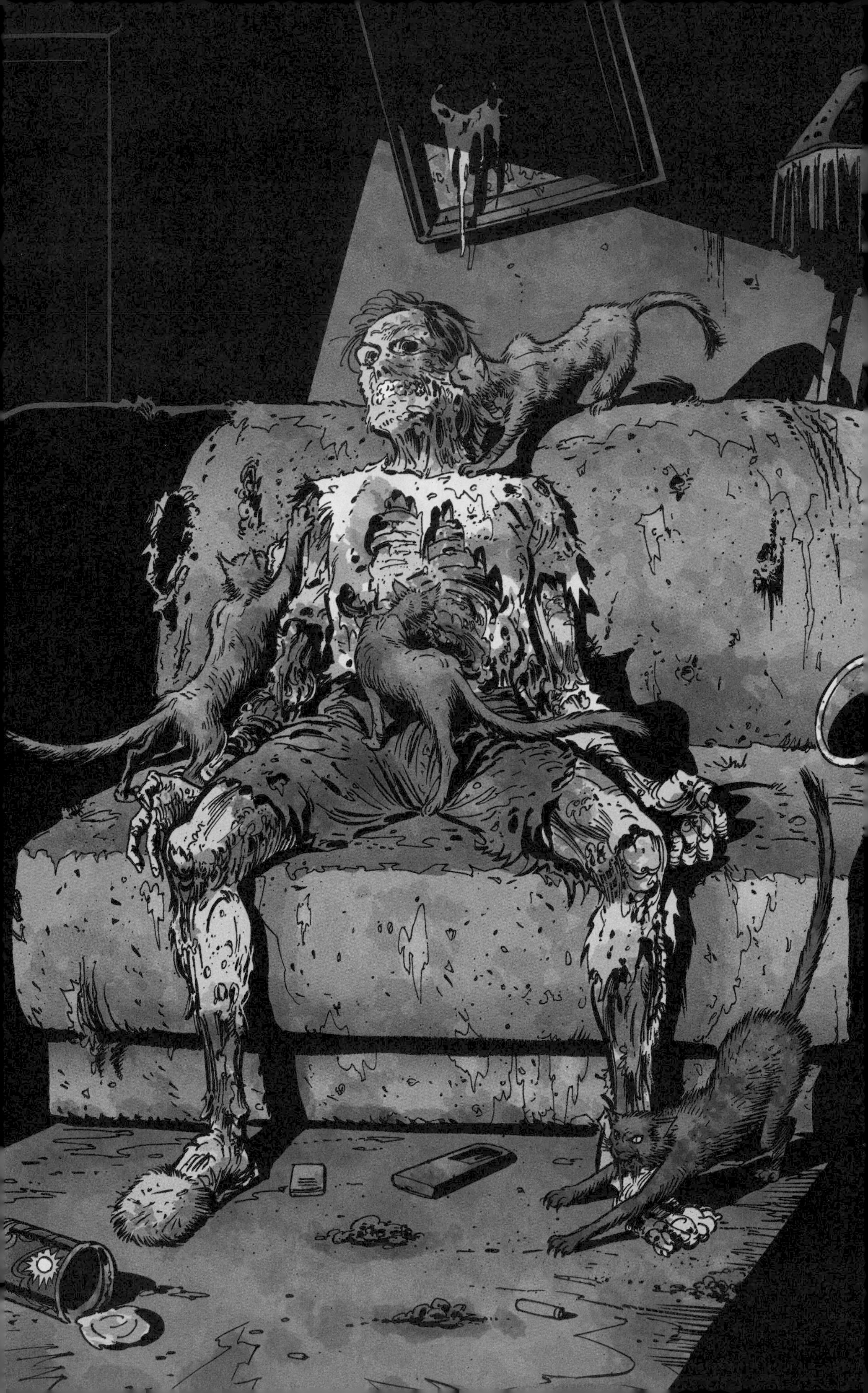

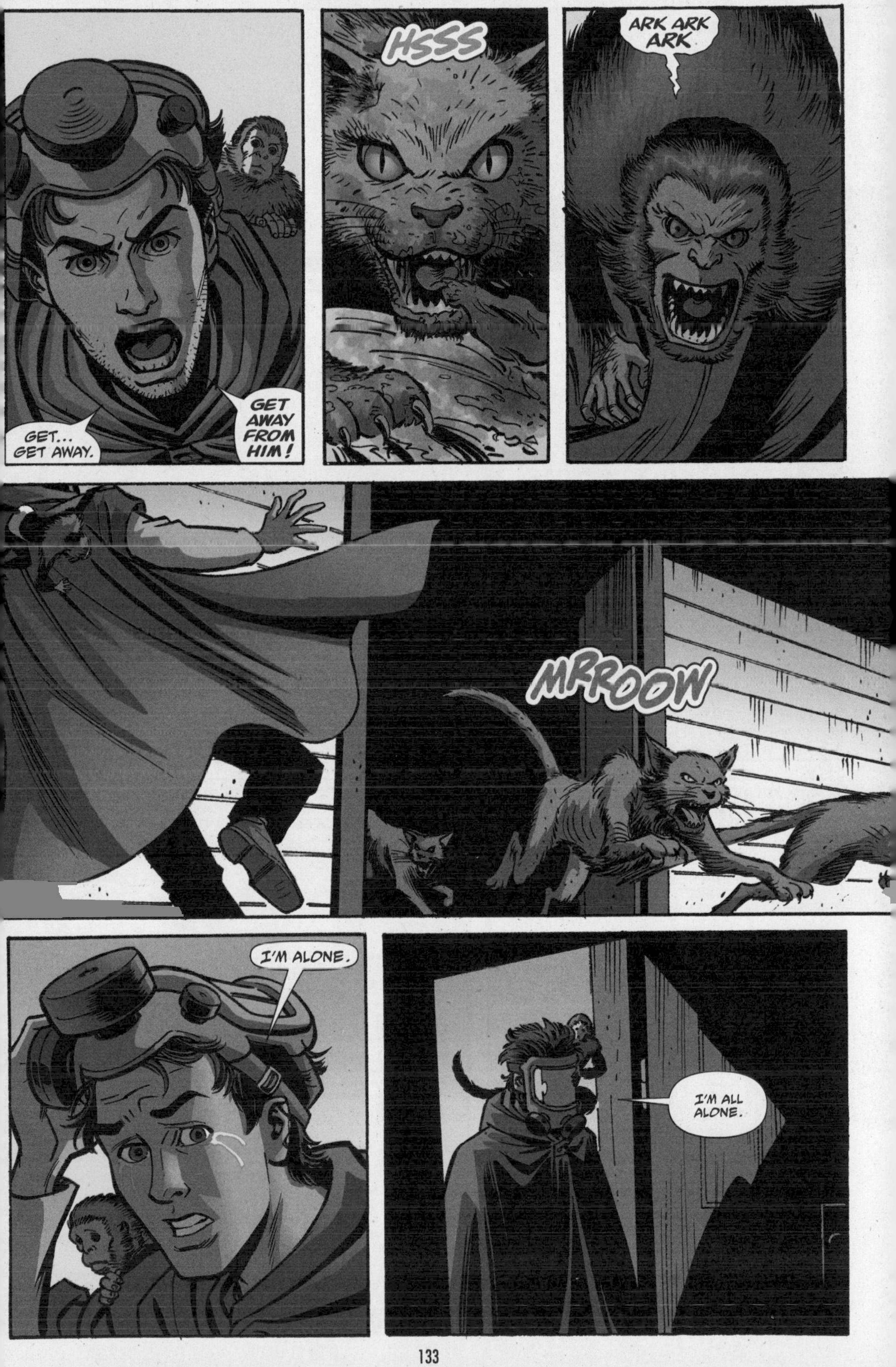
GET... GET AWAY.
GET AWAY FROM HIM!
HSSS
ARK ARK ARK
MRROOW
I'M ALONE.
I'M ALL ALONE.

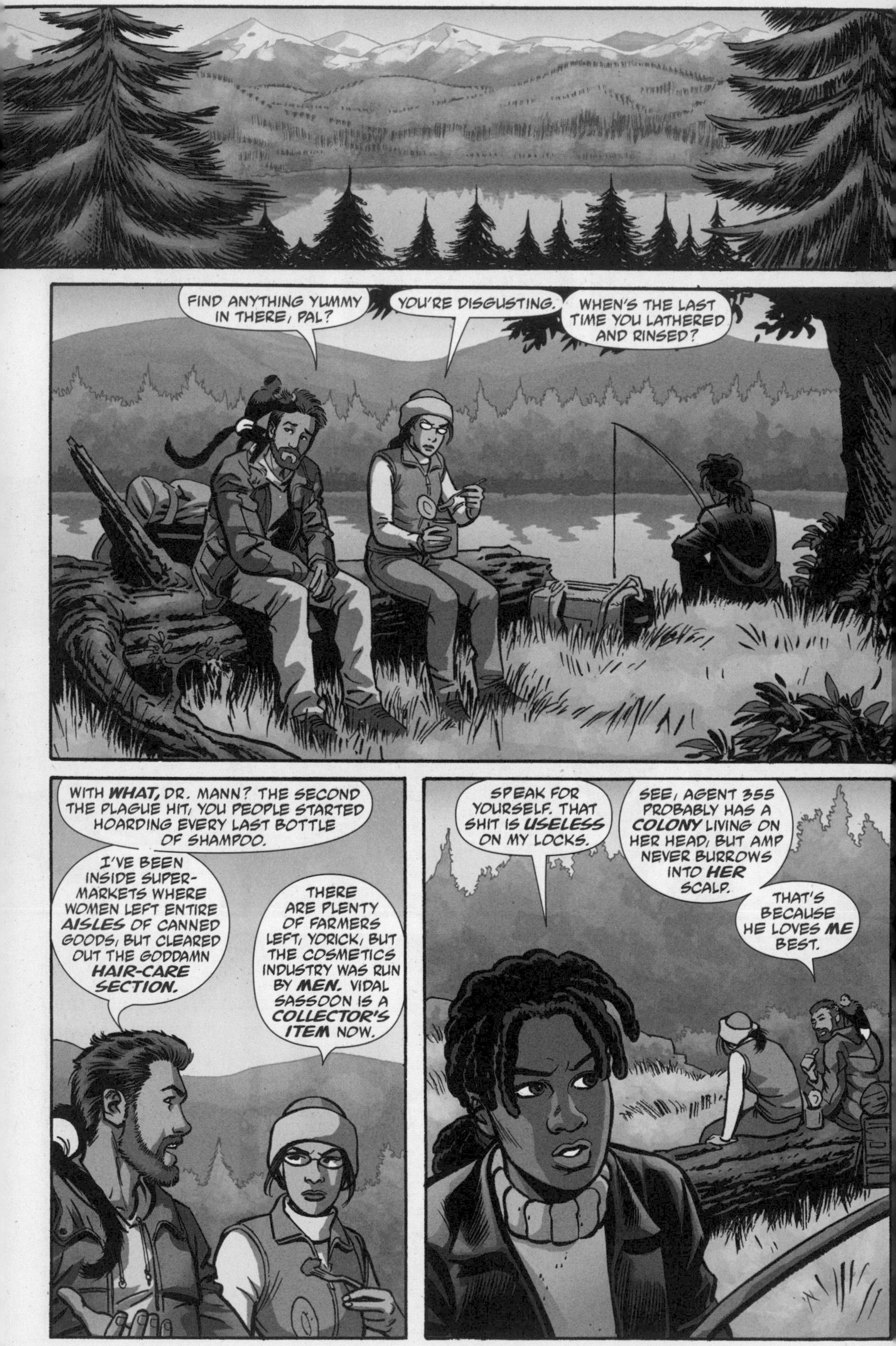
FIND ANYTHING YUMMY IN THERE, PAL?
YOU'RE DISGUSTING.
WHEN'S THE LAST TIME YOU LATHERED AND RINSED?
WITH WHAT, DR. MANN? THE SECOND THE PLAGUE HIT, YOU PEOPLE STARTED HOARDING EVERY LAST BOTTLE OF SHAMPOO.
I'VE BEEN INSIDE SUPER-MARKETS WHERE WOMEN LEFT ENTIRE AISLES OF CANNED GOODS, BUT CLEARED OUT THE GODDAMN HAIR-CARE SECTION.
THERE ARE PLENTY OF FARMERS LEFT, YORICK, BUT THE COSMETICS INDUSTRY WAS RUN BY MEN. VIDAL SASSOON IS A COLLECTOR'S ITEM NOW.
SPEAK FOR YOURSELF. THAT SHIT IS USELESS ON MY LOCKS.
SEE, AGENT 355 PROBABLY HAS A COLONY LIVING ON HER HEAD, BUT AMP NEVER BURROWS INTO HER SCALP.
THAT'S BECAUSE HE LOVES ME BEST.

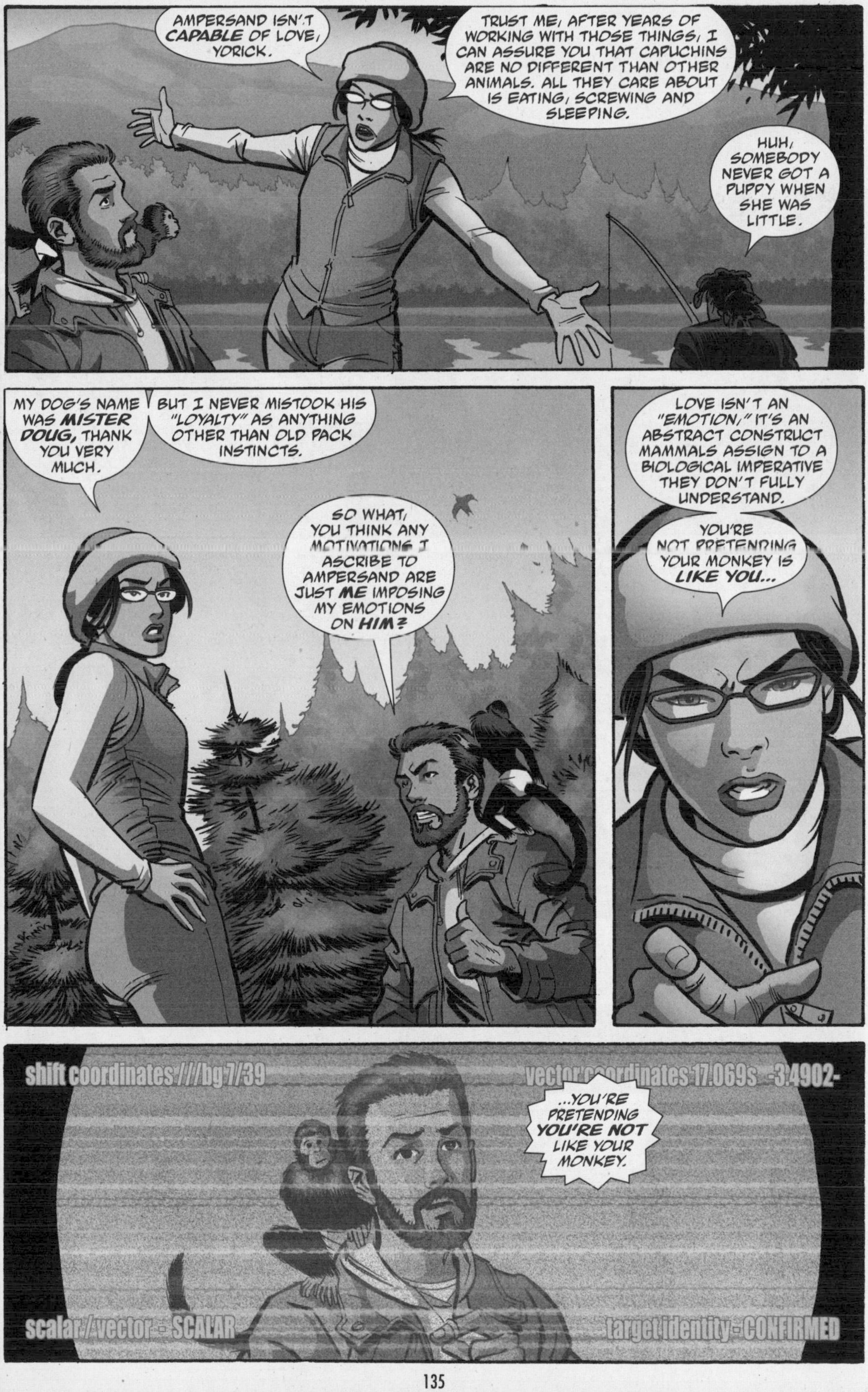
AMPERSAND ISN'T CAPABLE OF LOVE, YORICK.
TRUST ME, AFTER YEARS OF WORKING WITH THOSE THINGS, I CAN ASSURE YOU THAT CAPUCHINS ARE NO DIFFERENT THAN OTHER ANIMALS. ALL THEY CARE ABOUT IS EATING, SCREWING AND SLEEPING.
HUH, SOMEBODY NEVER GOT A PUPPY WHEN SHE WAS LITTLE.
MY DOG'S NAME WAS MISTER DOUG, THANK YOU VERY MUCH.
BUT I NEVER MISTOOK HIS "LOYALTY" AS ANYTHING OTHER THAN OLD PACK INSTINCTS.
SO WHAT, YOU THINK ANY MOTIVATIONS I ASCRIBE TO AMPERSAND ARE JUST ME IMPOSING MY EMOTIONS ON HIM?
LOVE ISN'T AN "EMOTION," IT'S AN ABSTRACT CONSTRUCT MAMMALS ASSIGN TO A BIOLOGICAL IMPERATIVE THEY DON'T FULLY UNDERSTAND.
YOU'RE NOT PRETENDING YOUR MONKEY IS LIKE YOU...
shift coordinates///bg 7/39
vector coordinates 17.069s -3.4902-
...YOU'RE PRETENDING YOU'RE NOT LIKE YOUR MONKEY.
scalar//vector - SCALAR
-target identity - CONFIRMED

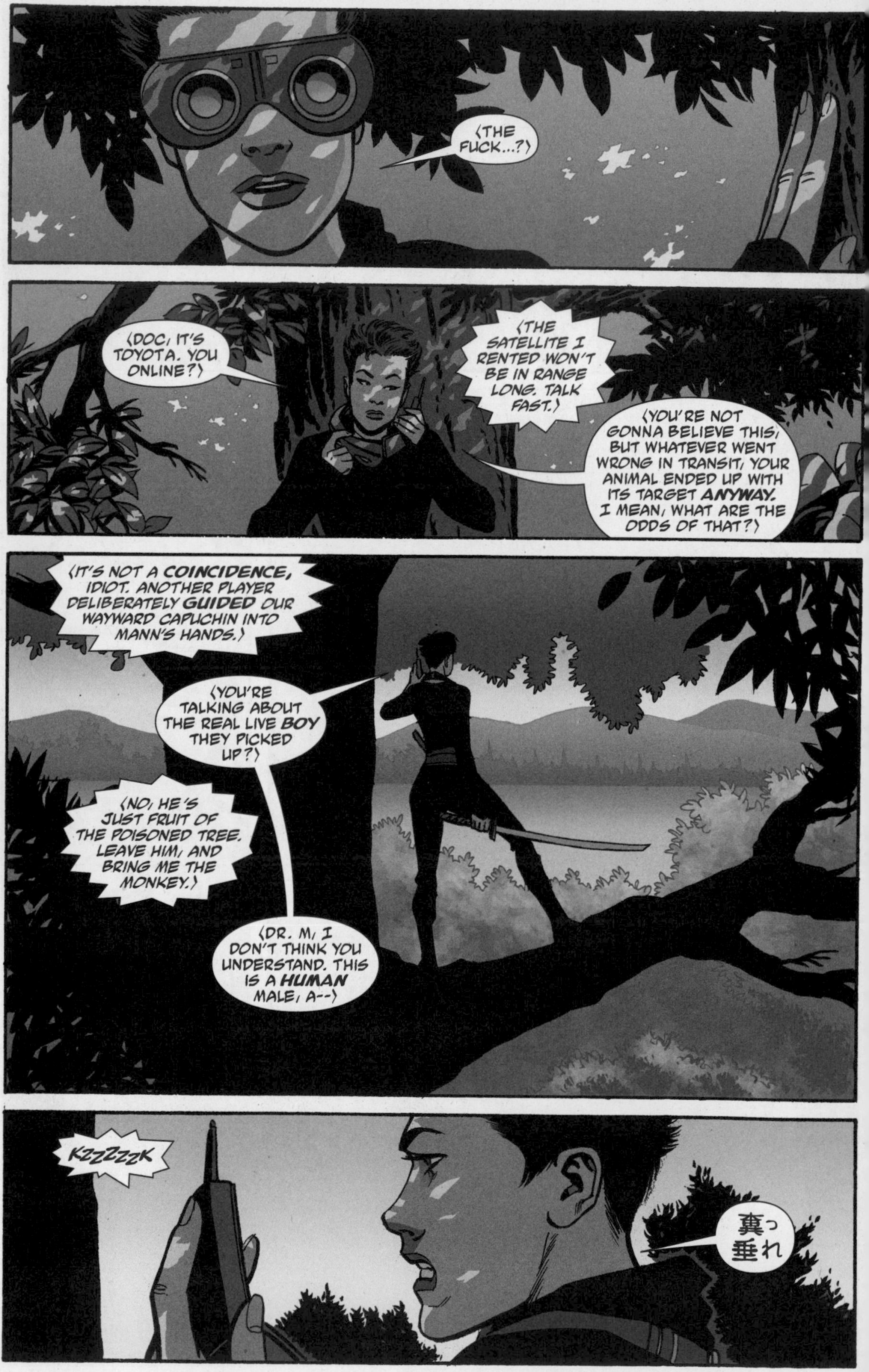

⟨THE FUCK...?⟩
⟨DOC, IT'S TOYOTA. YOU ONLINE?⟩
⟨THE SATELLITE I RENTED WON'T BE IN RANGE LONG. TALK FAST.⟩
⟨YOU'RE NOT GONNA BELIEVE THIS, BUT WHATEVER WENT WRONG IN TRANSIT, YOUR ANIMAL ENDED UP WITH ITS TARGET **ANYWAY.** I MEAN, WHAT ARE THE ODDS OF THAT?⟩
⟨IT'S NOT A **COINCIDENCE,** IDIOT. ANOTHER PLAYER DELIBERATELY **GUIDED** OUR WAYWARD CAPUCHIN INTO MANN'S HANDS.⟩
⟨YOU'RE TALKING ABOUT THE REAL LIVE **BOY** THEY PICKED UP?⟩
⟨NO, HE'S JUST FRUIT OF THE POISONED TREE. LEAVE HIM, AND BRING ME THE MONKEY.⟩
⟨DR. M, I DON'T THINK YOU UNDERSTAND. THIS IS A **HUMAN** MALE, A--⟩
KZZZZZK
糞っ垂れ

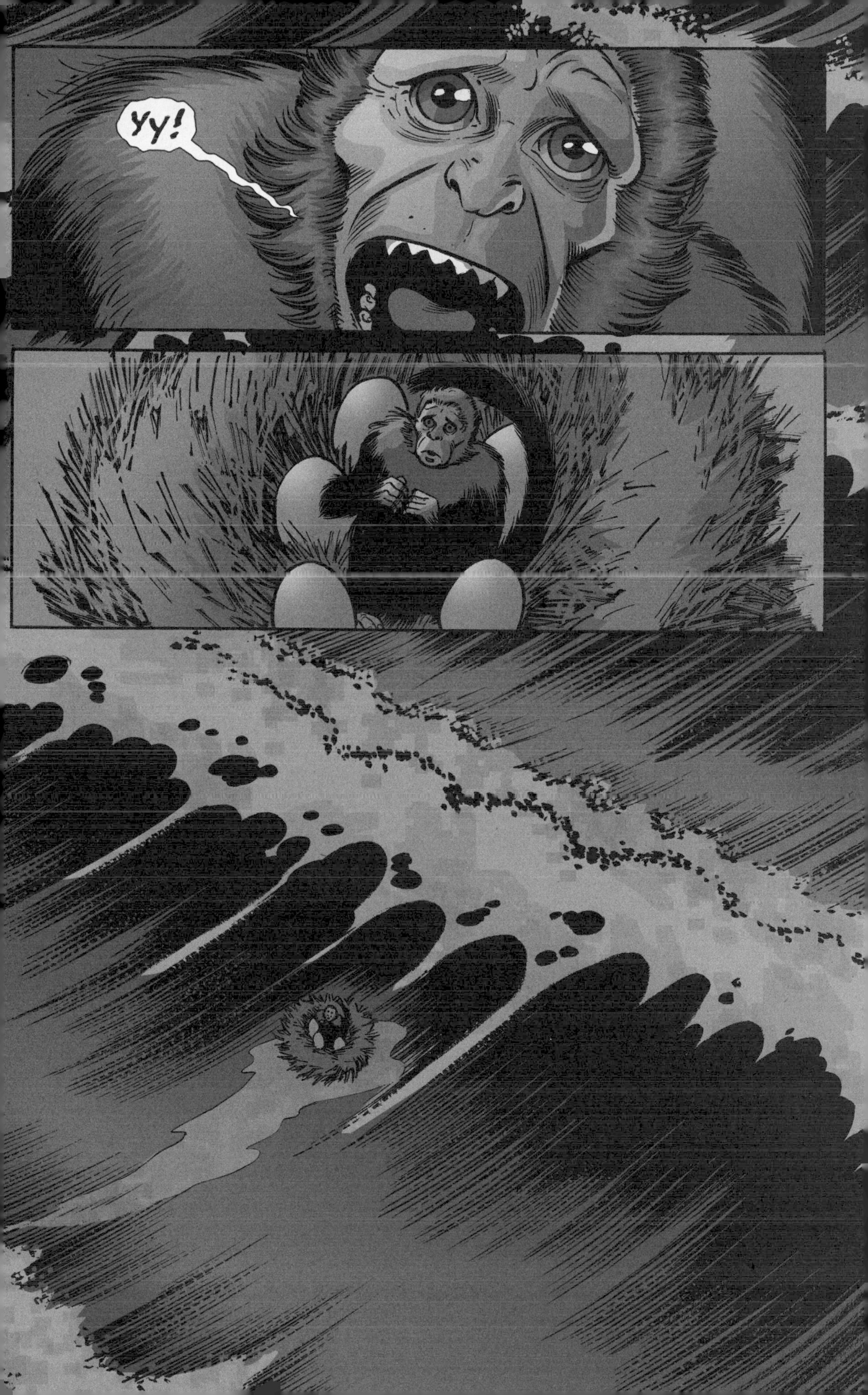
YY!

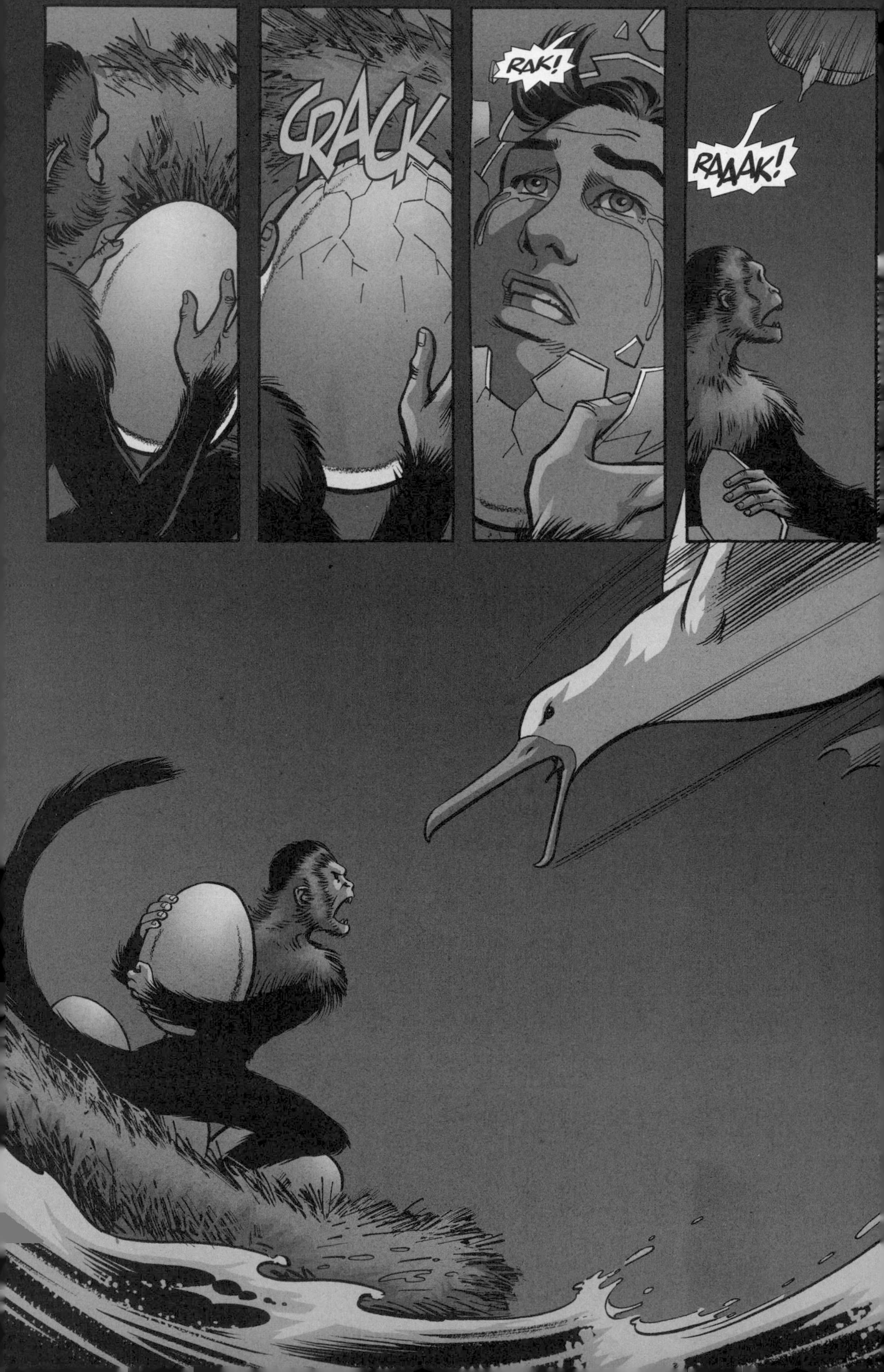
CRACK
RAK!
RAAAK!

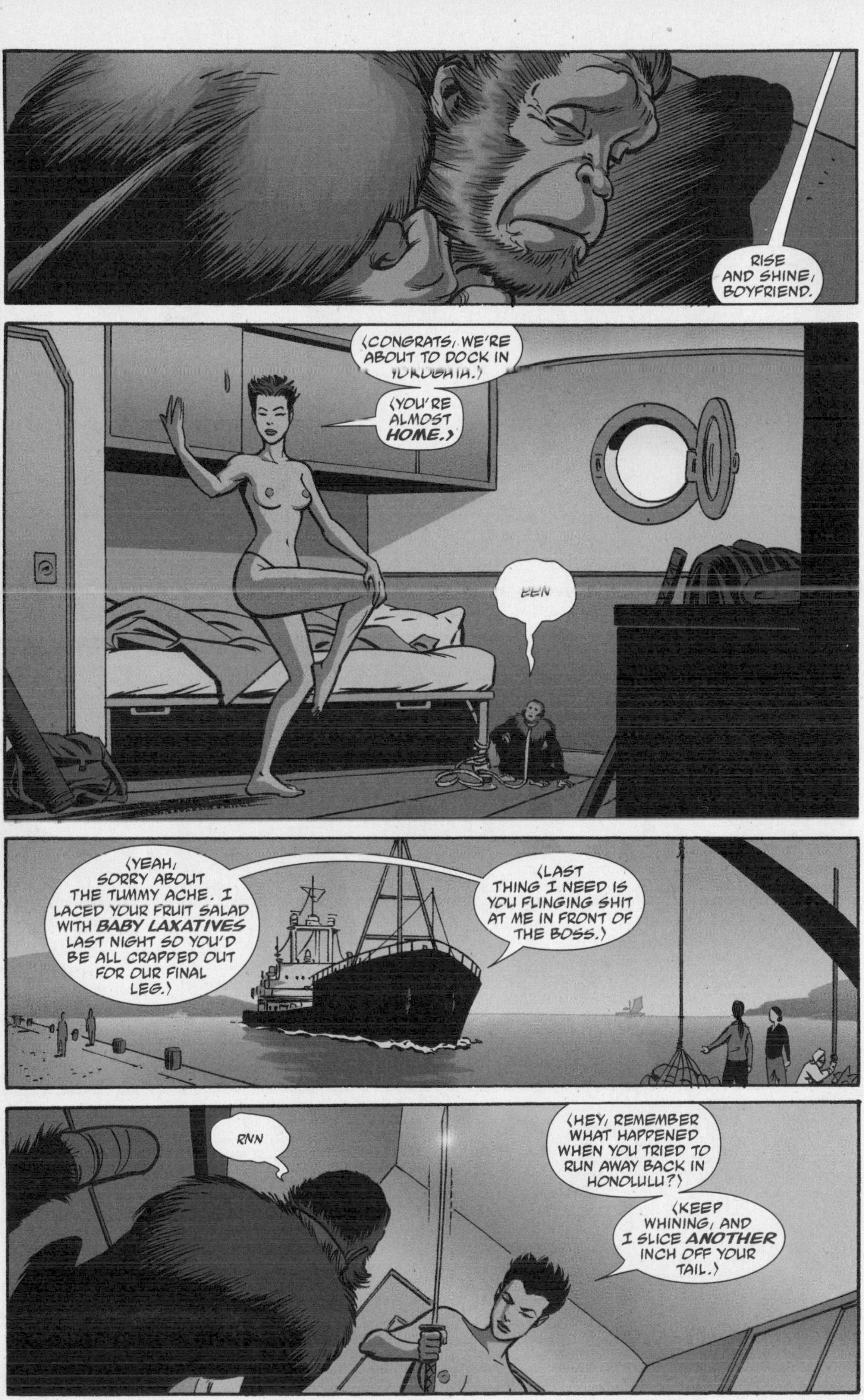
RISE AND SHINE, BOYFRIEND.
⟨CONGRATS, WE'RE ABOUT TO DOCK IN
⟨YOU'RE ALMOST **HOME.**⟩
⟨YEAH, SORRY ABOUT THE TUMMY ACHE. I LACED YOUR FRUIT SALAD WITH **BABY LAXATIVES** LAST NIGHT SO YOU'D BE ALL CRAPPED OUT FOR OUR FINAL LEG.⟩
⟨LAST THING I NEED IS YOU FLINGING SHIT AT ME IN FRONT OF THE BOSS.⟩
RNN
⟨HEY, REMEMBER WHAT HAPPENED WHEN YOU TRIED TO RUN AWAY BACK IN HONOLULU?⟩
⟨KEEP WHINING, AND I SLICE **ANOTHER** INCH OFF YOUR TAIL.⟩

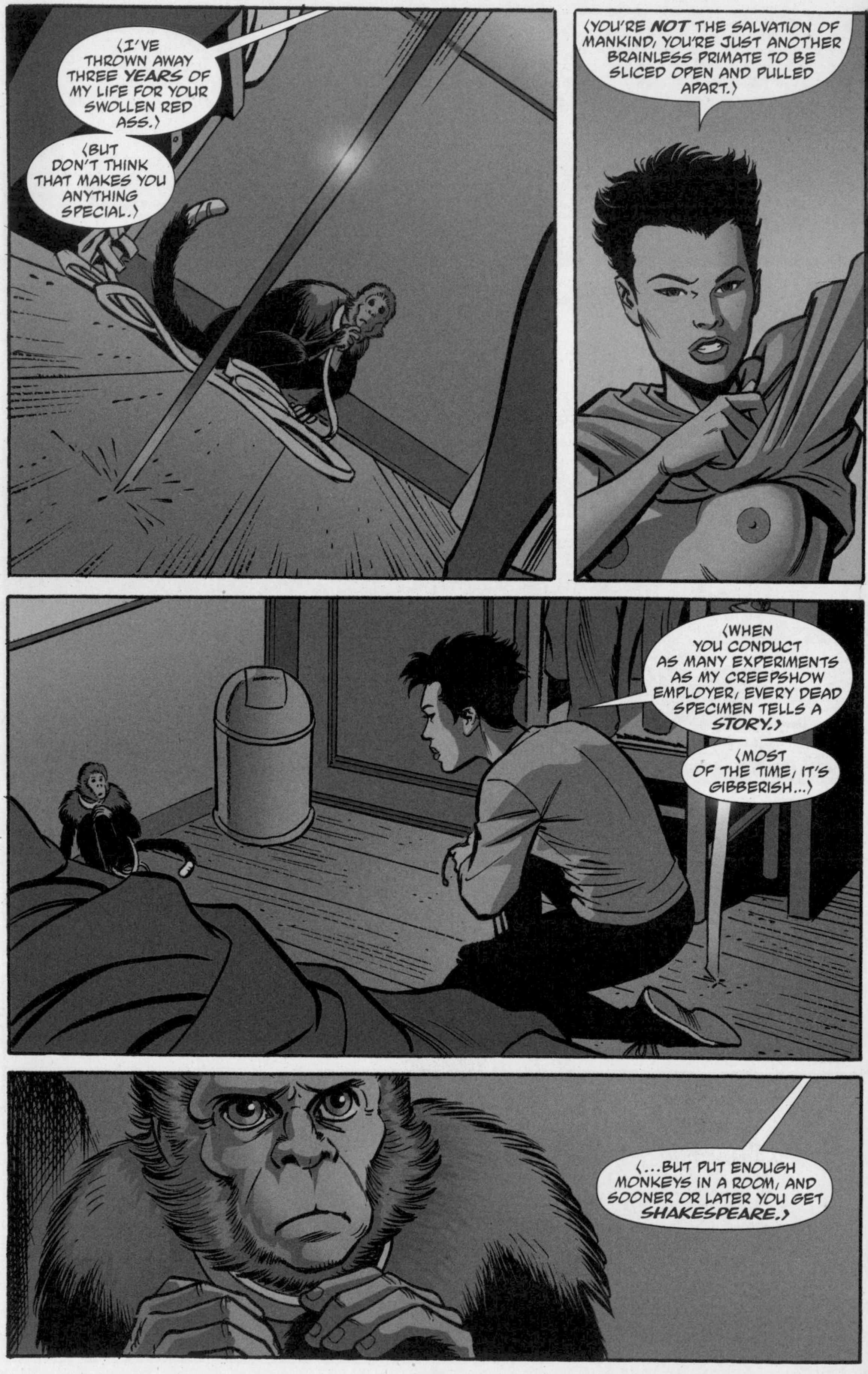
⟨I'VE THROWN AWAY THREE YEARS OF MY LIFE FOR YOUR SWOLLEN RED ASS.⟩
⟨BUT DON'T THINK THAT MAKES YOU ANYTHING SPECIAL.⟩
⟨YOU'RE NOT THE SALVATION OF MANKIND, YOU'RE JUST ANOTHER BRAINLESS PRIMATE TO BE SLICED OPEN AND PULLED APART.⟩
⟨WHEN YOU CONDUCT AS MANY EXPERIMENTS AS MY CREEPSHOW EMPLOYER, EVERY DEAD SPECIMEN TELLS A STORY.⟩
⟨MOST OF THE TIME, IT'S GIBBERISH...⟩
⟨...BUT PUT ENOUGH MONKEYS IN A ROOM, AND SOONER OR LATER YOU GET SHAKESPEARE.⟩

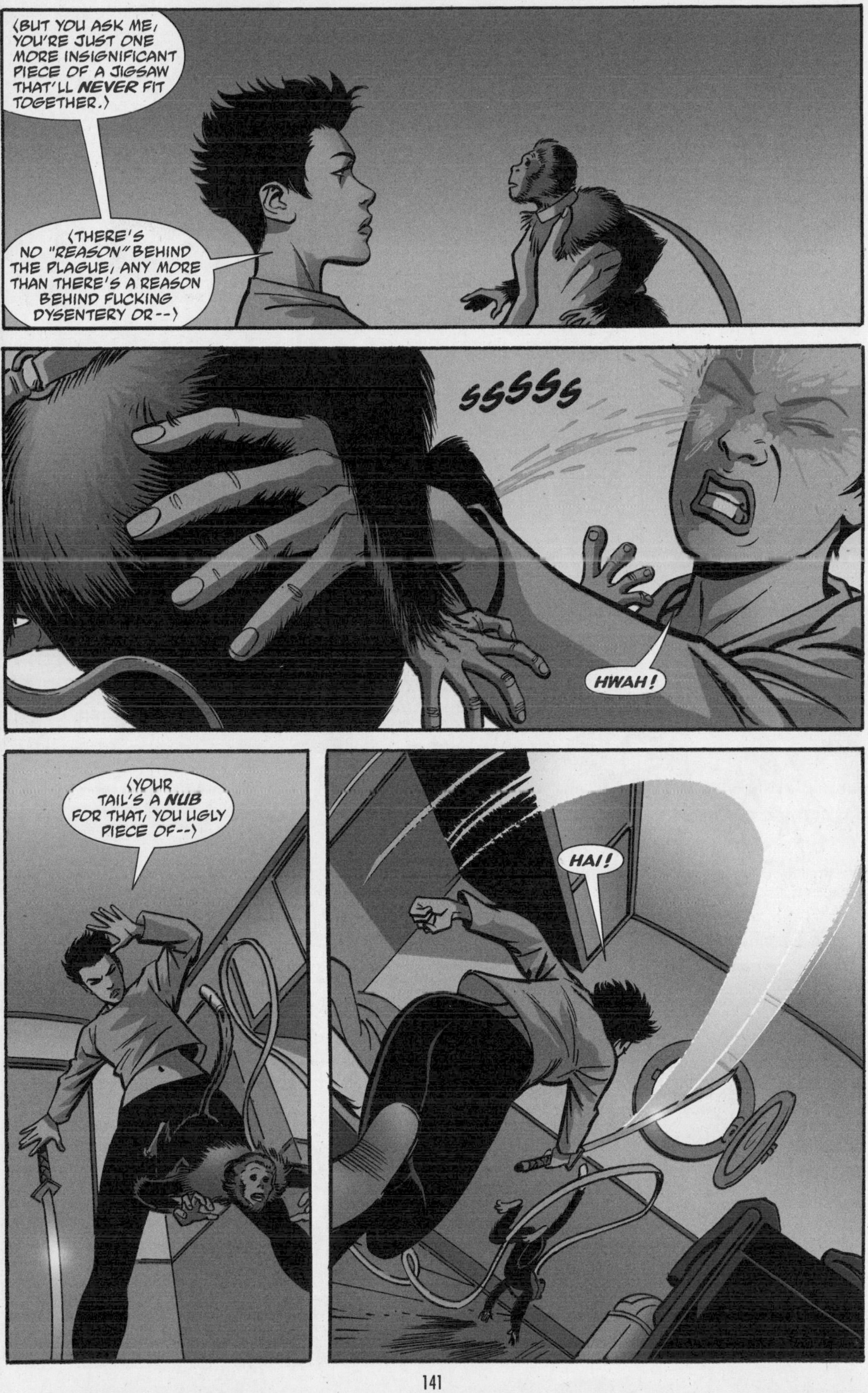

‹BUT YOU ASK ME, YOU'RE JUST ONE MORE INSIGNIFICANT PIECE OF A JIGSAW THAT'LL **NEVER** FIT TOGETHER.›
‹THERE'S NO "REASON" BEHIND THE PLAGUE, ANY MORE THAN THERE'S A REASON BEHIND FUCKING DYSENTERY OR--›
SSSSS
HWAH!
‹YOUR TAIL'S A **NUB** FOR THAT, YOU UGLY PIECE OF--›
HAI!

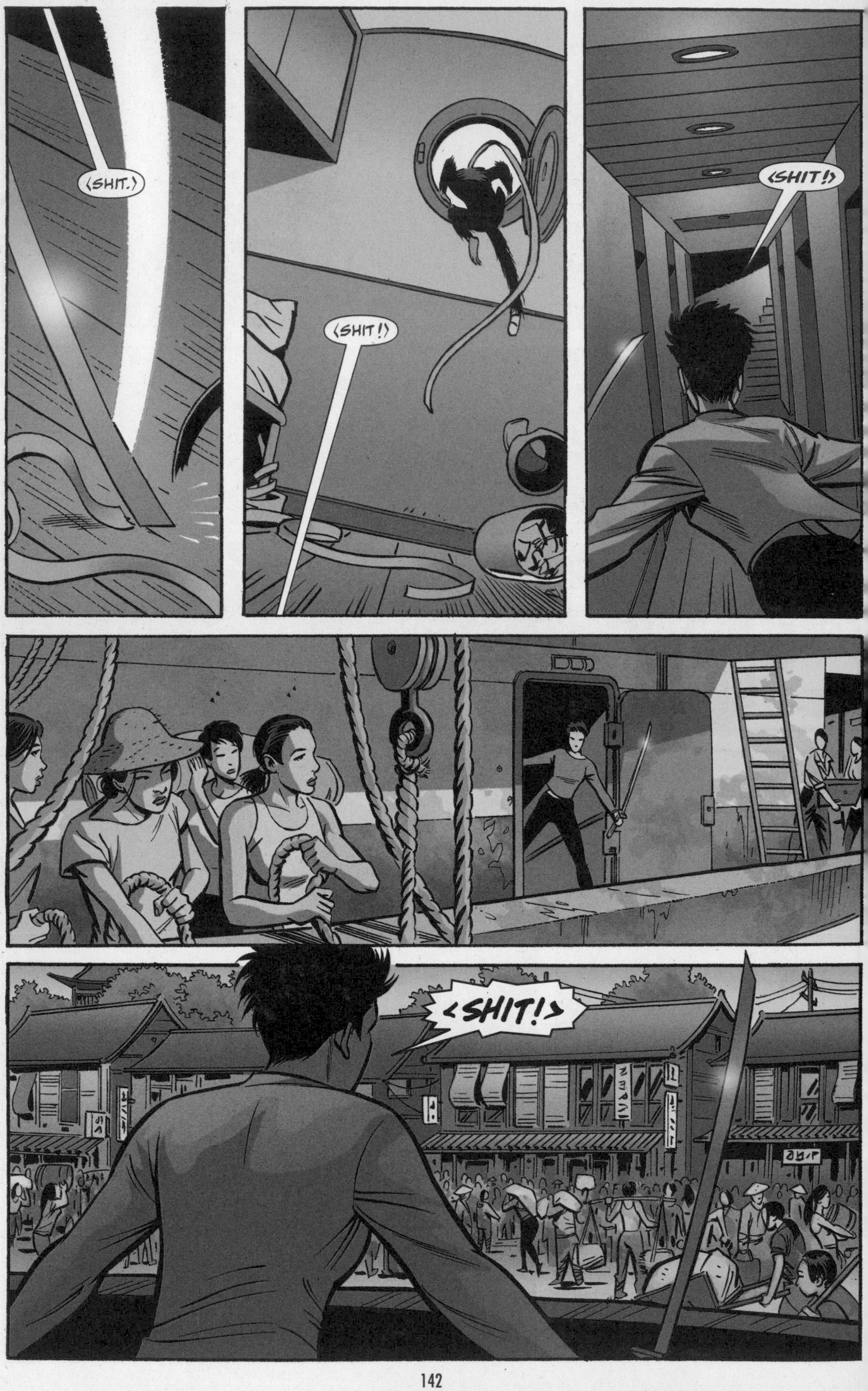
‹SHIT.›
‹SHIT!›
‹SHIT!›
‹SHIT!›

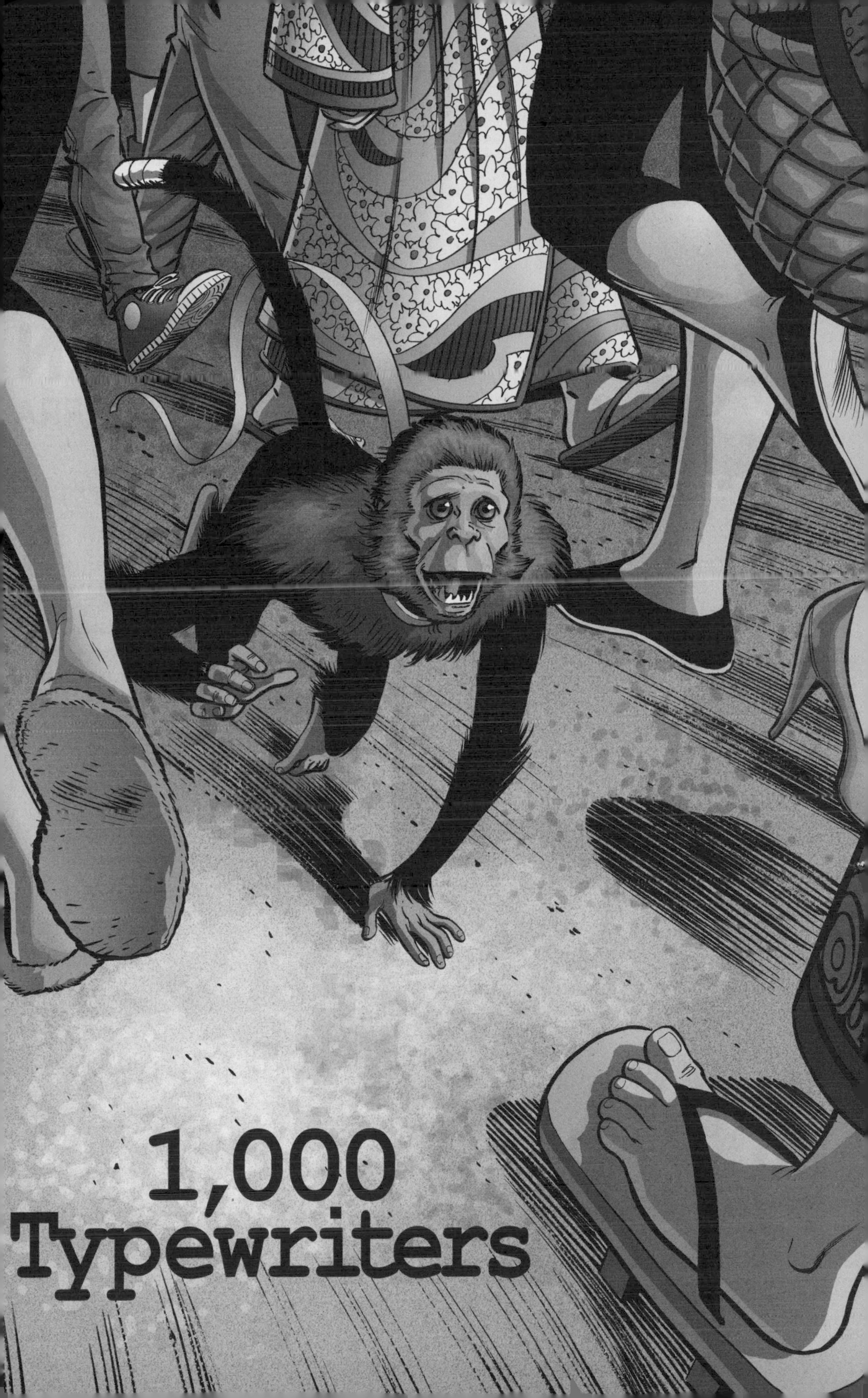
1,000
Typewriters